April 2010

To Victoria Bonilla-Arguda

With great appreciation for your work as a Merit
Panel member in assuring that what transpires in
our courthouse remains worth celebrating.

Vaughn C. Woodlock
V.S.D.J.

CELEBRATING THE COURTHOUSE

A Guide for Architects, Their Clients, and the Public

CELEBRATING
THE COURTHOUSE

A Guide for Architects, Their Clients, and the Public

Edited by Steven Flanders

Foreword by Justice Stephen G. Breyer

W. W. NORTON & COMPANY
New York • London

Facing page: Photo courtesy of Maura Moynihan

Copyright © 2006 by Steven Flanders

For information about permission to reproduce selections from this book,
write to Permissions, W. W. Norton & Company, Inc., 500 Fifth Avenue,
New York NY 10110

Manufacturing by Edwards Brothers
Book design by Gilda Hannah
Production manager: Leeann Graham

Library of Congress Cataloging-in-Publication Data

Celebrating the courthouse : a guide for architects, their clients, and the
public / edited by Steven Flanders; foreword by Justice Stephen G. Breyer.
— 1st ed.
        p. cm.
    Includes bibliographical references and index.
    ISBN-13: 978-0-393-73070-8 (hardcover)
    ISBN-10: 0-393-73070-0 (hardcover)
  1. Courthouses—United States—Design. I. Flanders, Steven. II.
Breyer, Stephen G., 1938–
NA4471.C45 2006
725'.15—dc22   2006022751

ISBN-13: 978-0-393-73070-8
ISBN-10: 0-393-73070-0

W. W. Norton & Company, Inc.,
500 Fifth Avenue, New York NY 10110
www.wwnorton.com

0 9 8 7 6 5 4 3 2 1

To Daniel Patrick Moynihan

1927–2003

CONTRIBUTORS

Justice Stephen G. Breyer was appointed to the U.S. Supreme Court in 1994 by President Clinton. Previously he served as judge and chief judge of the U.S. Court of Appeals for the First Circuit in Boston. With Judge Woodlock, he inspired and supervised the creation of the new Boston federal courthouse. Author of *Active Liberty* and other important volumes in diverse fields of the law, he has served in senior posts at the Senate Judiciary Committee and the Harvard Law School.

Paul Spencer Byard, F.A.I.A., has an active practice at Platt Byard Dovell White Architects in New York City, and is Director of the Historic Preservation Program at the Columbia University Graduate School of Architecture Design and Preservation. Author of *The Architecture of Additions,* his designs include the new 42 Studios near New York's Times Square, and master plans and renovations for Boston's Symphony Hall, New York's Cooper Union, and the Japanese Ambassador's Residence at the U.N.

Cathy Daskalakis, A.I.A., has devoted the majority of her professional efforts to the planning and programming of federal, state, and county courthouses. A graduate of the Cooper Union for the Advancement of Science and Art, she has served as chair of the A.I.A. New York Chapter Committee on Architecture for Justice. She is a partner at Gruzen Samton L.L.P.

George A. Davidson chairs the litigation department at Hughes Hubbard & Reed, L.L.P. of New York, and has tried cases and argued appeals throughout the United States. He is a fellow of the American College of Trial Lawyers and a member of the American Law Institute.

Steven Flanders is a consultant and author based in Pelham, New York. Author of numerous studies concerning judicial administration in the United States and many other countries, he was co-editor of *Cass Gilbert, Life and Work.*

He served as Circuit Executive for the Second Judicial Circuit of the United States, and previously on the research staff of the Federal Judicial Center.

Nathan Glazer is professor of sociology and education emeritus at Harvard. Author and editor of numerous books on American ethnicity, race relations, and social policy, his most recent is *We Are All Multiculturalists Now.* He wrote *Beyond the Melting Pot* with Danial P. Moynihan as co-editor, and both edited *Ethnicity: Theory and Experience.*

Frank Greene, A.I.A., Principal of Ricci Greene Associates, has over twenty-five years of experience in design and construction of courthouses at every level. He has received GSA Design Excellence awards for work on the federal courthouses in Scranton and Pittsburgh, Pennsylvania, and an A.I.A. Rochester Chapter Design Award for the Wyoming County, New York, courthouse.

Jordan Gruzen, F.A.I.A., has had a forty-year career in every design facet of justice. He led Gruzan Samton's design efforts first in correctional and public safety work, and for the last twenty years in courthouse design. A graduate of M.I.T., the University of Pennsylvania and a Fulbright Fellow, he has served as chair of the A.I.A. New York chapter Committee on Architecture for Justice and is a member of the A.I.A. National Justice Committee.

Peter Krasnow, F.A.I.A., has a forty-year architectural career that includes planning, programming, design, technologies, and project management for criminal justice projects (including courthouses) and other building types. His *Correctional Facility Design and Detailing* received international recognition.

Fredric I. Lederer is Chancellor Professor of Law and Director of the Center for Legal and Court Technology and the Courtroom 21 Project, "The Courtroom of

the Twenty-first Century," at William & Mary School of Law. The project includes, in the Law School's McGlothlin Courtroom, the world's most technologically advanced trial and appellate courtroom.

Andrea Leers, F.A.I.A., principal of Leers, Weinzapfel, Associates, is a national leader in courthouse design, having taught a Professional Development Seminar at Harvard on "The New American Courthouse" since 1992. She and her firm have received many design awards, among others for federal courthouses in Worcester, Massachusetts and Portland, Maine. International work includes fellowships and grants supporting research and publication concerning Japan, and residence at the American Academy in Rome.

Todd S. Phillips, Ph.D., A.I.A., is an architect and historian specializing in courts planning, programming, and design research. His work includes co-authorship of *Justice Facilities,* published in 2003, as well as service from 1992 to 2000 as Director, Professional Practice, at the American Institute of Architects, Washington, D.C.

Historian William Seale is co-author with Henry-Russell Hitchcock of *Courthouses,* and *Temples of Democracy: The State Capitols of the U.S.A.,* among many other books. He is co-author of the two-volume *The President's House: A History,* as well as *The White House: History of an American Idea.*

Judge Douglas P. Woodlock was appointed to the United States District Court for the District of Massachusetts in 1986. Author of numerous articles and addresses related to courthouse architecture, he was a guiding spirit with then-Chief Judge Breyer in the design of Boston's new federal courthouse. He received the Thomas Jefferson Award in 1996 from the American Institute of Architects.

CONTENTS

FOREWORD

JUSTICE STEPHEN G. BREYER

As the most recently appointed of our nine Justices on the Supreme Court until October 2005, I sat at the far corner of the bench in the courtroom that Cass Gilbert designed as a kind of Roman forum, intended to be open. Looking out across the room from that corner, I am conscious of a considerable responsibility: to understand, in depth, the particular case before me; to write judgments that are careful, workmanlike, and sound; and to remember that what I write affects not only the litigants but many others not before us, directly through instruction or indirectly through suggestion, metaphor, or symbol. The responsibility of a judge in this respect is not so very different from the responsibility of an architect as a creator of our public spaces. Public spaces also have great power to instruct or suggest, metaphorically or symbolically. Both in function and design, the buildings architects design will embody and reflect principles that tell the public who use or see them something about themselves, their government, and their nation. In doing so, those buildings can help us live together better as a community. Indeed, the story that a building tells through its design may be as important to the community it

serves as is its function. By shaping our thoughts about ourselves and our institutions, it will directly affect our efforts to work productively together.

The challenges are similar for those who work in government and for those who design the public space in which government works. How can our work better reflect several basic tenets of modern public life: first, the fact that, in our democracy, power flows from the people; second, the need to resist the technical, atomizing forces that divide us and to encourage those forces that unify and bring us together as a community; and third, the effort to prevent our government from being perceived as a hostile, alien entity, but rather to emphasize through participation that it can and should amount to no more than our nation's individual citizens themselves, each showing a "civic" face as each acts in his or her public capacity. Government officials and public architects alike are trying to rise to this challenge.

When I was chief judge of the first circuit, I worked with Judge Douglas Woodlock in helping our architect, Harry Cobb, create the Boston federal courthouse. Harry showed us a picture of the Hanover County Courthouse, which Vir-

ginia built in 1735—a picture that Harry kept taped to his mirror for inspiration (see fig. 6-1). That courthouse contains one single courtroom and a front porch. Its materials, brick and wood, are simple. Its location was a crossroads. Its portico offered space for the community's citizens to gather daily. It clearly was a public building with a governmental purpose. Its single courtroom plainly announces its important community function of dispensing justice. In eighteenth- and nineteenth-century America one could find many public buildings and public spaces that embodied or reflected similar ideals; of democracy, community, and participation.

We saw other pictures that suggested an unfortunate change in public architecture in the twentieth century. We saw some courthouses that looked not like significant public buildings but like faceless office buildings. Some looked like prisons. The architectural challenge, Harry said, was to create a building embodying certain civic virtues of the eighteenth century Virginia courthouse while simultaneously responding to our judicial system's twenty-first-century need for quantity—many courtrooms, many judges, many lawyers, many administrators—and the government's further need for security. That is a challenge that faces public architects today. Beautiful courthouses in Johannesburg, Jerusalem, and elsewhere have risen to that challenge. I discuss the Boston courthouse, however, because it is the project I know best (see figs. C-9 and C-10).

A successful federal courthouse must

be more than a courthouse. The Boston building occupies a beautiful site. Because that site now contains a public building, the site belongs not just to the judges or courts or lawyers but to the public as well. The site includes a public park that contains a continuation of the Harbor Walk. The inside of the building has meeting and exhibition spaces for use, in part, by community residents, as well as public spaces that will encourage visits by schoolchildren and other non-lawyers.

The object was to create a public building that provides broadly public uses. Courthouses traditionally were found in the center of a town; inside one found public notices, public records, and trials, where passersby sometimes watched the law in action; outside the public picnicked, celebrated the Fourth of July, set off fireworks in surrounding parks. Historically, courthouses were not office buildings.

The building design also tries to convey certain civic messages. A judge, for example, is a public servant, not a potentate. The courthouse and courtrooms must focus upon lawyers and their clients, and upon helping them to carry out their business. There can be no regal procession toward a judicial throne. The courtroom is the home of the *law*, not the judge. The law is objective, fair, and impersonal. It speaks through the judge, who wears a black robe in part to emphasize the comparative unimportance of his or her own personality. Better to treat the judge, at least a little, like the background objects or the law books that furnish the room.

Neither is a judge a bureaucrat, nor a courthouse a bureaucracy. A court, unlike a government agency, deals not with the public en masse but with the individual citizen who appears before it. It devotes as much time and attention to that individual's specific problem as the problem requires. In this modern age, when people fear government's dehumanizing tendencies, it is particularly important to emphasize that the judicial branch of government treats each citizen before it not as a member of a group but as a separate human being with a right to call upon the court's considerable resources to resolve his or her specific dispute with whatever effort that may take.

Through form and design the building tries to convey these messages. Its glass and windows bring the building into the park (see figs. 4-13 and 4-14); its ample natural lighting facilitates discussion and creates an atmosphere of openness; its courtroom plan focuses attention upon the litigants; its arches, rotunda, cupola, and other classical forms help convey a

FW-2. The Supreme Court Building at night. (Photo: Franz Jantzen, courtesy of the curator, United States Supreme Court)

sense of fairness, dignity, continuity, and equality in a public building In all these ways the building tries to meet our contemporary need for public buildings that reflect the ideals of democracy, that help to restore a sense of community, and that encourage public participation.

In helping to build the courthouse, Judge Woodlock and I learned that any building process today will typically involve different groups of people (clients, administrators, and architects) who should communicate with each other continuously and well, but do not always succeed in doing so. Without continuous communication, the client may simply list desires and priorities; the administrators may follow bureaucratic rules and practices when translating those desires and priorities and trying to implement them; and the architects may simply do the best they can with what they are told to do. The results, in terms of appearance, function, and neighborly relations, are not always happy ones. A better alternative is to build a team—a team that includes administrators, clients, and architects. Those team members must spend time together, trying to understand each other's problems and points of view, so that they can break out of the institutional pattern that too often cannot rise to the set of challenges described.

The team also needs to involve the public in the process. Our architect told us that not so many years ago, it took only a few phone calls to obtain the necessary support for an important building project. He told us this as we prepared for our *thirtieth* public meeting on the subject. The public building process today means government in its broadest sense, involving meetings with many different groups, ranging from state and local commissions (e.g., the Boston Civic Design Commission), to environmental groups (e.g., the Boston Harbor Associates), to neighborhood groups (e.g., the Citizens Advisory Group), and others. In my view, that interactive process of discussion, suggestions, responses, and more meetings worked well. It took time, but it also created understanding. It built support. It produced change. The result is a building that will better serve the public. This type of participatory process today is a necessity. and my experience suggests that that necessity has substantive, as well as procedural, virtues.

Jonas Salk once gave credit for his polio vaccine to the architectural design of the monastery in Assisi—he said that his stay there "was so inspiring" that he "was able to do intuitive thinking far beyond any" he had "done in the past." Public architecture cannot make everyone into a Jonas Salk. It does not even claim to have made Jonas Salk into Jonas Salk. But it did inspire him to do his best, to see things in a new way. Perhaps a building, indeed a government building, can have that kind of impact. If so, the design process, involving both the legal and design professions and involving the public as well, will not only build buildings but also help to rebuild trust in our public institutions.

PREFACE

Courthouse design became a troubled art and a troubled business in the course of much of the twentieth century. The ascendancy of the Bauhaus, Modernism, and the International Style beginning in the 1920s made traditional courthouses and every look that defined them—even new ones of the day—seem fusty and old-fashioned. By the postwar years, court projects held little interest either for important architects or for citizens. The constituency for courthouses and courthouse design was limited to judges and staff who needed a more capacious space in which to accommodate increased workloads. Courthouse design fell to journeymen architects who were willing to compete for jobs that usually went to the lowest bidder, so it is difficult to identify more than a handful of courthouse designs of any distinction anywhere in the world from the decades immediately following World War II.

Yet the final decade of the century saw a resurgence of interest in the distinctive issues a court project presents. As projects displayed throughout this book demonstrate, recent years have seen an astonishing diversity of solutions to the many problems of courthouse design.

There are many ways to create a courthouse that is less than satisfactory, but almost as many ways to create a good one. The unhappy image on the following page demonstrates what became the central problem for most of the twentieth century: it has become very hard to define what a courthouse is supposed to look like (fig. Pr-1). In the foreground is part of a shell of the old federal courthouse in Chicago, designed by Henry Ives Cobb and completed in 1905, under demolition around 1966. Looming behind it is its successor, a masterpiece but not as a courthouse: Mies van der Rohe's Everett McKinley Dirksen Federal Building and Courthouse. Though a successful building both functionally and aesthetically, there is nothing about the Mies structure that defines it as a courthouse until one is deep inside and finds the beautiful courtrooms. It is especially notable that this lack of definition is *not* a consequence of a court program that was newly overwhelmed by other uses. The old building was also a general federal building as well as a courthouse,

PR-1. Henry Ives Cobb's 1905 federal courthouse in Chicago, under demolition, c. 1965, with its successor looming in the background: the Mies van der Rohe Everett McKinley Dirksen Federal Building and Courthouse. (Photo: A. Y. Owen, *Life* Picture Service)

ment center or even a justice center was, in nineteenth-century America, nearly always the courthouse, with imagery to match. And its natural location was at the center of things. Many or most county seats outside the coastal Northeast grew around a central square adorned by a courthouse that accommodated most functions of county, and sometimes also municipal, government. For a combination of reasons that may offer a rich field for speculation, it no longer seems so natural that structures with a roughly similar mix of uses should be defined, in name as in imagery, by the court component. The matter of imagery becomes all the more amorphous if the location lacks definition as well. A courthouse that dominates the town square and much of the town beyond, with lawyers' offices hard by, defines itself in a fashion that is hard to replicate at a more remote location surrounded by malls or adjacent to freeways.

In significant part, credit for this reawakening goes to the late Senator Daniel Patrick Moynihan, the distinguished public servant and public intellectual to whom this book is dedicated. Not only did he inspire and support the Design Excellence Program of the federal General Services Administration, which has drawn the cream of the architectural and other design professions to federal work, but he also inspired a nationwide renewal of interest in good design for courthouses nearly everywhere. The many layers of obstacles to a satisfying and effective design are being addressed, sometimes fitfully, sometimes successfully—and sometimes hardly at all. Too late, an architect may find that the nominal client is neither well informed about project requirements nor a user in any sense.

and it served as Chicago's central post office. In the old building, perhaps even more than in the new one, most people who entered were on business that had nothing to do with courts.

Yet the mix of functions that court buildings are today asked to accommodate does indeed serve as a distraction from court-related imagery and presents a distinct design challenge. As William Seale shows in his historical survey of courthouse design in America (Chapter 1), what today might be called a govern-

The program—if there even is a serious effort to develop a program that addresses requirements systematically—may address only the most basic requirements of square footage and technical needs and reflect little understanding of courthouse imagery or of the subtle human dynamics of the courtroom and the spaces that support it. Mistakes in courthouse design can lead to everything from a "dispiriting and dysfunctional" structure (see Chapter 11) inconsistent with the operational as well as symbolic needs of the court, to spaces that induce a comedy of errors—jurors unable to see the witness properly, the short judge who disappears from view upon sitting behind the bench, the court reporter who is physically isolated from essential parts of the proceeding and can't hear or see well enough to take effective notes, and so on.

The purpose of this book is to inspire and inform the diverse professionals and laypeople who create courthouses. Many if not most central participants come to a courthouse project entirely fresh, without much (if any) previous experience with courthouse design. County commissioners, or others with funding responsibilities, may be confronted suddenly by the desperate need for expansion, modification, or even replacement of an existing courthouse. Citizens' groups and bar associations with a direct interest in achieving a successful solution to the practical needs of the courts may similarly have little or no experience locally with ways to confront the myriad special design features of a courthouse. And architects newly drawn into what was once a minor subspecialty of their profession, confined to a handful of practitioners, often need to learn very quickly about their new frame of reference and

what opportunities and special problems it presents.

Chapter 1 makes clear that the inheritance offered by the American courthouse as found in cities across the land is far from monolithic. Although occasional efforts have been made, especially by the federal government, to define an official style, all were fairly short-lived. The American inheritance of courthouse design is more interesting: courthouses, whatever their style, manifest a communal demonstration that justice matters via that style and their placement in their city. And this tradition continues; indeed, the succeeding chapters show that it remains possible to restate the centrality of the administration of justice in an American community, in a bewildering variety of styles and settings. Chapter 4, especially, shows that this centrality is being discovered and rediscovered outside the United States, as well.

No attempt is made in this book to prescribe a particular program for any model courthouse project. We live in too diverse a design world for that; courthouse programs are specific and distinct from one another. Rather, the contributors to this book bring together the skills and experience of architects, judges, administrators, and lawyer-users to illuminate the issues that must be addressed in creating a suitable and successful courthouse, and to offer a variety of solutions that can help readers solve the problems they confront in their particular settings. Moreover, these multidisciplinary authors see the world of the courthouse in different ways; no effort has been made to conform their views to one another. I hope that every reader's perspectives are enriched by this multiplicity of views and experiences. If we can inspire architects and citizens to enlarge their horizon to embrace and create a suitable solution, and to avoid some of the pitfalls they encounter along the way, then this book will have fulfilled its purpose

The value of this book rests upon the distinguished work of its contributors. And it rests especially upon the inspiration and guidance provided from the start by Judge Douglas Woodlock, who shaped the unfolding of this book at least as deeply as he did Boston's new federal courthouse. And Nancy Green, with her colleagues at W. W. Norton, have been essential to the realization of whatever strengths this book now has.

C-1. Cass Gilbert's United States Supreme Court Building, Washington, D.C., 1935. Photo courtesy of the Office of the Curator, U.S. Supreme Court.

C-2. Resolving a difficult urban site: the Edward W. Brooke Courthouse, Boston, Massachusetts, Kallmann McKinnell & Wood, 1999. (Photo: Steve Rosenthal)

C-3. Creating a civic ensemble: the Charles Evans Whittaker United States Courthouse, Kansas City, Missouri, Ellerbe Becket and Abend Singleton Associates, 1998. (Photo: Timothy Hursley)

C-4. Embracing the city hall: the United States Courthouse, Minneapolis, Minnesota, Kohn Pedersen Fox Associates and Architectural Alliance, 1997. (Photo: Don F. Wong)

18

C-5. A positive presence on the public park: the Mark O. Hatfield United States Courthouse, Portland, Oregon, Kohn Pedersen Fox, Associates, and Boora Architects, 1997. (Photo: Timothy Hursley)

C-6. A distinguished courthouse embedded in a dense residential neighborhood: Bronx housing court, Bronx, New York, Rafael Viñoly, 2000. (Photo: Jeff Goldberg © Esto)

C-7. In a small city, a large building is woven ingeniously into a difficult residual site. Robert C. Byrd United States Courthouse and Federal Building, Beckley, West Virginia, Robert A. M. Stern, Design Architect, SEM Partners, Local Architect, and Architect-of-Record Einhorn Yaffee Prescott, 1999. (Photo: Peter Aaron © Esto)

C-8. In a historic mill town, the canal that helped create it is a powerful shaping force for courthouse design. Fenton Judicial Center, Lawrence, Massachusetts, Leers Weinzapfel Associates, 1998. (Photo: Steve Rosenthal)

C-9. Combining court and public waterfront uses of a remarkable site: the John Joseph Moakley United States Courthouse and Harborpark, Boston, Massachusetts, Pei Cobb Freed and Partners, Jung Brannen Associates, 1998. (Photo: Steve Rosenthal)

C-10. Entrance to Judge Douglas P. Woodlock's courtroom, Moakley United States Courthouse, Boston, Pei Cobb Freed, 1998. (Photo: Steve Rosenthal)

C-11. Bridging the divide between two parts of the city: the United States Court-house, Orlando, Florida, Leers Weinzapfel Associates/HLM Design Joint Venutre, 2006. (Rendering: Advanced Media Design)

C-12. An iconic civic building for an expanded downtown: the Wayne L. Morse United States Courthouse, Eugene, Oregon, Morphosis and DLR Group, 2005. (Rendering: Morphosis)

C-13. Welcoming courtyard for a Mediterranean courthouse: High Court and Lower Court Building, Montpellier, France, Bernard Kohn, 1996.

C-14. The High Court, Bordeaux, France, with administrative block on the right and conical, raised courtrooms wrapped in cedar on the left. Richard Rogers Partnership, 1998. (Photo: Christian Richter)

C-15. An elegant porch with treelike steel supports marks this classically composed courthouse in Melun, France, Jourda and Perraudin, 1997. (Photo: Jean Marie Monthiers)

C-16. An austere porch and transparent façade are connected to the city center by a pedestrian bridge. Courthouse, Nantes, France, Jean Nouvel, 2000.

C-17. A serene new courtroom in Bohlin Cywinski Jackson's 1998 addition to the Scranton, Pennsylvania United States Courthouse and Post Office.

C-18. New York Appellate Division courtroom; America's finest room for appellate enlightenment, James Brown Lord, 1900.

C-19. Old Federal Courthouse, Worcester, Massachusetts, courtroom renovation of 1995, Andrea Leers. (Photo: Steve Rosenthal)

C-20. New courtroom, Worcester federal courthouse, Andrea Leers 1995. (Photo: Steve Rosenthal)

C-21. New courtroom, Portland, Maine federal courthouse, James Knox Taylor, 1903, 1933; courtroom designed by Andrea Leers, 1997. (Photo: Steve Rosenthal)

C-22. The Michigan Supreme Court's new courtroom evokes Native American sentencing circles. Albert Kahn Associates and Spillis Candella and Partners, 2002. (Photo: Justin Maconochie)

C-23. A riot of decoration: James Knox Taylor's Courtroom No. 1, originally a
trial courtroom when the building opened in 1905, now used by the United
States Court of Appeals for the Ninth Circuit, San Francisco. (Photo: courtesy
of the Ninth Circuit)

C-24. Courthouse with public plaza and discrete entrance pavilion, U.S. Courthouse, Denver, CO., Hellmuth Obata & Kassabaum and Anderson Mason Dale, architects, 2004. (Photo: Greg Hursley)

C-25. Detail of a public entrance pavilion at night, U.S. Courthouse, Denver, CO., Hellmuth Obata & Kassabaum and Anderson Mason Dale, architects 2004. (Photo: Greg Hursley)

C-26. Exterior plaza view at dusk, highlighting the transparency of the facility, New Queens Civil Court, New York City, Perkins Eastman, architects, 1997. (Photo: Chuck Choi)

C-27. View of Seattle Justice Center, on a dense urban site, NBBJ architects, 2002. (Photo: Christian Richter)

C-28. Exterior view from the curb at night of public entrance, Seattle Justice Center, NBBJ architects, 2002. (Photo: Christian Richter)

PART ONE

Placing the Courthouse in Its Community and History

ONE

American Vernacular: The Courthouse as a Building Type

WILLIAM SEALE

The most local of all buildings in the United States is the county courthouse.[1] No matter how closely it may pattern its windows or towers or columns on some past monument of civilization, it becomes notably local about as soon as the builders step away. History and use, more than architecture, make it important. Yet it is the architecture that we can readily see and touch that symbolizes the rest. Courthouses familiar to a community possess a power earned over time and for this reason, if this alone, have great value to the culture they represent.

What happens in and around courthouses and what they protect are basic to our lives. They are the scenes of the courts, the holders of land titles, of deeds, marriage licenses, divorce decrees, adoption, probate, and other legal papers of all kinds. Where natural disaster has not intervened—or, rarely in our fortunate country, war—the records may go back to the earliest days of the jurisdiction. Courthouses contain both the dynamics of ongoing life and the documents that prove life past.

Courthouses are thoroughfares of decision and inquiry. The meaning of the courthouse is nourished by daily life itself and validated by memory.

American courthouses are a distinguished lot of structures and merit a general review of their appearance and style, beginning with the early ones.[2] A few are notable for their architecture, as is Henry Hobson Richardson's mighty Allegheny Courthouse in Pittsburgh (see figs. 1-21, 4-2, 5-1, 5-2, and others), but most are simple or elegant or quirky piles that have earned public affection for the stability and continuity they symbolize. "It is *ours!*" citizens may rightly say of their one-of-a-kind courthouse. Take, for example, the squat, stubby-columned Ralls County Courthouse, built at the end of the 1850s in New London, Missouri, with its heavy, though soaring, cupola; do not overlook the old Roane County Courthouse in Kingston, Tennessee, built a few years earlier, boasting strange columned three-story porches and loggias. With such buildings as these, which nevertheless have a lot in common with other American courthouses, departures from the finer points of architectural practice are indeed often badges of distinction. Almost without exception, when one of

1-1. A classic early courthouse type, built of brick with wooden lantern atop, San Augustine, Texas. (Ambrotype, c. 1856, Jane Cartwright Weed)

1-2. American courtroom in the mid-nineteenth century. The room is simple in design and stringent in functional layout, an enduring pattern. *Harper's New Monthly Magazine*, 1852.

the old edifices has been pulled down and replaced with something suggesting an ice tray, or most anything different from what was there, the community takes the loss sadly. Beyond the county lines, a certain kinship in sentimentality unites them all, the courthouses of America. The old San Augustine, Texas courthouse (fig. 1-1) of 1840, or so, can represent its generation.

The initial motive in building has always been to provide shelter for official county work, but in the past, when the time and money could be found and history had passed from raw frontier to a measure of civilization, the designers sometimes had bigger ideas. That the building be fireproof is basic; that it have a courtroom is obvious; that it have some office spaces that are open every day is also clear—county sheriff often, county clerk, and other officials. Sometimes, but not usually, municipal offices are included. But at some point the builders faced the more abstract issue of the civic expression they were contemplating. This is a tough challenge and builders' eyes inevitably rove elsewhere for good examples or for a builder or architect, or both in one, who knows what to do (fig. 1-2).

The courthouse might seem to vary in magnificence according to the wealth of the county, but not necessarily. Poor counties, such as Shelby County, Texas, with its 1880s castle, could build thundering well (see fig. 1-22). Sometimes a grand courthouse came from a judge who thought he could do the job as well as any professional; perhaps the best known is Judge Harry S. Truman of Jackson County, Missouri, who built a "skyscraper" courthouse in Kansas City in the early 1930s and kept the project very

WILLIAM SEALE

much under his thumb (see fig. C-3). (In fact, Truman, then a county judge or county executive, built *two* courthouses: the skyscraper in Kansas City (1934) and a modest-scaled neo-Georgian county courthouse in Independence (1935), his hometown. (Jackson County, of which Independence is the historic county seat, was taken over by Kansas City; hence the unusual circumstance of two county courthouses.)

A resolute local official such as Truman was likely to order up something that was right to his eyes, for good or for bad. Most courthouses reflect that reality. How well a judge communicated with his appointed building commission and the architect and/or builder himself was important to the result; yet the judge really held the authority. An excellent model he saw in a city somewhere might translate into something quite different on a knoll in a small county seat. The White House was patterned on the palace of the Duke of Leinster in Dublin (one must squint a bit to see similarities). The dome of the United States Capitol is patterned on the iron dome of St. Isaac's Cathedral in St. Petersburg, Russia; however, the result is far different, less academically correct, but so wholly satisfying locally that as a symbol, it has a power that overwhelms any shortcomings of design. A county courthouse, influenced by the state's new capitol, does its job well in much the same way. "Sensible accident" describes the designs of some of our most appealing courthouses (fig. 1-3).

Courthouses are rooted deeply in the traditions of the American landscape. Years ago, when people traveled by foot or horse, they approached a county seat slowly and the buildings of the town

1-3. Montgomery County Courthouse, Dayton, Ohio, under construction. A highly significant Greek Revival building that was intended to be fireproof, it was built entirely of masonry, with vaulted interiors. (Daguerreotype, c. 1853, Montgomery County Historical Society)

were low, except for the steeple of a church, perhaps, and the upward quarters of the courthouse. An example of such a classic American vernacular courthouse is that in Alcorn County, Mississippi in the town of Rienzi, its date of 1854 seeming very late for the look of the structure (fig. 1-4). Yet the then century-old style, so reflective of its type, would survive at least half a century longer in such buildings as the Hinsdale County Courthouse, built in 1877 in Lake City, Colorado, and as late as 1931 in the Kent County Courthouse in Hindman, Kentucky. Monumentality is relative, and courthouses vary. Late eighteenth- and early nineteenth-century examples were typically little more than boxes,[3] cubes, or rectangles, such as that at Alcorn, made outstanding from the other boxes lining the streets by standing alone on a square, crowned with a cupola. The cupola heralded the approaching citizen, announcing the official purpose of the building, and, more abstractly, the overall power and security of life brought by the law. There has never been a more succinct expression of purpose.

1-4. Alcorn County Courthouse, Rienzi, Mississippi, a rural seat built in 1854, somewhat resembles the courthouse in fig. 1-1. (Photo: Geoff Winningham, Seagram's Courthouse Project, Library of Congress)

1-5. Old Washington County Courthouse, St. Stephens, Alabama, 1850, drawn in 1935 by N. H. Holmes for the Historic American Buildings Survey. The simple Gulf Coast public building was restored from this drawing in the 1990s. (Holmes & Holmes Architects)

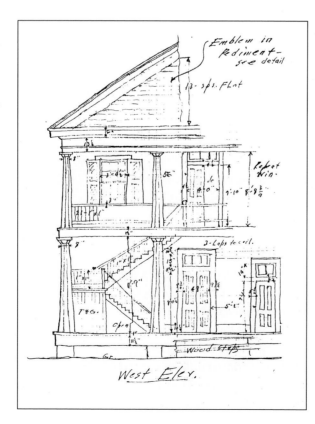

Little of this centrality was inherited from the British Isles or Europe. The equivalent town halls where the courts usually sat were not dominant; churches were. The old market house in the middle of the public square in Fayetteville, North Carolina, built Gothic Revival style by the Englishman William Nichols about 1840, recalls the English town hall, claiming little dominance from afar, with its official purposes housed above and the open market below.

In America it was not to be the church that dominated the town but the courthouse. This is not difficult to understand, considering that there was no state church to represent God, and the institution in law of individual freedom had replaced it. The yearning for visual symbols of this freedom was naturally addressed in the courthouse, as the principal public edifice; it housed the basic mechanics of citizens' rights, and tax revenue paid for the building. Most early courthouses looked not much different from houses, the distinction nearly always marked by a vertical element of some kind, either a lantern or cupola, sometimes a roof platform, which made the courthouse a public building, more important than a house.

Eighteenth-century courthouses in America, especially in colonial Virginia, varied from these simple vernacular buildings to structures decidedly reflective of formal architecture in England. Take, for example, the small, superbly Georgian brick courthouses at Smithfield, Isle of Wight (about 1750), Hanover (about 1735; see fig. 6-1), and King William Counties (about 1725); all are one-story, built of brick in the finest techniques, and decidedly akin to the monumental public buildings that adorned Williamsburg—Capital, Royal Governor's Palace, college, and church, all four commissioned and begun in 1699 in the reign of William and Mary and following the Dutch-flavored Renaissance forms one might expect in that time. More typically, fine colonial courthouses resembled dwellings, such as Lincoln County Courthouse (1761) in Dresden, Maine (fig. 1-6). The Chowan County Courthouse (about 1767) in Edenton, North Carolina and the Charleston County Courthouse (rebuilt about 1788) in South Carolina could easily have come from any of a number of British "how-to" building books on dwelling houses published in the eighteenth century. The Old Colony House (1734–41) in Newport, Rhode Island, one of the finest and most effectively ornamental American buildings of the colonial period, boldly proclaims kinship to English town halls of the time.

Such fashionable architecture was the exception for courthouses well into the nineteenth century. Another exception was the remarkable Culpeper County Courthouse, remodeled about 1809 and demolished over a century ago, in Fairfax (later Culpeper), Virginia, with the exotic touch of its added tower (fig. 1-7). A typical example of the more common pattern was the Washington County Courthouse (1814–16) in Springfield, Kentucky (fig. 1-8). Although remodeled extensively, its boxlike early character is still very clear. Beyond the box, however, it boasted more than a cupola; it had and retains a festively ponderous tower-like climax, mounted in the center of the roof. This feature was probably inspired by the long-vanished late-eighteenth-century statehouse at Frankfort, Kentucky, which had a similar whimsy on top.

1-6. Lincoln County Courthouse, Dresden, Maine, built c. 1761 in a domestic vernacular that makes it difficult to differentiate from a typical New England mansion of the time. (Photo: Douglas Baz, Seagram's Courthouse Project, Library of Congress)

1-7. Culpeper County Courthouse, Fairfax (later Culpeper), Virginia. Records on this building are not clear. It may be an eighteenth-century building to which the bell tower was added about 1809, or the main block may have replaced an earlier building. In any case the exotic tower was added to an existing building, providing a sort of monumentality not unfamiliar in eighteenth-century Virginia and Maryland. One of the few photographs of the building, which was demolished in 1870, this was taken by Timothy O'Sullivan in 1863 and shows Union soldiers hanging out their washing in the upper loggia. (Library of Congress)

1-8. Washington County Courthouse, Springfield, Kentucky, built in 1816 as a traditional box made of brick, crowned by an ambitious cupola that proclaimed the county seat from afar. (Photograph made in 1936, Library of Congress)

what the courthouse itself lacked. For example, if the courthouse was built of wood, the county clerk's archives might be maintained in a "fireproof" built on one corner of the square or flanking the courthouse, balanced by a similar structure on the other side containing a brick jail.

From all accounts, venturing into any of these early courthouses was to see somewhat the same scenes. On the lower floor offices were open weekdays. Here the county clerk and tax collector presided, unless the clerk was both, or the sheriff was also the collector. The ground-level rooms were low and dark, with stark plaster walls and wood doors and windows sometimes protected by iron rods. Office furniture, as such, was not invented as yet. Documents, folded and stored upright, were banded by subject in ribbon (usually red) and lined up on shelves or in boxes. A stair of more or less importance led to the upper floor, where the courtroom could be anywhere: along one side, down the center, across the front, or occupying nearly the entire space. A small corridor of a lobby was typically partitioned off to receive spectators, if necessary, before they entered the chamber and to block the open stairwell against drafts; more critically, it prevented a chimney effect if the building caught fire. As one entered the chamber, the judge's bench was directly across the room. Before it were the lawyers' tables and the bar. A door beyond the bench opened into a robing room for the judge; a second door gave into a room for the sergeant-at-arms, which might double as a jury room. Sometimes a third door accessed a room for holding dangerous prisoners on trial.

The courtroom was the only stately

Buildings of this sort, and very often plainer ones, were all over the early republic. Few survive, except on the eastern shore of Virginia and Maryland and in Delaware. Built nearly always of brick, so as to be fireproof containers for valuable records, they seldom stood more than two stories. Often outbuildings sharing the square supplemented

WILLIAM SEALE

interior of the building, but even this seldom betrayed much generosity with public money. A big space, with perhaps a little broader wood trim around the windows and a higher ceiling than other rooms, gave an impressive setting for the work of the court. Light came mostly from the windows, which were often tall, like those at a church, or there were two rows of small ones, up and down, in the same room. If court met late enough at night to justify it, oil lamps and candles provided artificial light; if spectators were numerous, sometimes the safer illumination of a chandelier with a dozen candles or oil burners might be offered, suspended just over their heads. Some cabinetwork up front created a judge's bench, witness stand, and jury box, with a railing or bar separating the spectators from the court's work. This arrangement was securely attached to tradition everywhere, with the judge prominent and others notably secondary. Plaster walls, woodwork grained with paint to look like mahogany or oak, and raw floors scrubbed to a silvery smoothness and spattered with tobacco spit completed scenes well known to America's early jurists. In such settings Andrew Jackson, Abraham Lincoln, and many more, even a generation after them, held forth. A late building of this character, permanent (meaning fireproof), still stands: the Genesee County Courthouse in Batavia, New York, built smooth-walled of masonry, the structure squarish with louvered cupola. Built in the early 1840s, it is a familiar courthouse image for its time. Works Projects Administration (WPA) and other photographs taken in the 1930s show that little change had taken place in such courthouses over time, though raw light bulbs dangle

down in the large, open court rooms.

Some judges traveled, as many still do, holding court in different places, the lawyers following in a caravan. They camped out or perhaps stayed in farmhouses, the judge occupying the available bed, the lawyers on straw in the barn. Sometimes taverns served both as courthouse and accommodation. By contrast, how luxurious some of the permanent county courthouses of the first half of the nineteenth century must have seemed.

A whole generation of early courthouses stood solid across America. Nearly every new county first built a temporary courthouse of wood and then replaced it with something more fireproof, more commodious. Few of these survive, but we can seek out the old buildings in documents filed with the county clerks. Sometimes what the buildings looked like can be pieced together in the construction papers, down to the types of bricks and colors of paint. So the plain, early buildings are not entirely lost.

Where architectural style was concerned, variety was usual in the more ambitious "permanent" courthouses, which could be second but were more often third in succession. The Old Windham County Courthouse in Brooklyn, Connecticut, is a late Georgian or Federal building constructed about 1820 and made of wood, a cupola distinguishing it from the fine houses of New England merchants of the same time. Less emphatic in its Federal style and more typical is the Burlington County Courthouse in Mount Holly, New Jersey, completed 1796 (fig. 1-9), as much a Georgian building as the Chowan County Courthouse in North Carolina, from

1-9. Burlington County Courthouse, Mount Holly, New Jersey, completed about 1796. It suggests in its design the New Jersey Statehouse at Trenton, of about the same time, but this is a much finer building, with its sensitive blocking, the thin skin of the walls, and the ample, well-articulated openings. (Library of Congress)

which it is distinguished by its arched windows with their Gothic mullions.

The first architectural style to influence American courthouses in a big way was the Greek Revival. Pattern books reduced the style to formulae. Any builder who could build a house could enrich his repertoire with lessons from the books of Asher Benjamin and his contemporaries. Because most courthouses were built by local builders under the direction of the judges, and probably a committee of citizens, pattern books were an indispensable guide. The building commissioners appointed to direct the project had doubtless seen or heard about what was being built in the city. They had their impressions of what was stylish. *The Country Builder's Assistant*, by Benjamin, a Boston builder and

1-10. Barnstable County Courthouse, Barnstable, Massachusetts, interior of the court room, showing Greek Revival elements and preserving neoclassical elements of the original construction, 1831–32, which was expanded later. It is a notable adaptation, not restoration, of a courtroom in a historic building. (Photo: Nicholas Nixon, Seagram's Courthouse Project, Library of Congress)

WILLIAM SEALE

supplier, seems to have inspired the design of most courthouses from the late 1790s until the Civil War. It put into common language the modified British neoclassicism with which Charles Bulfinch had transformed Boston. Doorways, windows, brickwork, columns—all the elements were described in geometrical and mathematical terms, so that a builder could plot out, on board or paper, how to realize his, or the commissioners', design. Clients unfamiliar with building naturally had faith in the teachings of a practical builder who could prove his ideas with numbers. Benjamin did not invent the new Greek Revival fashion any more than Bulfinch did the Anglo-American mode, but he became its most popular promoter in print, especially at the grassroots level where most courthouses were built. The Barnstable Courthouse (1831) in Barnstable, Massachusetts (fig. 1-10) adapted the Doric order from the Parthenon, which had appeared just four years before in Benjamin's sixth edition of 1827. Already in South Carolina half a dozen Greek Revival courthouses were being built by Robert Mills, who had studied with James Hoban in Charleston and Washington and had been a draftsman for Jefferson at Monticello. Mills made the Greek Revival his own in South Carolina (even though scholars today attribute some of the original courthouse designs to the Englishman William Jay, then living in Savannah).[4] Mills's courthouses were delightfully proportioned, seeming smaller than they were, fronted with pediments and colonnades, Ionic or Doric, with important external stairs— some paired and curving, some straight —to the second, courtroom level. Offices and the brick-enclosed iron-strap vault—

1-11. St. Louis County Courthouse, St. Louis, Missouri, a remarkable Greek Revival pile intended probably to lure the state capital from Jefferson City. When built in the early 1830s it was the grandest courthouse in the United States. (Photo: c. 1900, Missouri Historical Society)

either jail or safe or one of each—were on the floor below.

The monumental portico of the Barnstable Courthouse shadows dressed-stone walls, and the exposed walls of the rest of the building are quarry-faced. This building is more architecturally correct than most that were to follow. By the time the Grecian idea reached St. Louis a decade later, the judges were so smitten with it that they removed a very fine courthouse in more or less the British "plain style" of John Soane to make way for the Greek Revival courthouse (1839–61) that still stands, facing the great arch and park (fig. 1-11). It is fully developed in the American Grecian form—box with portico—that was to characterize public buildings for half a century.

At St. Louis the structure rambles overflowingly, but somehow it remains logical because the basic plan is clear enough (see fig. 6-4). The central block

1-12. Claiborne Parish Courthouse, Homer, Louisiana. A neoclassical structure completed just before the Civil War, it resembles some of the planters' houses of the region, not quite any single style, but decidedly in a local vernacular. Rising from a flat terrace, the "Tuscan" columns are built of shaped brick, as are the walls, and are also covered with stucco. (Phoro: Louisiana Historical Commission)

follows the temple form with fluted Doric columns and pediment on both river and town front, protruding sufficiently so that the large side wings recede. A lofty and rather heavy dome is mounted at the crossing of wings and main block. When built, it was the primary landmark of St. Louis, flying high over all. The columned rotunda inside rivaled those in most state capitols of the time.

The American Greek Revival had some of its most satisfying expressions in courthouses of lesser aspiration. Within their Grecian confines they can be playfully free. Powhatan County Courthouse (1848–51) in Powhatan, Virginia is an example: Doric columns in antis beneath a deep "Doric" cornice of triglyphs form a chaste front, and pilasters executed in uncovered brick belt the sides, suggesting a temple form of ancient Greece without belaboring the point. The monumental Warren County Courthouse (1858–61) in Vicksburg, Mississippi, built just before the Civil War, overlooks the

Mississippi River unshrinkingly, presenting massive Ionic facades in plastered brick more gigantic and toppling tall than chaste, with a cupola/clock tower in stacked, columned stages. It is a magnificent building. In East Feliciana Parish, Louisiana, at Clinton, the parish courthouse, flat on the ground, has a surrounding colonnade that is like some of the famous plantation houses of the region, not temple style at all, yet another instance of the plasticity of the Greek revival. A smaller, equally delightful version of this type of columned building is found at the Claiborne Parish Courthouse (1850) in Homer, Louisiana (fig. 1-12).[5]

Greek revival courthouses were never more spectacular than that in Petersburg, Virginia (no county, an independent city), built 1838–40 (fig. 1-13). Set on a high hill, approached by broad steps, the courthouse features a Corinthian colonnade in antis, surmounted by a pediment. On the roof a steeple—it could be called nothing else—soars to thrilling height.[6] A somewhat similar example is the Old Orange County Courthouse (1841-42) at Goshen, New York, where most of the elements of the Petersburg Courthouse are present, but on a much less soaring scale and more weighted to the ground. It is a very satisfactory Greek Revival building in the temple style, surmounted by a slender adaptation of the Choragic Monument of Lysicrates. The relatively small courthouse (1847–50) at Dayton, in Montgomery County, Ohio (see fig. 1-3), follows the same general mode, with certain creative turns—such as the freestanding columns at each end of the rear elevation, set into niches created by scooping out the square corners—but is more academically Grecian. A marvel of fine materials, the entire structure is built of bearing stone vaults, with an inner dome. A tomblike solemnity pervades the dark interior.

The ultimate expression of the flexibility of the Greek revival is the Ross County Courthouse in Ohio, known as the Chillicothe Courthouse (1855). One even hesitates to call this sprawling pile Greek Revival, for although symmetrical, it otherwise flaunts the builder's bold liberties with plasticity, using shallow arches, heroic columns but not of an order, and ornament in a rococo vein. It seems almost a foreshadowing of the neo-grec of the later 1860s and 1870s, yet it is not. However, seen in the long line of nineteenth-century courthouses, it can be called transitional. The Chillicothe Courthouse sides up to one main street, on a corner, and faces another in a broad-armed, sprawling composition that must have seemed odd to the eyes of the 1850s. It contained all the county offices. The courtroom upstairs is a splendid space, occupying the central section of the main building, rich in florid ornamentation in plaster, wood, and cast iron, with gilt and elegant paint.

Departures from the Grecian norm were well underway as the walls of the Chillicothe Courthouse were rising. Most of these departures represented strains of style more than taste-changing innovation. Fredericksburg, Virginia (also an independent city) built a Gothic-style courthouse in 1851–55. A similar courthouse, looking rather more like a church, was built 1854–60 in Decatur County, Greensburg, Indiana. Real change came, however, with the Civil War and the spread of a new stylistic viewpoint toward building. Like most

1-13. Petersburg Courthouse, Petersburg, Virginia, was built in the 1830s and presented on its hilltop a dramatic announcement of the city it serves. The lantern pulls the building dramatically from the earthbound and is also a tower for viewing the countryside. It is surmounted by a zinc statue of Justice. (Photo: Mathew Brady, 1865, Library of Congress)

new tastes, the new one was partly a reaction against the Greek Revival and a more general supposed rejection of "imitative" styles of the past. This style also took its cues, however, from the past and traditional architecture as interpreted anew in other countries, notably the Gothic and various vernaculars inspired by Italian modes.

More significant was the architecture of the French empire of Napoleon III. During the Second Empire France underwent an explosion of public building, providing a sumptuous series of models for Europe and America. Inspired by the glory of the past, French architects, working in a time of great prosperity, looked to create a new architecture. It was a mixture drawn from historic

1-14. Philadelphia City Hall, John McArthur, Jr., 1872. (Etching by Joseph Pennell, 1912, Library of Congress)

cially in larger towns and cities.[7] It reached its popular apogee, perhaps, in Alfred B. Mullet's State, War & Navy Building in Washington, built to combine those three departments under one roof next to the White House.[8] Although this mighty building of granite that fills its site so heavily was out of style almost by the time it was finished, it cast a long shadow in public building even as it was being built. Mullet's federal courthouse and post office in New York, now demolished, and John McArthur Jr.'s Philadelphia City Hall (also a courthouse, fig. 1-14), which remains standing, both from the 1870s, join State, War & Navy as being the most opulent expressions of Second Empire France, as interpreted in America.

The response of the courthouse to the Second Empire mode in architecture was typically conservative yet representative enough of the fashions of the day to show that the architects were selling it well as "modern," and thus progressive, design. In Jacksonville, Illinois, the Morgan County Courthouse (ca.1868–69) was more loyal to French rules than most, in its pair of great mansard towers and the rich neo-baroque surfaces of its facades (fig. 1-15). An awkward version of this design was found in the Bartholomew County Courthouse (1871–74) in Columbus, Indiana, with one very heavy tower and a second, higher and thinner, both with mansard roofs and very tall. With this style the architect's imagination was freer to take flight than with the archeological styles, taking designs into the fanciful, yet with little apparent understanding of the parent concept conceived in France.

In the last third of the nineteenth century the immense population increase in

themes in design that created the building art and interior design of the Second Empire. In the United States the popularity of this approach was seen before the Civil War mostly in private houses. However, its appearance in the Boston City Hall just after the close of the war, and the masterful way in which that building fit the existing urban scene, addressing the street, not the skyline, fixed the style in civic architecture from the late 1850s until the early twentieth century, espe-

WILLIAM SEALE

the United States and the breakup of old counties into smaller ones, as well as the creation of new counties in new or newer states, set off a boom in courthouse building that resounded loudest in the Midwest and West. It was to last well into the twentieth century. A history of Nevada, written in 1881, asked, "A King without a kingdom, a general without an army, a county without a Court House—What are they?"[9] Towns, perhaps even more than the counties they crowned, wished to proclaim their importance through a fine courthouse and gain the economic boon of county-seat designation. Some flamboyant, highly decorative courthouses made their appearance in this period. In a sense the old situation still applied: Some were built by accomplished builders and architects whereas others, indeed very many, were vernacular echoes of formal style, built by entrepreneurs eager to make money from a costly building project. In both cases the designs were likely to be interesting, and age, which is kind to most buildings, makes them more so.

The "Victorian" courthouses, 1870s– early 1900s, are the most recognizable of all American courthouses. Still, the variety among them is greater than with any other architectural genre. After a century and more, particularly the western ones still speak of pioneer optimism and the glorious triumph perceived in the settlement of the frontier. These courthouses ornament their town squares, often heavily decorated outside with stone trimmings, colored slate roofs, towers, and carvings, and far less ambitious interiors. They were nearly all originally one courthouse under one roof, with no annexes, except perhaps the jail. The grounds around them were scattered

with monuments by several generations of people who loved commemorative monuments, be they to the Revolution, the Civil War, or, later, the wars of the twentieth century.

Most of these are found in the Midwest, Southwest, and West, especially Illinois, Indiana, Michigan, Iowa, Texas, Colorado, Nevada, and California. They stand tall on the landscape, even today when they are buried or crowded by tall commercial structures. A beau ideal of these vernacular courthouses, one that speaks for them all, is the Tarrant County Courthouse in Fort Worth, Texas, completed in 1894 (fig. 1-16) Its design is an intense but orderly mix of Second Empire and the later "free classic" of the 1880s and 1890s. Placed at one end of Fort Worth's restored downtown, it still sounds a bold voice, even among later, larger buildings. This kind of statement is what courthouses were always meant to make.

1-15. Morgan County Courthouse, Jacksonville, Illinois, begun c. 1868, was built of quarry-faced limestone and is an early example of the massive architecture that would characterize courthouses for the balance of the century. (Photo: Lewis Kostiner, Seagram's Courthouse Project, Library of Congress)

Victorian courthouse styles varied, but there were regional concentrations. In Shelbyville, Texas, in the thick forests near the western border of Louisiana, the Gothic Revival Shelby County Courthouse (see fig. 1-22) is worthy of 1840 but surprising to find near turn of the twentieth century, when it was actually built. The splendor of the Marshall County Courthouse (1884–86) in Marshalltown, Iowa—Second Empire is probably the closest name for it— approached the palatial, a monumental house of justice and administration fashioned in various textures of stone, topped by a square clock tower that

1-17. Old Ramsey County Courthouse and City Hall, St. Paul, Minnesota, Edward Payson Bassford, c. 1895. The courthouse presented a highly vertical rendition of the late-nineteenth-century mode and announced its public purposes from a distance, but up close it had the feel of a commercial building. The style is a pumped-up version of what was rendered in smaller courthouses all over the West. It was demolished in the late 1920s, before anyone even considered restoring such Victorian structures, and was soon replaced by a more modern building (see fig. 1-32). (Minnesota Historical Society)

1-18. Salt Lake County Courthouse, Salt Lake City, Utah, begun 1891, is a colossal spectacle even in a city commanded by a magnificent state capitol. The massive pile of stone seems to borrow from the Mormon tradition of stupendous architectural showmanship, not least from the soaring temple not far away. Immense and romantic, the courthouse is notable among American public buildings. (Photo 1904, Library of Congress)

greeted the railroad trains from across the land. Castlelike Whitley County Courthouse in Columbia City, Indiana, seems a reversion to the past, although the oak woodwork and colorful tiles of the interior unmask its 1880s construction period. The frothy Merced County Courthouse in Merced, California, 1868, is an echo of the then new state capitol in Sacramento, and thereby also reflects the national Capitol in Washington.[10]

These are exceptions. The Victorian courthouses were typically romantic piles that formed irregular outlines and were made of stone, preferably, or brick. It is difficult to label most of them by

1-19. Van Wert Courthouse, Van Wert, Ohio. Built in the middle 1870s in the style known usually as Second Empire, it shows the triple towers popularized in the New Louvre in Paris (1852–57). Courthouses in this style could be ornamental, like this one, or very plain. The original entrance here has been removed and new access created through the ground floor. (Photo: Lewis Kostiner, Seagram's Courthouse Project, Library of Congress)

improved printing technology. They described important buildings then being built, such as the Petit Palace in Paris and the Victor Emmanuel II monument in Rome. Several journals, in particular *The American Architect and Building News* (founded 1876), *Architectural Review* (1891), and *The Architectural Record* (1891), kept apace with the latest in architectural style and planning. Still, one rarely knows the actual source of design of a courthouse—a puzzle all the more mysterious for those built without schooled architects, whose ideas are usually easier to anticipate. Henry-Russell Hitchcock found the courthouse in Van Wert County, Van Wert, Ohio (1874–76) more akin to the buildings of the time of Louis XIII than of Napoleon III, which were apparently the models in mind (fig. 1-19).[11]

A Second Empire strain was evident in some Victorian courthouses well through the later nineteenth century. The effect could be quite whimsical, as in the Hancock County Courthouse, which made an alien sort of appearance in the early 1880s among the antebellum Greek Revival mansions of Sparta, Georgia (fig. 1-20). Completed in 1883, the building thrusts a bold pedimented centerpiece forward from a squarish, mansarded block; above the tall mass of the structure emerges a cupola—a rather exotic piece in itself—certifying that this is a courthouse instead of an opera house, perhaps, or a hotel.

Sometimes heavy external arches used in Victorian courthouse design make us call the buildings "Richardsonian," after the work of H. H. Richardson in the East, with their heavy stone construction and grand arches, all contained within a massive body. Richardson's

style. The influences are European, distantly, in an American tongue then fairly general to other sorts of public buildings. One can speculate safely that most of the designs bear heavy influences from what the architect or builder or judge had seen built somewhere else; the image might have transferred vaguely, with no demand for formal exactness. Books, magazines, and journals on architectural subjects were available in the later nineteenth century, increasingly more clearly illustrated thanks to

Allegheny County Courthouse in Pittsburgh, by which the architect hoped the world would remember him, was completed in 1888, after his death, and is true to his form (fig. 1-21; see figs. 5-1–5-4). Its rich, arched stonework, boldly structural, creates a sort of wrapping for a distinctly civic building, yet one with the romance of an abstract sort of distant past, a certain gloom and mystery. It is extremely exciting architecture set in the dense downtown of Pittsburgh.

The courthouse vernacular of the late nineteenth century was rich in towers, arcades, various patterns of windows, and stone (or brick, if not stone). Interiors as rich as the county could afford featured ceramic and encaustic tiles, polished oak woodwork carved to the budget's limit, ironwork, stained glass, fine brass gas lights, and maybe custom-made public-building furniture from the factories of Chicago. Architects moved

1-20. Hancock County Courthouse, Sparta, Georgia, 1881–83, combines several architectural styles, notably the Second Empire and Italianate of about twenty years earlier. The lofty courtroom occupies the second floor with the tall windows. It appears to have been designed as it was built, and time has given it charm, set in an old town filled with early houses. (Photo: Jim Dow, Seagram's Courthouse Project, Library of Congress)

1-21. Allegheny County Courthouse, Pittsburgh, Pennsylvania. The masterpiece designed by H. H. Richardson was definitive of his style. Completed in 1888, well after Richardson's death, the courthouse makes a firm statement: fortresslike, to protect recorded history, and overpowering, to emphasize the superiority of law. This detail shows a Richardson device inspired by the Bridge of Sighs in Venice—a closed passageway spanning the street between the courthouse, where justice was dispensed, and the jail. (Photo: William Clift, Seagram's Courthouse Project, Library of Congress)

1-22. Shelby County Courthouse, Center, Texas, completed in 1885, a "castle" where one might least expect whimsy, especially in a public building, is set in the deep forests of a small East Texas county seat. It is built of brick and is of a type more familiar in the 1840s. (Photo c. 1912, University of Texas Library)

1-23. World's Columbian Exposition, Chicago, Administration Building, Richard Morris Hunt, 1893. (Library of Congress)

from county to county selling these ideas. Elijah E. Myers of Detroit must surely have been the most flamboyant. Designer of state capitols, train stations, asylums, and churches, he also designed courthouses in Illinois and Michigan. His tastes seem to have been seeded when he worked as a carpenter under the tutelage of the imaginative Samuel Sloane of Philadelphia, architect of the Lancaster County Courthouse in Lancaster, Pennsylvania, and original architect of the Philadelphia City Hall before he lost to McArthur in two competitions. Myers brought rich and varied adornment to many buildings; he was an artist of sorts, with the checked-suits-and-spats approach of a traveling salesman.

A more prolific designer of Victorian courthouses—if, however, no rival to Myers as a designer—was J. Riely Gordon, headquartered ultimately in San Antonio, who first built Richardsonian sorts of courthouses, then branched out. These two architects, and many more, were building the first civic expressions in architecture in most of the places to which they were drawn. The lure of the courthouse market in a vast and newly settled land was irresistible. With fleet feet provided by the railroads, they conducted their work in many states, foreshadowing the "national" architectural practices of the century to come.

Style is fickle in the popular eye. No event in American architecture ever made a more profound impression upon the general public than the World's Columbian Exposition of 1893, commonly remembered as the Chicago World's Fair (fig. 1-23). The event was housed in a great visionary "city" of plaster that was an essay in how civilized a real city might be—a City Beautiful. Absent were the muddy, dark streets and rank odors of waste common to American cities; clean, pure, bright electric light fell upon the fair's spotless streets and walkways, clipped lawns, and inspiring monuments. The architecture was predominantly neo-Renaissance in character and deemed appropriate to civic architecture by both citizens and architects. Hundreds of thousands of Americans went home with the image of the White City burned in their memory. The architecture of the fair was quickly applied to courthouses.

It was not that neoclassical courthouses were not built between the late 1860s and the 1890s, for they were. The Tuscarawas County Courthouse (1882–85) in New Philadelphia, Ohio, with its large dome/clock tower, is certainly neoclassical. Vanderburgh County Courthouse (completed 1891), in the old steamboat manufacturing capital of Evansville, Indiana, is dramatically neoclassical. But these buildings are what was called in their time "free classic" and should not be confused with the academicism of the fair buildings. The Evansville courthouse—one of the finest in the nation—makes every effort to be French, and its academic details are many, yet the composition has an animation that is more characteristic of the Victorian courthouses, of which, chronologically at least, it is certainly one.

The neoclassical architecture of the fair is identified with the Ecole des Beaux-Arts in Paris, a leading institution for the training of architects at the time. "Beaux-Arts" does not technically identify one style but refers to the adoption of motifs and ideas of the past into new architecture. In the eyes of its practitioners it was not an antiquarian approach.

1-24. Dallas County Courthouse, Adel, Iowa, completed 1902, provides a compromise between the many-faceted Victorian courthouse and the European proclivities of the Beaux-Arts. The building essentially is a rendition of the chateau style of smooth planes and towers; its tower block bears little relation to the rest, is far more ornamental, and simply says *courthouse*. (Photo: Robert Thall, Seagram's Courthouse Project, Library of Congress)

Its era was one of almost incredible technological improvements in transportation and human comfort. Buildings offered greater convenience than ever before, a convenience achieved through machinery. The Beaux-Arts ideal espoused acceptance of every modern innovation, reconciling these improvements with what its creators judged the best designs of the past. Moreover, the Beaux-Arts architects welcomed collaboration with painters, sculptors, and other artists and craftspeople.

French aspects of the Beaux-Arts courthouses were well represented at the turn of the century in the chateau-style Spokane County Courthouse (1895) in Spokane, Washington and the pared-down, vastly simplified version of about the same thing in the Dallas County Courthouse (1902) in Adel, Iowa (fig. 1-24), both suggesting architecture in the French style known as Francis I. Monroe County, Rochester, New York gained an

1-25. Essex County Courthouse, interior view, Newark, New Jersey, Cass Gilbert, 1902–7. (Photo: Stephen Shere, Seagram's Courthouse Project, Library of Congress)

The large architectural firms in New York and Chicago, in particular, maintained offices and drafting rooms peopled with young men, and sometimes women, often educated at the Ecole des Beaux-Arts. To have even suggested calling them "historical" architects or characterizing their designs as "historical" would have been an affront. Somehow, in their curious credo, they were able to escape believing that they leaned heavily on the past. Principals of these firms, well versed in the idea, spent considerable time marketing for courthouse projects. Yet the influence of the famous architectural firms upon the design of courthouses was greater than their actual involvement. They went after the large courthouse jobs, but the long and costly processes of negotiation proved impractical, and they usually lost anyway in the local political antics that naturally accompany expensive public building projects.

An exception was Cass Gilbert, gifted designer of the Gothic Woolworth Building in New York and of the Corinthian colonnaded white marble Supreme Court in Washington, D.C. A very aggressive businessman, he was still a young architect from the Midwest, just after the turn of the century, when he gained the job as architect for the granite Essex County Courthouse in Newark, New Jersey (fig. 1-25). The result is typically Gilbert; an opulent neo-Renaissance building sumptuously decorated inside with murals by Edwin Blashfield, Kenyon Cox, and others. James Gamble Rogers, in his day as well known as Gilbert, designed the Shelby County Courthouse in Memphis, Tennessee, a near copy of Robert Mills's 1830s United States Treasury in Washington, D.C., although to call it Greek

Italian palazzo (completed 1896) beautifully executed in stone. World's Fair neoclassicism dominates the domed Allen County Courthouse (1897–1902) in Fort Wayne, Indiana, an urban building, very heavy and intense in its academic detailing. The Utah County Courthouse (1899) in Provo, Utah is a less ambitious but more typical Beaux-Arts courthouse, with its tranquil Ionic portico and academic stone trimmings, together with a tympanum framing a parade of allegorical sculptures.

revival in the pure "Grecian" sense of
the treasury is a stretch (fig. 1-26). In his
Beaux-Arts framework he might suggest,
but never copy exactly.

Other architects who had national
reputations made Beaux-Arts marks on
courthouses around the country. J. Riely
Gordon, designer largely of western
courthouses, could be called a "courthouse architect." He adopted the Beaux-
Arts mode in 1900 when he designed
the august McLennan County Courthouse in Waco, Texas, with its neofederal
echoes of New York's old city hall.
Twenty years later he carried the general
idea to the Cortland County Courthouse
in Cortland, New York (fig. 1-27). Cumberland County Courthouse in Portland,
Maine, a stately marble pile in the
French Louis XVI tradition, was designed
by George Burnham with the assistance
of the well-known Boston architect Guy
Lowell (fig. 1-28).

Frederick DeLongchamps (or DeLong-
chant), designer of seven courthouses in
Nevada and two in California, was a distinguished architect without formal
training.[12] A mining engineer, he turned
to architecture when he served as an
apprentice draftsman in the rebuilding of
San Francisco after the earthquake. His
design of the Modoc County Courthouse
(1914) in Alturas, California is as fine as
any of the period, and, in the Beaux-Arts
way of thinking, not a copy of anything.
It is an octagonal, colonnaded building
of limestone crowned by a shallow
dome. It was natural, given the Beaux-
Arts philosophy that local building traditions might appear on public structures;
this had been the practice at least since
the 1880s in the East and was underway
in the West by the twentieth century.
The colonial revival had captured the

1-26. Shelby County Courthouse, Memphis, Tennessee, 1908, is based on Robert Mills's United States Treasury Building in Washington, D.C., which had been restored recently. The model recalled Jacksonian America and satisfied the modern taste for neoclassicism inspired by the Chicago World's Fair. (Tennessee State Archives)

1-27. Cortland County Courthouse, Cortland, New York, early 1920s. Resembling less a courthouse than a small state capitol, this courthouse follows the Beaux-Arts classicism popularized at the World's Fair in Chicago thirty years before and not entirely gone from American taste by the twenties. (Photo: Patrick Linehan, Seagram's Courthouse Project, Library of Congress)

1-28. Cumberland County Court House, Portland, Maine, 1910. The interior presented a civic statement with its allegorical murals and classical detailing. (Library of Congress)

1-29. Santa Barbara County Courthouse, Santa Barbara, California, 1927–29, in the "Spanish" style inspired by the Santa Barbara mission. (Photo: Tod Papageorge, Seagram's Courthouse Project, Library of Congress)

suburban eye, and "Cape Cod cottages" were only less likely to appear in Montana than in New England. Spanish colonial design was all over California and the West.

Subsequent world fairs introduced different regional designs. The Jamestown, Virginia, three-hundredth anniversary fair in 1907 featured replicas and adaptations of historic houses. At San Diego's 1914 Panama–California Exposition the main architectural motif was the Spanish style of the eighteenth-century mission chain Spain had built along the Pacific.[13] Rich in stucco massing and stone trim, with tile roofs, the mode was seldom more charmingly expressed than in the Santa Barbara County Courthouse (fig. 1-29). Built 1927–29 immediately following the seminal restoration of Mission Santa Barbara, mission and courthouse gave the town of Santa Barbara its design key, which it has assiduously maintained. Frederick DeLongchamps designed such a structure for the Nevada State Building, only on a larger scale. His was a long, serene tile-roof edifice that had arcades stretching to pedimented wings with classic Spanish frontispieces to the main windows.

Nativism became an important theme in courthouse design in the 1910s and 1920s, reflecting a certain hunger for the regional and local traditions that had seemed obliterated by the European leanings of the Beaux-Arts. The growing urban character of some county seats heralded the appearance of the skyscraper—most not really as tall as the word suggests, but high downtown buildings nonetheless. The vertical look had excited public architecture, as manifested in such buildings as the Nebraska State Capitol, introduced in 1919 and

WILLIAM SEALE

completed in 1932. Because the idea seemed modern and practical, it gained support in the Depression years as an appropriate civic architecture. Rather apologetically, the skyscraper courthouse was always accompanied by a nativist art program, usually calling for murals representing Indian and pioneer life. These were very popular in the western courthouses, but were present to an extent everywhere.

First to make the skyscraper effort was Sioux City, Iowa, where Woodbury County commissioners, in 1918, completed a five-story square structure crowned by a central "skyscraper" of seven more stories plus a penthouse (fig. 1-30). This building, which actually slightly predated the better-known and highly influential Nebraska capitol, was heavily adorned within and without in the nativist way. It presents a memorable interior indeed, using Roman brick and somewhat Sullivanesque carvings. Maricopa County Court House in Arizona, built ten years later, gave Phoenix some semblance of a skyscraper in nine stories. Jefferson County Courthouse (1935), in Beaumont, Texas, executed in orange brick with decorative plaques in limestone and detailing in bronze and aluminum, is a skyscraper courthouse that an oil-rich community made more splendid than most county courthouses (fig. 1-31). The skyscraper idea continued, although not in profusion. Inevitably, the commercial tone of the skyscraper clashed with the traditional idea of a courthouse; skyscrapers seemed related to the money crowd and not philosophically aloof, as would befit a seat of justice.

Beaux-Arts tradition persisted in courthouse design through the Depres-

1-30. Woodbury County Courthouse, Sioux City, Iowa, interior view, William Steele, 1918. (Photo: Robert Thall, Seagram's Courthouse Project, Library of Congress)

sion, when federal funds were lavished upon public buildings both to help localities and as symbols of nationalism in a system commanded from the top more than ever before. By this time the Beaux-Arts usually was served up in a variation stripped down to simplicity of line and form, divesting itself of any identifiable historically imitative elements. Through this process, courthouse architecture had a brief flirtation with Art Moderne. The Colonial Revival was its arch rival. Moderne and the geometrical Art Deco ornament that was likely to accompany it

1-31. Jefferson County Courthouse, Beaumont, Texas, 1935, followed the Art Deco idea for an all-inclusive county building. The skyscraper form is styled in a slightly pyramidal form here, with the massing serving a broad base and telescoping to heighten the effect of the tower. Little interior function is expressed externally. Courtrooms were on the lower floors, along with county offices, and the tower was crowned with a jail. (Mildred Powell Hall)

were entrenched by the late 1920s and became mixed in courthouse design during the Depression. Art Moderne in character but slightly pre-New Deal was the Ramsey County Courthouse (1931–32) at St. Paul, Minnesota, which is also the St. Paul City Hall (fig. 1-32). The dimly lighted grand corridor, with its shimmering white statue and dark, shiny, marble walls reminds one of the stark white-on-white fantasy sets from some movies of the time.

Cochise County Courthouse (1931) in Bisbee, Arizona followed the Art Moderne mode, with details in the decorative style of the Art Deco, its external form suggesting the contour of the mountain that rises behind it. Orleans Parish Courthouse (completed 1931) in New Orleans houses the criminal courts in a rather formidable and severe building of similar

character, reflecting the era of Governor Huey Long, who made the Moderne his unofficial style. The Colfax County Courthouse (1936) in Raton, New Mexico gives the usual Moderne a quite compatible, slightly pueblo look, whereas the Wakulla County Court House (1949) in Crawfordsville, Florida, with its restrained, reeded pilasters and simple planes, represents a style that had become nearly universal in public building but had faded by the early 1950s.

Modernism made its first appearance in remodeling rather than new construction in the later 1950s. The San Diego County Courthouse, in San Diego, California, begun at the end of the 1950s, for example, is a vast structure with low towers at each end of a long expanse of white building, varying pierced concrete with vast blank planes. This design is a mild version of the International Style, which was usually simply called "Modern." The style held sway particularly in the 1960s and 1970s, and many an earlier courthouse suffered from the intrusion of unhappy additions. Indeed, by the late 1950s there was almost a mania for this Modern style, rivaling that for the Victorian buildings a century before. As though an echo of the Marshall Plan of 1948–1952, with which it was for a time contemporary, Modern architecture favored clearing the site and starting over. At times the Modern mentality carried a religious sort of fervor, with its commitment to the certainty that modern meant improvement. Its adherents were likely to turn on their rare critics, such as Lewis Mumford, with all the liberality of Father Torquemada toward heretics during the Inquisition.

Plain often to coldness, Modern public buildings featured expanses of marble panels, marble or terrazzo floors, smooth plaster, and windowless courtrooms paneled in flush sheets of mahogany, walnut, and other woods. Frank Lloyd Wright spoke his piece in the Marin County Courthouse in California, an impractical but compelling building strongly in the Modern vein but with Wright's characteristic personal turn of design (fig. 1-33). Visually it is more varied and thus more interesting than most. Few counties are willing to come up with the money, however, for so artistic a building; few busy judges will tolerate such a mercurial artist.

Modern courtrooms, and particularly Modern ceremonial interiors, were seldom satisfactory; of course, today they suffer the handicap of being just lately out of style. The state supreme courtroom (1970) in Columbus, Ohio, a con-

fection in red, had a fine interior with a theatrical quality in a strict adherence to Modern maxims (a successor is shown in fig. 1-34).[14] In Los Angeles the courtroom made familiar by the O. J. Simpson trial is more typical of the Modern genre—indeed, rather a vernacular—and, broadcast all over the world, illustrated very clearly the weaker points of Modern design in a courtroom. In the 1980s a strong reaction against these courtrooms came particularly from the judges of the federal courts. The public, it seems, could not "read" in these Mod-

1-32. Ramsey County Courthouse and City Hall, St. Paul, Minnesota, completed 1932, replaced an earlier Victorian structure (see fig. 1-17). The interior is highly dramatic, clothing the Beaux-Arts forms in the fashionable Art Moderne and Art Deco of the 1930s. Expensive materials and contrasting textures combine with lighting effects to create good theater indeed, but while such effects are not unusual in civic architecture, these seem ephemeral, at least for a courthouse. (Photo: Frank Gohlke, Seagram's Courthouse Project, Library of Congress)

ern courtrooms the formal layering of authority of court persona; the designs of the rooms actually led to confusion, which hampered proceedings. A Massachusetts judge ordered his courtroom rebuilt to resemble, large scale, a colonial courtroom, which he said was better suited to the conduct court business than any other form he knew.

Others have agreed. The architectural community, or that part of it privileged to design courthouses, hurried to try to accommodate the new point of view. When in 1990 the General Services Administration of the federal government began a ten-year $10 billion project to build fifty to sixty new federal courthouses, the race was on. The first effort was focused on the federal courthouse on

Boston Bay, a curved, ten-story structure of brick in which all the courtrooms, although themselves windowless, open on glazed terraces, gathering places for spectators, overlooking bay and city (see figs. C-9, 4-13, 4-14). Henry N. Cobb was the designer, and two federal judges, Douglas P. Woodlock and Stephen G. Breyer (contributors to this book), were intimately involved in the design and wished for the new building to embody the traditions of the past, no matter its style. The architect was inspired by the Royal Courts of Justice in London (1874–82), where the various courtrooms open at levels off a grand general concourse.[15] The building, nevertheless, is essentially Modern, and it remains to be seen if innovation here will serve practicality sufficiently to make this a model for other courthouses.

Beyond question, the most interesting court buildings today are not in the United States. Japan's Supreme Court in Tokyo is a formidable rock of a structure, rising from the busy city's heart and seeming almost like a natural outcropping, its interior well within the rugged protection of masonry confines (see fig. 4-18). The Supreme Court building of Israel at Jerusalem, with its powerful references to ancient Roman architecture in the Holy Land, may be one of the most beautiful courthouses of our time (see fig. 4-19)—though it may be borne in mind that a supreme court's requirements are not as complex as those even of a county court or of other lower courts. However, a supreme court building or courtroom, with its emphasis upon symbolism, may cost more. The new American federal court buildings also cost hundreds of millions and must have the everyday capacity to house

1-33. Marin County Courthouse (Marin County Civic Center), San Raphael, California. Designed by Frank Lloyd Wright and completed in 1964 after his death, this was considered a work of art from the outset. It is a fascinating building; from one perspective it is rather like a great bridge crossing a valley, but as a courthouse it is inconvenient, and structurally it has presented endless problems. (Photo: Pirkle Jones, Seagram's Courthouse Project, Library of Congress)

WILLIAM SEALE

almost unimaginable loads of work, with many courtrooms, chambers, and offices. To that must be added present-day requirements of security. To compare them with the relatively diminutive courthouses of the American past is difficult outside the courtrooms themselves.

As with most American architecture today, the trend toward historic preservation has identified the courthouse as a major monument to preserve for both its architecture and its use. Public approbation and federal and state funding have empowered the conservation and preservation of hundreds of courthouses. The results are not always felicitous. Qualified restoration architects and builders are very few in the United States, although the claimants are many. Uninformed clients hire the latter unknowingly and are led down a primrose path. Buildings "restored" too often show that their practitioners were unaware of, or did not comprehend, the nuances of the original architecture, and buildings are bent into something they never were in the past. This misdirection can happen in ways subtle and in ways bold, but in any case the result should be labeled *remodeling*, not restoration or preservation. Modern and inappropriate details of material, lighting, finish, and other elements too often diminish the historical impact of the courtrooms and corridors, the wish for which led to the restoration in the first place. However, for all the shortcomings one sometimes encounters in the preservation of courthouses, the American courthouse is safer from demolition today than ever in its past. Natural disaster seems the greatest threat, as in the January 1999 destruction of the Clarksville, Tennessee, Courthouse by a tornado and the 2001

1-34. Supreme Court Chamber, Columbus, Ohio. Housed in a former office building completed by the state in 1932, this former hearing room was adapted for the Supreme Court of Ohio 1999–2004. The Venetian-flavored Art Moderne style of the room was retained and restored by Schoole–Caldwell, Associates, architects for the renovation.

destruction by fire of the plain old castle courthouse in Newton, Texas.

What one hopes for when courthouses are brought to modern standards is that the integrity of the existing building is defined sufficiently to maintain it at all costs. This is not a difficult challenge. The key is a sensitive level of understanding of the building and how it evolved. Key also is a keen perception of how the building speaks to citizens—what are its greatest extant attributes? Most of what we lose in our courthouses is lost through ignorance. In the twenty-first century, it happens that most of our courthouses are old ones, built far enough in the past to represent history, with the elements of tradition usually intact. They have been expanded by annexes of nearly every imaginable kind, for they are very often too small to serve their various purposes alone. Some are used only as a seat for the court, with other functions elsewhere. Yet remaining in use or reused and restored, the old courthouses seem to fulfill the needs of the jurisdiction. Most of all they enjoy a warm rapport with the citizens.

The only real and enduring formal ceremony in American society is attached to the courts of law. We are otherwise a culture that threw out ritual forms more than two centuries ago. Yet court ceremonies are stringently maintained because ceremony is practical and useful in a courtroom. It represents order and discipline, of course, not pomp. The judge's unchallenged author-ity demands a visual framework that expresses the hierarchy of the judicial process. Others below him or her perform in a prescribed, stratified framework. Even the United States Congress lacks staging as carefully defined as the courts. By world standards, the American system of government is very old; traditions in our courts have roots far predating the nation itself. New York's courts, for example, celebrated their three-hundredth anniversary several years ago. American life has been shaped to an extent in courtrooms, largely on the local level, physically close to the citizen. The response of successful courthouse builders to the challenge of housing this basic part of the system of government has taken forms less surprising in their variety than in their adherence, no matter the costume or style, to what has been established before. If we have learned one lesson about courthouses in the last half of the twentieth century, it is this.

TWO

The Image of the Courthouse

FRANK GREENE

The image of the American courthouse, "musing, brooding, symbolic and ponderable," in Faulkner's words, has become a more complex expression that reflects the dynamics of our ever-changing society. Once simply a symbol of the lofty regard of the citizenry for its instrument of public order, the design of a courthouse today must resolve paradoxes of security and openness, privacy and public gesture, grandeur and economy, stasis and change. No longer simply the Temple of Jupiter aloof on its acropolis, as in Cass Gilbert's United States Supreme Court (see figs. C-1, FW-1, and FW-2), the courthouse has now become, in many ways, the Marketplace of Due Process in the agora with the masses (fig. 2-1).

Many new courthouses are being designed by leading architects, with often-spectacular results. Although it remains to be seen just what degree of public acceptance will greet the more daring of these new buildings, many of the current crop of courthouses challenge traditional assumptions about the form of public buildings and perceptions of the nature of the justice system. The sheer quantity of new courthouses recently completed and in development today is unprecedented, and the ambition of their designers surprising, even astonishing.

With the advent of Richard Rogers's 1998 addition to a historic courthouse in Bordeaux, France (see figs. C-14, 4-22, 4-23, and 4-24), the boundaries of what has heretofore been considered appropriate imagery have been swept aside. In their place are new opportunities for expression of the values that our society associates with our justice system and its embodiment in the courthouse. These values may be characterized as principles of *transparency, accessibility,* and *civic engagement.*

The philosophy driving this work is an outgrowth of a tradition of modernist experimentation that has occupied artistic energies for the last century. Postmodernism's withering critique of midcentury modernism for its sterility and antihumanism reinvigorated rather than destroyed the Modern movement, leaving it renewed and richer in expres-

sion. From an experiential point of view these new buildings seek to delight their users; magical qualities of light, materiality, and spatial variety appeal to the senses and the intellect. The best of the new buildings serve as potent metaphors of public institutions that value their relevance to current concerns of fairness, environmental responsibility, and urban revitalization.

Thus the reasons for the excellence of the best of the new work are far more than a matter of style. The new structures can be seen as self-referential sculptures, interpretations of existing precedents, or even abstractions of landscape features; yet they exhibit a common awareness of the need to address the principles fundamental to the rule of law in a democracy. I hope to demonstrate how such disparate buildings, including those that employ traditional architectural languages, may be understood as wrestling with the same issues and aspirations.

Transparency

More than simply glass walls, the phenomenon of transparency, both literal and symbolic, is a defining metaphor of a critical need in gaining public trust in the judicial system. With an alienated populace in many cities in long-simmering conflict with the law enforcement and judicial systems, the legal process itself has suffered diminished stature to much of the public. With the testimony of police officers often discounted by juries and most convictions arrived at through plea-bargaining deals, overcrowded, obsolete buildings themselves embody a justice system that lacks the resources to fairly weigh evidence and provide due process to citizens.

The traditional elements of American courthouses—their massive masonry construction, opacity, blocklike massing, and heroically scaled public porticos, staircases, and sculptural elements rendered in the authoritative language of neoclassical architecture—expressed the power of the law but did little to communicate concern for the place of citizens in the workings of the process. Grandeur has often overwhelmed humanism, and overcrowding and deterioration of the building due to deferred maintenance often amplify the sense of being in the presence of an uncaring, aloof, and unaccountable bureaucracy.

To help address this crisis of confidence in the Bronx, New York, Rafael Viñoly Architects was retained to design a new criminal courthouse. Located on the Grand Concourse, the site is near the forbidding limestone pile of the Merola Courthouse of 1934, which was the setting for the climax of Tom Wolfe's *Bonfire of the Vanities.* The new courthouse is intended to relieve the Merola Courthouse of its criminal caseload (fig. 2-2).

The project goals included (1) symbolizing the dignity and traditions of the judicial system, (2) delivering services with renewed efficiency, and (3) communicating a new openness and accountability of the court to its community. In the initial enthusiasm for this initiative, community groups proposed the inclusion of ground-floor retail, a day-care center, community access to the jury assembly hall for public functions, and incorporation of a high school for careers in the justice system. The initial design schemes included many of these features, and the design of the 75-courtroom building that emerged was low-rise, spanned a city street, and was entirely clad in glass, allowing daylight to penetrate all spaces of the building.

With the events of the Oklahoma City and first World Trade Center bombings, concerns for the vulnerability of civic structures forced the resetting of these ambitions. In response, Viñoly's redesign included closing the street and eliminating nonjudicial uses from the program,

2-2. Street-level view of the new Criminal Courthouse in Bronx, New York, Rafael Viñoly Architects, 2005. (Photo: Rafael Viñoly Architects)

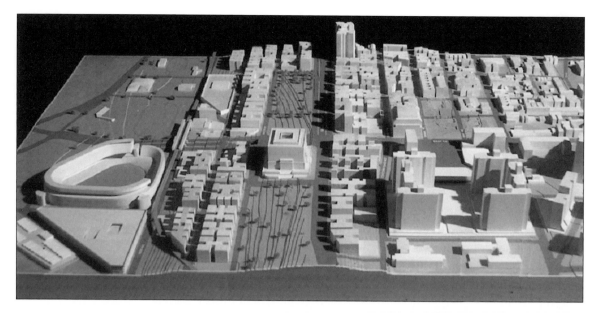

but the glass skin was retained. It was hardened to a ballistic-resistant level, and its literal transparency transformed to gradations of clear, transparent, and opaque. Thus, the essential message of the new Bronx criminal courthouse—a justice system open to public scrutiny, inclusive of public participation, and dependent on the support and protection of its community—remains unchanged (figs. 2-3 and 2-4).

Given the requirements for security, the secret nature of jury deliberations, and the private and contemplative nature of the intellectual work of the court, such as consideration of written

FRANK GREENE

briefs, the notion of an all-glass court-house might seem an overreaction to the call for openness and accountability. Many new courthouses have exploited the contrast between their transparent and opaque programmatic elements in an expression that creates a narrative that more accurately represents the workings of the process.

Such a duality of expression charac-terizes Henry Cobb's design for the fed-eral courthouse in Boston, a result of extensive public debate about site, orien-tation, and amenities (fig. 2-5). The major design gesture is a concave glazed public hall that both presents the court-room entrances to downtown Boston, just across Fort Point channel, and sym-bolically brings the downtown into the courthouse by making it visible from within that public hall. The body of the building is a brick masonry exercise in neighborly congruence with the historic urban context of rapid gentrification of formerly industrial buildings. The figural space created by the building is a combi-nation of the glazed public hall and the public park bounded by the hall's sweeping arc. What the massive brick walls of this structure frame is not a just a symbol of the power of the institution, but of the participation of the citizens in its exercise (fig. 2-6).

In a more traditional architectural expression, yet with a similar motiva-tion, Robert A. M. Stern's courthouse in Youngstown, Ohio places a glazed curv-ing colonnade at a gateway intersection at the edge of the central business dis-trict (fig. 2-7). This glass wall, convex where Cobb's is concave, and rendered in an interpretation of Youngstown's industrial roots, employs transparency to reveal the public circulation system of

2-5. View of new Boston Federal Courthouse from the waterfront park, Pei Cobb Freed & Partners, Architects, 1998. (Photo: Steve Rosenthal)

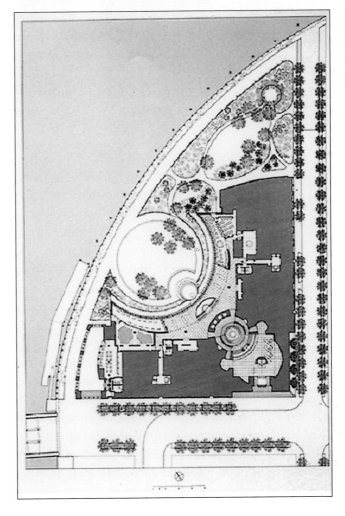

2-6. Site plan of the Boston Federal Court-house, showing rela-tion to the waterfront park.

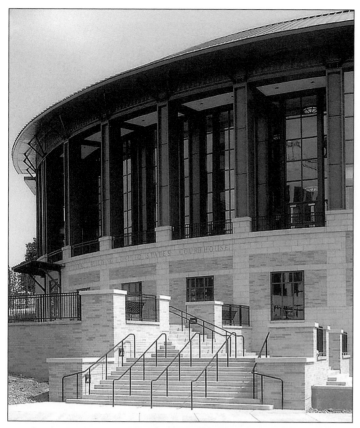

2-7. Entry stairs and portico of the United States Bankruptcy Courthouse in Youngstown, Ohio, Robert A. M. Stern, Architects, 2004.

2-8. Public stair, Bankruptcy Courthouse, Youngstown, Ohio.

the courthouse and to connect the experience of entering the courtroom to the main public impression of the building from curbside. The connection between exterior plaza, interior stair, great hall, and, finally, courtroom ennobles the public experience of movement through the building and, by extension, the place of the public in the process (fig. 2-8).

In an exquisitely crafted exercise in balancing transparency with opacity, Bohlin Cywinski Jackson's design for the new federal courthouse annex in Scranton, Pennsylvania both repeats the blocklike massing of the older building and inserts a light-filled glass atrium between the two blocks (fig. 2-9). Ricci-Greene's collaboration with Peter Bohlin and Frank Grauman resulted in a plan

built around an atrium that contains the public circulation for both buildings, allowing existing corridors to be used for private and secure circulation (figs. 2-10 and 2-11). Its transparency, as seen from the courthouse square across the street represents an invitation for public use. Its exaggerations of circulation elements within the atrium, a Piranesian array of stairs, bridges, overlooks, and glass elevators, signify a celebration of the public use of the courthouse.

Other recent examples of transparency used as a metaphor of openness include the design for the Wyoming County Courthouse in Warsaw, New York, where the addition of a new wing to a historic courthouse is defined by its rotunda and its "front porch," which faces a green

FRANK GREENE

2-9. View from Lackawanna County Courthouse of the new annex (*left*) to the United States Courthouse in Scranton, Pennsylvania, Bohlin Cywinski Jackson, Architects, RicciGreene Associates, 1998. (Photo: Michael Thomas)

Below left:
2-10. Public atrium, Scranton federal courthouse.

Below right:
2-11. Entry lobby linking new and old buildings, Scranton federal courthouse.

2-13. View of entry rotunda, Wyoming
County Courthouse, Warsaw, New York.

commons linking the major public buildings of this rural county (fig. 2-12). The duality of the solidity of the older building and the transparency of the new heightens the attraction to the public zone of the new building, especially in the evening hours, when the public space glows. The views out from the public hall include the buildings and green spaces of the adjacent historic district, further reinforcing the link between the new building and its historic forebears (fig. 2-13).

New courthouses constructed as additions or adjacent structures to grand courthouses of distinguished architectural quality and high public regard must contend with the standard set by those structures, despite the diminished financial resources of many declining urban areas. In Syracuse, New York, a prosperous manufacturing center in the early part of the twentieth century with a suitably grand Beaux-Arts courthouse, the opportunity to construct a new courthouse to address the burgeoning needs of the criminal and family courts was

FRANK GREENE

nonetheless constrained by a severely limited budget. Through an exacting process that separated wants from needs, the program was reduced to its absolute essentials while retaining the generous circulation areas needed for the large number of users and for the separation of private and secure circulation streams from the public (fig. 2-14).

The budget still could accommodate only the most basic exterior and interior materials and building systems; a "stucco and sheetrock" courthouse. Presented this way to the county legislature and the public, the proposal generated an outcry that added monies to provide for a cast-stone masonry exterior, impervious finishes in the public areas, and infrastructure for present and future technology installations. The public demanded a courthouse that "looked like a courthouse, not a bus station."

The resulting building shares many features with the grand old building, such as its use of the stairs as a major architectural element. These are in the center of the old building and at the front edge of the new building to encourage use of the stairs and also to communicate the public nature of the building and its function. Both buildings have a portico at the front entrance. The old building's entry, elevated at the piano nobile level, is rendered useless by the Americans with Disabilities Act (ADA) requirements and the necessity for continual snow removal in winter months. The new building's portico is at grade, encompassing a glass entry hall, and makes a statement of convenience and openness. The enduring value of the renewed old courthouse is complemented by the state-of-the-art functionality of the new building, as are the complemen-

2-14. An entrance portico at grade that complements a distinguished structure of the previous century; addition to Onondaga County Courthouse, Syracuse, New York, Ashley McGraw Architects / RicciGreene Associates, 2004.

tary symbolic messages of the two structures: one grand, aloof, difficult to enter, but beautifully crafted, the other more modest, accessible, and easy to navigate (figs. 2-15 and 2-16).

Accessibility

The ADA codified the principle that buildings should not present architectural barriers to their use by physically disabled persons. Its enactment profoundly changed the character of civic buildings. In particular, it made an anachronism of the ancient architectural device of elevating important floors above street level and celebrating the transition through dramatic stairs.

Parallel with this influence on courthouse tradition, the proliferation of civil litigation, the drug-fueled rise in criminal

2-15. The Syracuse Beaux-Arts predecessor courthouse, as seen from the new building's entrance staircase, a feature shared with the older structure.

2-16. More modest and accessible and easy to navigate: the new Syracuse structure as a whole.

caseloads of the 1960s through the 1980s, and the explosion of domestic and juvenile court matters meant that courthouses were experiencing far greater usage rates than ever before. Even the federal courts experienced an exponential increase in business, as Congress extended the federalization of criminal matters and as the federal courts were used more frequently in civil rights cases.

A third factor, the introduction of weapons-screening technology at the entrances of courthouses, combined with the vast increase in numbers of public visitors, created a bottleneck in buildings not designed to handle these two opposing forces: demand for access to process, and constriction of the flow to allow access. The ubiquitous queues that clog our airports today have long been the norm in courthouses. New building designs have increased the space allocated to the lobbies outside the security zone to accommodate waiting, entry, and exit in an organized fashion. The consequence of this requirement in the hands of designers with vision is spaces that welcome visitors to the building, dignify them with a gracious first impression, and communicate the importance and stature of the judicial institution.

In the federal courthouse in Islip, New York, designed by Richard Meier & Partners/Spector Group, the space outside the security station is a rotunda that might be expected at the center of a traditional building (fig. 2-17). Pulling out this interior form from the body of the building serves to mark the entry to the building, to create a moment of awe and emotion before the inevitable indignity of the security screening process, and to offer a transition for visitors, who must

FRANK GREENE

turn 90 degrees into the public atrium and halls of the courthouse. The visual connection of all twelve floors of the building that is experienced in the atrium, along with the immediate prominence of a monumental stair that leads to the ceremonial courtroom, communicates a solicitude for first-time users in the functional organization of this enormous structure (fig. 2-18).

Compare this to a courthouse of equivalent size, such as the Moynihan federal courthouse at Foley Square, New York, or its Cass Gilbert predecessor (see fig. 2-21), or the new Eagleton building in St. Louis, Missouri (see fig. 3-20). In these more conventional configurations, visitors enter a lobby, punch an elevator button to gain access to any of the functions within the building, and find their destinations through building directories located in elevator lobbies.

The new federal courthouse under construction in Brooklyn, New York, by Caesar Pelli/HLM, utilizes a six-story atrium to great effect in linking the new tower to the existing midrise courthouse (figs. 2-19 and 2-20). The size and scale of the atrium communicate a concern for the scale of the user and orient public visitors. Similarly, in the annex to the federal courthouse in Scranton, Pennsylvania, the atrium serves not only to make functional connections between new and old buildings but also announces the public access to the judicial process in a dramatic array of stairs, bridges, and galleries (see figs. 2-10 and 2-11).

Civic Engagement
The best new courthouses share the values displayed in the best of their historic forebears: prominent siting,

2-17. Evening view, Alfonse D'Amato United States Courthouse, Islip, New York, Richard Meier & Partners/Spector Group, Architects, 2000.

2-18. Entry rotunda, federal courthouse, Islip.

2-19. Model of new
United States Court-
house, Brooklyn, New
York, Cesar Pelli/HLW
Architects, 2006.
The low-rise building is
the existing courthouse.

2-20. Section through
model of atrium, federal
courthouse, Brooklyn.

FRANK GREENE

2-21. Daniel Patrick Moynihan United States Courthouse, New York, from Foley Square. The New York State Supreme Court (Guy Lowell, 1925) is on the left and the Thurgood Marshall United States Courthouse (Cass Gilbert, 1936) on the right.

meaningful public space design, and important public art programs. With sites for new buildings in downtown civic districts at a premium, federal and local governments have gone to tremendous lengths to secure appropriate ones. The construction of a new building on a constrained urban site, with visual and functional relationships to adjacent structures that often are landmarks, requires a careful and sensitive urban design approach, a talented designer, and a courageous development agency to bring it off.

Among the outstanding new courthouses that have been fitted into existing urban ensembles are the Daniel Patrick Moynihan Courthouse (fig. 2-21), the two new federal courthouses in Brooklyn (see figs. 2-19, 5-12, and 5-13), the new criminal/family courthouse in Brooklyn, and the annex to the Prettyman courthouse in Washington, D.C. Each of these was inserted into a site barely adequate

to the program, with little opportunity for site development, setbacks, parking, or consideration of the urban impacts. The overriding critical nature of the essential adjacency to existing courts facilities forced the hand of the planners and designers to choose these sites.

The effects of such intense development on urban districts can be muted by sensitive site treatments, but in the current climate of heightened security concern, what civic zone remains can become cluttered with blast and intrusion barriers. At the Moynihan courthouse the limited public space around the courthouse that once provided an amenity for the nearby Chinatown community (it is graced by a Maya Lin sculpture commissioned by the government) now is surrounded by barricades and delivers a message of separation rather than engagement in the civic realm.

Other courthouse projects have taken on greater roles than are implied simply

by the basic functions of housing and symbolizing the judicial system: they engage in a positive dialogue with their neighbors. Some new courthouses have been called upon to repair a rent in the urban fabric—sometimes one left by arrested urban renewal projects.

The new Edward F. Brooke state courthouse in downtown Boston is a conspicuous success in locating a large new courthouse in a prominent downtown location (see fig. C-2). On a site originally intended for a new tower to complete a futuristic 1970s government office complex designed by Paul Rudolph, the building is as cool, urbane, and satisfying as its earlier neighbor is raw, affected, and disturbing. Designed by Kallman, McKinnell, & Wood, the new courthouse makes whole an urban wound that lay open for nearly thirty years, stands up to its flamboyant neigh-bor without prejudice, and makes a truly memorable urban space with its great top-lit atrium (figs. 2-22 and 2-23).

New courthouses that serve as sponsors of new development or as anchors for urban redevelopment schemes include federal courthouses in Alexandria, Virginia, Kansas City, Missouri (see fig. C-3), and Boston, Massachusetts (see figs. C-10, 2-5, and 2-6), and a children's court in Dublin, Ireland (fig. 2-24). Although courthouses do not have the clientele, streetscape activity, or hours of operation of more conventional urban redevelopment anchors, they nevertheless have stable uses that tend to generate a host of service and commercial neighbors, including law firms, that can help to stabilize a neighborhood, lend it panache, and provide a 24-hour presence that helps make the neighborhood more secure.

FRANK GREENE

The development of a new courthouse should always be linked to an urban context, existing or anticipated, and when possible, on "the most beautiful site possible," as Judge Douglas Woodlock has urged. There is a disturbing trend, particularly in state and county government, to avoid the risk, cost, and public controversy of obtaining high-quality sites. But sites that are selected on the basis of low (or no) cost, proximity to the detention center, or convenience to the freeway exit lend little to the urban cohesion of a community and are unlikely to become the cultural landmarks that our historic courthouses represent.

A renewed trend in courthouse design is also outreach to local traditions and even to local landscape features to increase community connection. For example, the lack of significant civic structures coupled with the spectacular nature of a nearby mountain range caused Antoine Predock to relate his

2-23. The atrium of the Edward F. Brooke courthouse.

2-24. The new Dublin children's court building in its urban environment.

2-25. Watercolor of United States Courthouse, Las Cruces, New Mexico, Antoine Predock, Architect.

design for the new federal courthouse in Las Cruces, New Mexico to the craggy peaks of the Organ Mountains. Here the dialogue between open and closed is exploded in this geode-like building, with the geometry both accepting of the rule of the urban grid as well as the dramatic opening to the view of the mountains. The symbolism of this federal courthouse thus is more related to natural law than abstractions, to the place rather than to the nation (fig. 2-25).

These courthouses deliver a message of celebration of the power of the landscape in settings where nature still is a dominant presence; they constitute a vivid metaphor for the basis of the law as rooted in traditions beyond memory, yet immediately identifiable and relevant to local circumstances. In a major metropolitan area, a new courthouse, even a

million-square-foot-tower, may be lost among other similar-sized buildings and may not have real visual impact beyond its immediate district. In smaller communities, however, these new buildings are not only larger than most, if not all, of the adjacent buildings, but are often of finer quality than those that surround them. The new building in Las Cruces towers over adjacent one-story adobe homes, and the only comparable context is the mountainous landscape. In Las Cruces, a city that has witnessed the introduction of many architectural expressions—pueblo, Spanish mission colonial, Victorian, mid-twentieth-century modern, and periodic revivals of historic styles—an authentic architectural expression may be rooted in a picturesque depiction of its heroically scaled natural "skyline." Predock's design not

FRANK GREENE

only defers to the Organ mountains in form and materials, but his orchestration of the pattern of public movement places the grand public hall on a platform directly facing the mountains and framed by two splayed wings of the building. Thus the architectural strategy places the building in the unusual role of paying homage to a greater power than that of the court and the law—of nature and its laws.

At a finer grain, the civic investment in public art in courthouses has recently gained in sophistication since midcentury efforts, many misguided, to rekindle the tradition of didactic works of art in public buildings. A commonplace component in classical buildings, often so integrated with the building that the boundaries between fine art and artisan were blurred, new public artworks have progressed beyond abstract lumps of metal in plazas and often take the form of glass windows, skylights, murals, plaza designs, and even lighting installations. Remarkable recent work includes a ceiling lens in Richard Meier's courthouse in Phoenix (fig. 2-26), the colored glass block wall in Bohlin Cywinski Jackson's addition to the Scranton courthouse (fig. 2-27), and exquisite color panels by Ellsworth Kelly in Pei Cobb Freed's Boston federal courthouse. Less than heroic, even modest in their ambition, these pieces are effective in engaging the public imagination about the message of these buildings and enriching the architectural framework with their color, scale, and texture.

This review of the characteristic features of the generation of courthouses should give some encouragement to those concerned for the "dignity, enterprise, and

2-26. Ceiling lens by glass artist James Carpenter, United States Courthouse, Phoenix, Arizona, Richard Meier and Partners/Langdon Wilson, Architects, 2000.

2-27. Colored-glass block wall by artist Paul Housber, federal courthouse, Scranton, Pennsylvania.

stability" of our governmental institutions, as Mr. Moynihan put it long ago, and long before he became a senator (see Epilogue). That these dynamic new courthouses express the enduring vitality and timeless nature of the law and the institutions responsible for its administration should not come as a surprise. That they express as well a new sense of openness and responsiveness to their communities is a bold statement of the legitimacy of the authority of a democracy, its expression of the will of the people. A nation that can build such structures to symbolize its most precedent-bound institutions can indeed endure for another century, or even a millennium.

FRANK GREENE

PART TWO

Solving the Distinctive Problems of a Courthouse Project

THREE

The Geometry of a Courthouse Design

JORDAN GRUZEN,

WITH CATHY DASKALAKIS AND PETER KRASNOW

The design of a courthouse presents a unique challenge for the architect: to find an expressive form and geometry that gives appropriate dignity and social significance to this special element of our democratic justice system. Today we are in a period of great invention and variety in building forms and functional relationships that are possible in the design of courthouses. New images are replacing traditional courthouse designs and gaining judicial as well as popular support.

As illustrated here (fig. 3-1) and in Chapter 1, courthouses have been immediately recognizable as such in the townscape due to their distinctive style, scale, and location. However, in the middle of the last century many large government office buildings were programmed to contain new court complexes, and these became virtually impossible to recognize directly as courts from any visual, symbolic elements (fig. 3-2). Visible expression of this third branch of government as separate from the legislative and exec-

utive branches is an important symbolic consideration in perceiving government.

A recent architectural resurgence of building forms has given greater recognition and importance to the judicial institution. The new geometric arrangements, which are taking a great variety

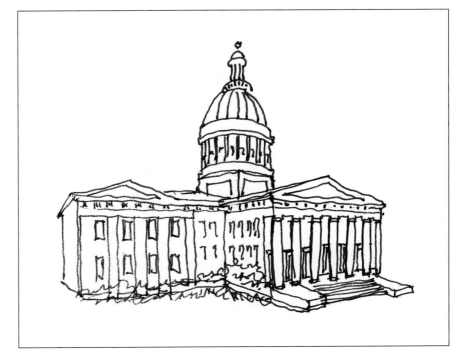

3-1. Old St. Louis courthouse ("Dred Scott Courthouse") of the 1830s, renovated c. 1862, exterior view. This and other drawings in this chapter are by the author, assisted by Cooper Cary of Gruzen Samton.

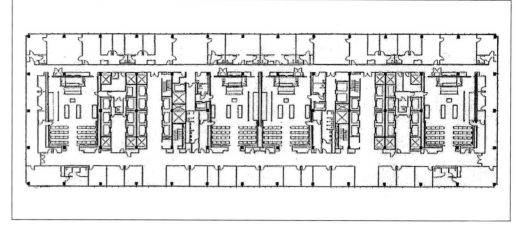

3-2. Dirksen Federal Building and Courthouse, Chicago, exterior view and plan, Mies van der Rohe, 1966.

of forms, are recognized and appreciated anew as the community's courthouse. The creative federal courts program, administered as part of the Design Excellence program initiative of the U. S. General Services Administration and assisted by the Administrative Office of the United States Courts (AOC), has demonstrated an extraordinary range of building designs that answer the functional requirements of the AOC Design Guide, our most detailed specification for new facilities. Since the early 1990s, the resulting work has demonstrated what can be done even within tight budgetary constraints. At the federal, state, county, or city level, new courthouses are being built utilizing all the traditional geometries and styles that were prevalent one hundred years ago. Each community has used this building type to project its preferred progressive or traditional architectural vocabulary and make a statement about its own values.

This chapter explores the external factors of site conditions and the inner relationships of program elements that architects manipulate in finding their particular solution as they apply their art

to the distinct problems presented by courthouse requirements.

Pre-Architectural Design and Strategic Planning

A "needs assessment" study is critical to the success of a courthouse design. The jurisdiction usually initiates the assessment of need for increased or modified space requirements. The need typically results from pressures within the system for an increase in the number of judges and courtrooms, because of the pressure of caseloads, needed improvement in disposition times, or security problems that generate judicial and political pressure for change. Ideally, a sophisticated needs analysis by an experienced court planner results in a preliminary program and consequent construction estimate. This program should provide the relevant authorities with the information needed to appropriate (or perhaps withhold) funds for the next step in solving pending needs.

Many government entities require a prospectus development study before engaging the final professional design team. Alternatively, developing a prospectus may be the first task for the selected professional team. These reports develop at a macro level the general bulk of the program, diagrammatic relationships, site requirements, and preliminary cost estimates.

The approval procedure for courthouse construction funds often does not rank high enough in the priority system of authorizing bodies, whether they are county commissioners or state or national representatives of the executive or legislative branches, or a combination. The full range of persuasive powers of the client and their design professionals is often needed, with early design representations created in order to secure funding.

Siting

The site selection process for a courthouse, as for most government buildings, begins with either the search for a site or with the study of a predetermined site provided by the client. The selection of an appropriate site for a courthouse requires a comprehensive list of goals and design objectives agreed upon by the architect and the client. Site selection is not always governed by a diagrammatic plan solution or by cost. The size of a given site relative to the size of the court program is a determining factor affecting the design solution. An urban site with limited acreage may dictate a high-rise solution; an open and generous suburban parcel may present a totally different opportunity for a low-rise, spread-out solution, with more area for surface parking and landscaped settings. The size of the program also influences the courthouse plan, in that the number of courtrooms per floor has a direct impact on the three circulation systems that commonly are required:

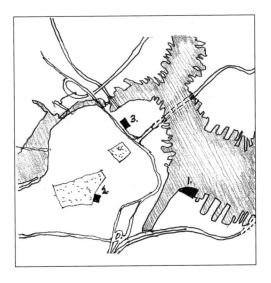

3-3. Boston courthouse sites: the selected site is at #1, facing the harbor at "Fan Pier."

public, judicial, and detainee movement. A search for a site is often the first task that officials and their architects face after they have completed the needs assessment and programming of a project (fig. 3-3). The site choice may be based upon internal organizational needs, or urban planning factors may be more dominant, with the internal relationship of the court parts accommodated to fit the characteristics of the site.

The next chapter discusses some diverse solutions that made excellent use of the opportunities a particular site presented. With a good site in hand, an experienced architect can develop a number of acceptable plans that will respond to the site's features. Examination of the results of recent architectural competitions sponsored by federal and local agencies demonstrates this: radically different solutions are found for the same program and the same site. For the federal courthouse project in Suffolk County, New York (see figs. 2-17, 2-18, and 5-12), Gruzen Samton managed an architectural competition on a large suburban site that produced notably different solutions; three contrasting examples

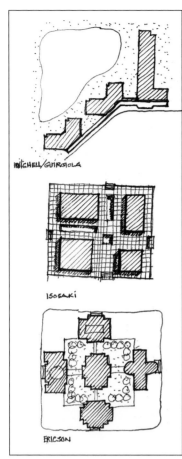

3-4. Contrasting solutions on a large, open site: Central Islip, New York.

appear in the sketches in figure 3-4. Each solution illustrated that a strong point of view about internal planning would come first in establishing the overall plan. A site found independently can then accommodate this preferred layout of the program's components.

The following principles and issues face an architect as practical matters of site size, convenient location to transportation, and proximity to other structures within the justice system are addressed. An urban site places the courthouse in juxtaposition to other buildings, to street patterns, and to existing public spaces. In locating the courthouse, the project's team will find alternatives and possibilities for orienting the structure with the following characteristics:

Symbolic central position within the city plan, as the object set apart in space, is a frequently used approach to siting a courthouse (fig. 3-5). As churches or town halls were the centerpieces of cities in past centuries, so has the courthouse become a symbol for cities more recently. Whether isolated or part of a larger governmental complex, the courthouse is often regarded as the symbolic

underpinning of people's image of justice in a democracy and thus deserves a prominent architectural position.

Whether the courthouse is on axis with major streets or other government buildings, the centerpiece of a public park, or visible along a prominent waterway, its position can magnify its importance.

The building as a street wall and/or outdoor space container is another site option for consideration (fig. 3-6). Court buildings can become part of a city's fabric in several different ways. They can become part of a street wall that maintains the integrity of a judicial square, or they can, if large enough, contain within their wings a public space, plaza, or park. Some sites present an opportunity to create a meaningful, usable outdoor public place for access to the courthouse as well as a place for social gatherings during breaks in court activities. The public space in front of the courthouse has become an important location for trial participants' public presentations to the media.

The view potential of natural or city landscape may drive the choice of a strong location (fig. 3-7). Siting a build-

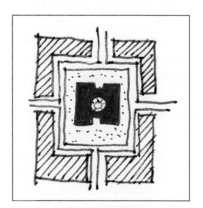

3-5. Symbolic central position.

3-6. Building as street wall.

ing for particular views has influenced many architectural solutions. Views of a river, a city skyline, or distant mountains are factors. Whether the views should be favored for the judiciary or the public or for both is central to siting and architectural configuration.

Connection or relationship to existing or proposed related facilities, in a campus setting, is also a consideration (fig. 3-8). Adjacency to an existing courthouse, administrative support building, attorneys' building, parking garage or an existing or proposed detention holding facility may determine the location. This factor gives rise to issues of old versus new and the balance between them.

A courthouse can create a significant route between destinations because it may be a hub connecting related offices and its placement and design may offer opportunities to strengthen the urban fabric. Courthouse arcades have taken form as linear containers of circulation through the city. Circulation patterns around a building, as well as through a multi-element complex, should be considered during the initial siting. However, new and tighter security regulations may limit this approach to allowing circulation—pedestrian and vehicular—not related to the courthouse only to pass adjacent to the contained spaces.

Site potential for proposed future expansion is essential to a well-planned facility design. In today's rapidly changing society, planned future expansion is critical to the design of any courthouse. Properly sized programs that support the future addition of courtrooms can be challenging. Providing expansion of both courtrooms and support spaces has direct impact on the initial design, which may require leaving an open-ended plan

arrangement for these future additions. Often, new courtrooms are anticipated and provided for by displacing offices that are temporarily housed in spaces with the correct structural bays and ceiling heights for these future courtrooms.

The Program
The net-to-gross ratio is the ratio of occupied space to nonoccupied space. It is strongly influenced by alternative approaches to the geometry of a floor plan and the size of the principal spaces and support systems. Net-to-gross ratios are one indicator of courthouse efficiency. In trying to find the right balance between economy, function, and architectural expression, court facility architects are inevitably concerned with construction budget constraints expressed in pressures to maximize this ratio.

Net-to-gross factors are often controlled by regional or national government agency planning guidelines, but project-specific factors determine the actual size of the courthouse (fig. 3-9). Although net-to-gross factors are applied to all building types, the complex geometry of a courthouse project is an underlying factor that creates less efficient ratios than in office buildings, schools, and other municipal projects. The federal courts have established guidelines for estimating the total gross area of federal courthouses. The net area is enlarged by an additional 12 percent circulation factor to create the "occupiable" area. This occupiable area typically accounts for 67 to 72 percent of the eventual gross area.

Guideline ratios, if religiously adhered to, can be very limiting of innovation. However, persuasive expression of a compelling design idea that requires increased area may win out in the end if

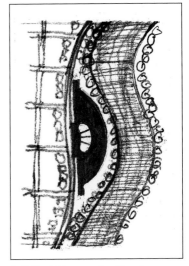

3-7. Exploiting an attractive site.

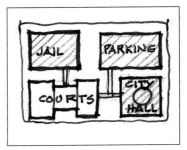

3-8. Connections to other facilities.

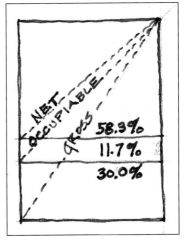

3-9. Net-to-gross factors in federal projects.

the client and the architect join in their support of the idea's validity and its consequences for the budget.

Five factors influence the efficiency of courthouse design: *configuration, modularity, population, circulation,* and *security configurations.* Configuration, modularity, and circulation are physical properties; population, circulation, and security are use factors that impact physical design. The site size and shape also affect efficiency.

Configuration

A building with a great number of courtrooms can be efficient if a consistent geometric configuration of the courtset—courtroom and adjacent ancillary facilities—is adhered to by repetition. This solution implies a concept of modularity. Courthouses also require considerable additional space that is basically office space. Courtroom space is more rigidly configured than office space. Therefore a courthouse is necessarily a mixed-use building, with courtroom floors having a specific geometry and office space adapting to this geometry.

Modularity

Modular design is possible when courtset dimensions are standardized, allowing for a stacking of courtsets. Even in courthouses that have a seemingly free articulation of form, courtroom modularity is the backbone of the design and construction approach. The proportion of courtrooms and the relationship of courtrooms to nearby spaces set the module. A large courthouse will have many different types of courtrooms: standard jury courtrooms, nonjury courtrooms, and perhaps ceremonial courtrooms, appeals courtrooms, hearing

rooms, and so on. These differ in size and height, and in their associated spaces and specific adjacencies. In many jurisdictions all courtrooms are designed as trial courtrooms, with specifics factored into a module, a set of standard dimensions that can accommodate the differences among types of courtrooms. Although this approach may initially appear wasteful in principle, because some courtrooms are larger than necessary to permit adaptation to future uses, often it can be justified through inventive assignment of spaces not required by a nontrial court use.

The number of courtrooms and the size of judicial support spaces have the most impact on the solution of a courthouse design. A four-courtroom facility is quite easily designed as a horizontally adjacent series of court parts. A forty-court program will certainly develop into a vertically stacked series of court floors, which may range from two per floor (the Mark O. Hatfield federal courthouse in Portland, Oregon; see fig. C-5) to ten or more per floor (the state courthouse in Wilmington, Delaware) (fig. 3-10). The arrangement of public waiting, judges' chambers, and prisoner-handling functions can be more complex in smaller horizontal facilities because they can be specially fashioned; there are few repetitive floors or none, and support elements at the lower levels can be placed with complete flexibility. When clustering numerous courtrooms per floor, the size of the public corridor to handle the assembly functions must be kept in mind.

Population

The large number of public visitors distinguishes courthouses from most other

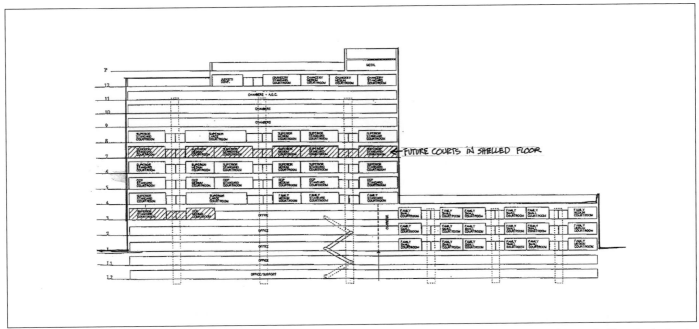

types of public buildings. A large courthouse may have thousands of visitors each day, accommodating many people who arrive at the same time. Entry spaces, corridors, escalators and elevators, restrooms, fire stairs, and other elements must be generously sized.

Circulation

Circulation patterns normally require three separate paths within a courthouse, and these form the skeleton upon which the courtset modules are fixed. How different users move to and from the courthouse, through its interior, and whom they meet, or must avoid meeting, are the result of the careful arrangement of key program components.

Different users of a courthouse have distinct patterns of movement. These distinct patterns are in notable contrast to most office buildings, where the prime traffic is composed of office workers who go to specific offices and remain there for the day. In the courthouse the judiciary (and impaneled jurors) are sep-

arated from public visitors until they arrive at the courtroom. Clerks move from their offices to the courtrooms, detainees are transported to and from the secure holding areas, and the public moves through the courthouse as a case moves through the judicial process. Prisoner circulation must be kept entirely separate (fig. 3-11).

It is often remarked that court proceedings involve a great deal of waiting. This waiting takes place in many locations: at the building entrance, the clerk's office, the detainee holding area, outside the courtroom, and again inside the courtroom. Proceedings are conducted and documented, and referral services are located in numerous other locations, so traffic among these locations must be accommodated. The trend toward creating "one-stop shopping" at courthouses locates many services under one roof, which leads further to increased public circulation. Although zoning a courthouse to create proper adjacencies and limit travel distances may cut down on

3-11. One layout providing separate courtroom access from public, restricted, and secure circulation areas.

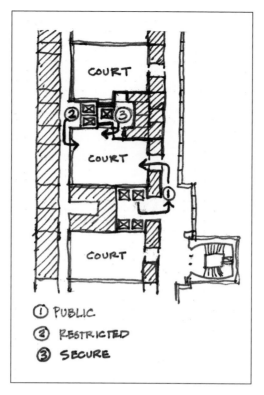

① PUBLIC
② RESTRICTED
③ SECURE

circulation, the trends are toward increased movement.

Security

To design a secure courthouse, configuration and security technology go hand in hand. The segregation of a courthouse building population into three distinct and separate zones—public, restricted, and secure—drives the geometry of the building. Separate public, judiciary, and detainee elevators are required; a courthouse has many elevators and complex vertical and horizontal circulation patterns, which affect the net-to-gross ratio of a courthouse and its cost. Designated and assigned spaces for security personnel, equipment, and vehicles further increase the square footage. Judicial personnel should not be seen, even when in their separate circulation systems.

When the public enters a lobby area through a security inspection area, tension may already be produced. Many potentially stressful transactions follow, whether with a clerk or in a court proceeding. Effective and thoughtful architectural design can help mitigate the stress of these encounters. Moving people quickly may be efficient, but giving them time to experience a successful courthouse design may have a calming effect. The public needs to have generous waiting areas that are brightly lit and comfortable. Most vertical courthouses are zoned to place the high-volume areas accessible to the public, including clerk functions, jury assembly, or motions courts, closest to the point of entry, on the lower floors. Stair and escalator access to these floors takes the load off the elevators.

Judicial participants—judges and their staffs—should be completely separated from the public. The courtroom is the only place where all three user groups interact: public, judiciary, and detainees. If public or attorney access to judicial suites is required, it can be accomplished through restricted and secure corridors containing controlled entry points. Common standards require that judges be provided with separate circulation both horizontally and vertically, from their automobiles to their chambers to the courtroom. There are two basic choices for the location of the judicial suite. One is on the court floor, allowing corridor access to the courtrooms; the other is on a separate, "collegial" judicial floor from which access to the courts is via elevators and/or stairs. Judges' access from parking utilizing secure entrance passes (card reader devices) requires separation from other users.

Detainees are brought to the courthouse under secure conditions via vehicles and/or tunnel or bridge connections from holding facilities. After their initial processing upon entering the central holding area, they are brought to smaller, secure holding rooms (which also require observation and control) located adjacent to each courtroom. Sheriff deputies or court bailiffs (security officers of the court) escort detainees from the holding rooms to the defense area within the courtroom or to the witness box, and remain to ensure discipline.

Security control is located at several points of access to and within a courthouse. First, public access from the lobby to secure interior space requires magnetometer and personal screening. However, waiting rooms are often the scene of confrontations and possibly even violence between contesting parties. Even after initial security checks people must be closely supervised in certain types of courthouses, particularly family courts and similar institutions that handle domestic disputes. Security within a courtroom—detainee entrance/exit as well as public access to the "well" of the courtroom and to the participants—requires containment and controlled movement. Judges' access from chambers or robing rooms must be secure. Finally, restricting passage from public areas to judicial areas requires control points where only authorized admittance is permitted.

Lighting

A courthouse has distinctive lighting requirements that must be addressed thoughtfully if it is to function effectively. Carefully designed natural lighting is desirable within the courtroom, the public areas, and the judges' areas, not only as a defining quality of space but because there may be positive psychological effects on litigants and other participants. Working, deliberating, or waiting in a courthouse can be very stressful. Natural light provides a positive environmental and emotional boost and may positively influence the decision-making process. However, modern courtroom circulation requirements tend to limit the amount of natural light that can be provided.

Ideally, those working in the courthouse should experience the changing quality of the light of day or the passage of time through openings to the outdoors. Often thought of as a potential distraction, natural light can enhance individual focus. However, architects must be cautious about siting windows facing populated buildings both for security reasons and to avoid distractions to the jury or others. In the extreme case, a mistrial could result if jurors were to see something that could influence their decision, whether displayed intentionally or not.

Natural light in a courtroom provides the feeling of normalcy, a feeling that is especially important in long trials, particularly when a jury is sequestered. To subject a long-sequestered jury, already living in a highly artificial environment under severe restrictions, to a windowless environment for the full working day is an extreme and unnecessary further disability to them. Light can be brought in with windows, skylights, borrowed light over lower-height adjacent spaces, or high clerestory windows (fig. 3-12).

Clerestory windows located high above eye level can provide the desired natural light source without compromis-

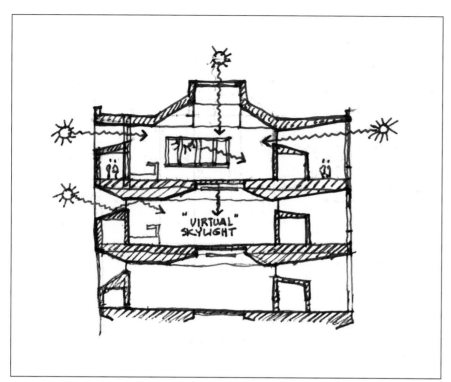

3-12. Clerestory windows, skylights, and virtual skylights.

all parties to a judicial proceeding require accurate observation of each other's features in order to judge their behavior and emotions. Artificial lighting in courtrooms must be controlled by dimmer switches.

Introducing natural light into the jury deliberation room will ease the fatiguing effect of long deliberations. Common placement of jury rooms is across the secure corridor on the outside wall or flanking the courtroom. The latter makes access to natural light more difficult, except in low buildings or tall designs with two or four courts per floor, in which the jury rooms are placed on the outside.

Successful design solutions have provided natural light in public waiting areas where this light, as well as pleasant views, help people pass long waiting periods (fig. 3-13).

The Entry
Public entries to the courthouse have evolved in form over time as our views of the building type and its role as both a functional and symbolic public space have changed. The public nature of the courthouse is apparent in the architectural expression of the entry.

As discussed in Chapter 1, historically courthouses were combined with other civic uses. The post office often was located on the ground floor of federal courthouses. In county courthouses much of the documentation of daily life—marriage licenses, deeds, record copies of newspapers and genealogical records—was maintained. Access to the courthouse was entirely open. Typically a grand interior space was directly linked to the exterior with an entry vestibule. Functionally the courthouse

ing security or outside communications. Clerestory light can be achieved from windows above lower adjacent perimeter corridors or meeting rooms and therefore may be set back from the exterior building walls to enhance security and further limit distraction. Glare can be avoided if the light is directed to adjacent walls or ceilings, which act as reflectors.

Skylights are frequently used on top-floor courtrooms in connection with vaulted ceilings, giving increased height and focus to the "well" portion of the courtroom. Often a "false skylight," employing artificial lighting, is created in multilevel stacked courtrooms to give the illusion of skylights. However, placement of courts adjacent to the outside wall is the most direct way to achieve natural lighting. Light wells in a large structure can achieve similar results with side lighting.

It is important to avoid glare, because

entry now requires a secure sequence of spaces for movement that include a queuing area, a screening area, and a lobby area. Entries have become deeper, with increased security, and a greater distance for visitors to penetrate. The delay in entry necessitates the provision of more weather-protected space outside of security.

Although much of the queuing and security screening poses a barrier to free movement, the courthouse entry still has a great potential for memorable architecture. Recently designed courthouses use highly evocative spatial and sculptural elements to bring a sense of ceremony to what can easily begin to feel like a terminal arrival point. (Useful examples treated elsewhere in this book include Richard Meier's federal courthouse rotunda in Islip, New York, illustrated in figs. 2-17 and 2-18; Hellmuth Obata & Kassabaum's new Denver federal courthouse in fig. 10-4, 10-6, and elsewhere; and NBBJ's federal courthouse in Seattle, fig. 10-5, 10-11, and elsewhere.) Associated spaces that may include security offices, public information counters, and highly public functions such as jury assembly help to focus the public path of activity.

The Courtset

The courtset is the building block of a courthouse design. Its basic element is the courtroom. The arrangement of the courtroom, once fixed, influences the dimensions of the entire building, particularly in large courthouses with numerous side-by-side courtrooms. The geometry of this space must be analyzed from the inside out, with the placement of each element of the room thoughtfully considered and the location of entries for

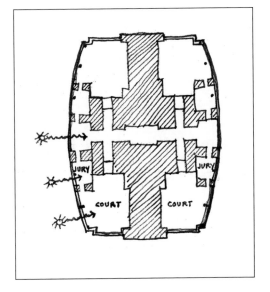

3-13. A configuration for four courtrooms per floor that allows natural light to the jury room, public hallway, and courtrooms.

the public, judge, jury, litigants, and detainees established. Dimensions are critical, because court proceedings rely upon views of evidence and witnesses from fixed vantage points. Needed also is a significant—often a prescribed—distance between litigants, the defendant, the prosecution, the witness, the judge, and the public. The need for proximity between the jury and the witness, the judge and the witness, and placement of the court reporter, the courtroom clerk, and the witness in relation to all participants must be balanced by the architect. Optimizing these dimensions, while taking advantage of technology to enhance court proceedings, is a critical preliminary task to be developed in consultation with the client agency, judges, court staff, and technology consultants. Inseparable from the courtroom design is that of adjacent spaces used in concert with the courtroom and critical to court proceedings. Courtrooms may be joined with separate sound locks to other spaces, including jury deliberation rooms, judges' offices, clerks' offices, conference rooms, detainee holding

3-14. Two approaches to locating judicial chambers.

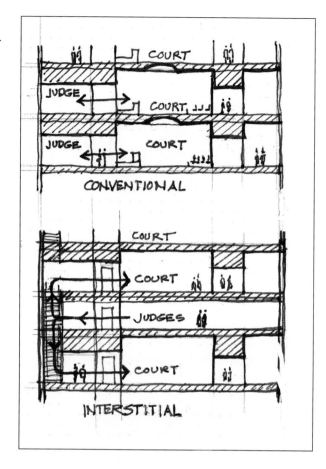

COURT
JUDGE   COURT, JJJ
JUDGE   COURT
CONVENTIONAL

COURT
COURT
JUDGES
COURT
INTERSTITIAL

In either case they can maintain their individual chambers, but the sharing of other areas, such as the library, conference rooms, and support-staff accommodations, can have operational benefits. A separate floor devoted to chambers, located either above or below the courtrooms or on a more distant floor, is referred to as a collegial floor. Often this collegial floor is located at the top of the courthouse to enhance security and to provide panoramic views. In a very tall courthouse several collegial floors can be distributed interstitially, near the courts they serve (fig. 3-14). Consolidation of chambers can allow efficiencies in the form of a higher net-to-gross ratio and, more important, facilitate interaction between judges and their staffs.

Specific criteria for court programming include many elements that are common to federal, state, and county courthouse design. Some states have extensive guidelines or requirements. Each jurisdiction has unique requirements, which are often articulated in a set of specific guidelines. Consult your local jurisdiction for the criteria (and local precedents and preferences as well) that govern your project.

A diagrammatic program outline for the state court in Wilmington, Delaware represents by example the space needs of a large state or county system's courthouse (fig. 3-15). This typical program illustrates the variety of different spaces in a large, complex courthouse.

The type of court and its work determine the nature of each court part. Court types, covered in Chapter 8 and elsewhere in this book, determine unique as well as common characteristics that influence design. Security of circulation patterns is one area of usual

areas, and evidence storage. Pairing courtrooms around a fixed vertical detainee elevator helps to achieve separation of the public from the restricted and secure circulation systems. It is, in fact, impossible to design only in two dimensions for a plan that has three paths that must not cross.

Judges' Chambers

The relationship of judges' chambers to courtrooms is achieved either by consolidated or dispersed elements. Traditionally, federal judges are assigned to a particular courtroom, so their chambers are best located nearby to provide speedy access for trial proceedings. Many state and county systems rotate the courtrooms for various judges' use.

JORDAN GRUZEN

commonality. Jury or nonjury courtroom and trial or appeals courtroom layouts have obvious differences. Identifying these issues in detail during the planning/programming phase provides the foundation for informed design decisions that follow. Designing a courtroom with or without jury boxes presents different issues. When a jury's movement to and from the courtroom is eliminated, the impact on the layout and all supporting spaces adjacent to the courtroom is considerable. The spatial relation among the elements in the courtroom may also change. Recent increases in alternative proceedings, such as alternate dispute resolution (ADR), which requires no jury, change the spatial relationships and the cost of the complex.

Although architects have generally maintained a traditional arrangement of interior elements of courtrooms, understanding the details of operations and proceedings and the interactive nature of events within a courtroom can lead to exploration of new arrangements and forms. A basic understanding of each element's role and position in trial proceedings can germinate alternative geometries.

A public waiting area with courtroom access is an important design element for both the exterior and interior environment. Once people are screened through security control upon entering the courthouse and find their way to courtroom floors, waiting areas become a very important design ingredient to the success of operations. People awaiting trial proceedings are often tense, anxious, and required to wait long periods of time. An architect should design the waiting spaces to assure comfort and quiet. Waiting areas, often designed in a linear fash-

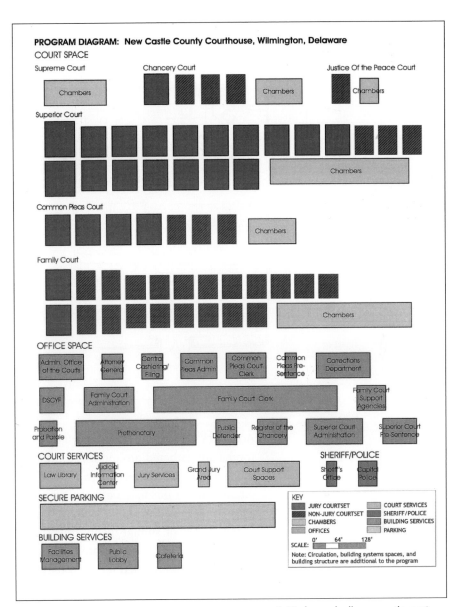

3-15. A sample diagrammatic court program.

ion parallel to the courtrooms, should be inviting, naturally lit spaces with ample and comfortable seating. Waiting areas need to be located close to courtrooms to assure all participants' timely, perhaps immediate, access to proceedings. Conference rooms have traditionally flanked the courtroom entrance, with their position defining the vestibule into the courtroom and providing an acoustical sound lock for control of the courtroom interior.

3-16. An example of a corner-bench arrangement, from a courtroom plan for a United States Magistrate judge.

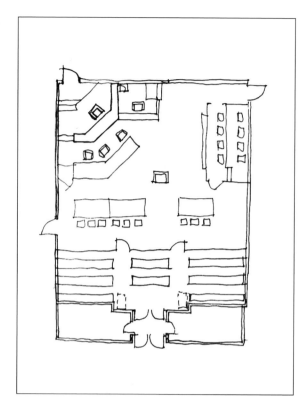

decisions are made, including scheduling and assignment of new cases. In smaller courthouse designs, an elevator and ceremonial stair are often adequate means of moving people to a second floor.

Courtroom Elements

The position of the judge's bench—centered or cornered—is one of the decisions to be made during the initial design phase. A centered and raised bench—the norm for federal courtrooms—confers on the judge an authoritative position and aesthetic dignity. A corner bench, more usual in state courts, can provide improved observation for the judge of all courtroom participants. The view of the witness box is improved for the judge, jury, and litigants (see fig. 3-16).

Handicapped accessibility regulations require that ramps be provided for judges. Electric lifts generally require more space. The bench in several court types, not only criminal, is often designed with bullet-resistant material, giving the judge extra protection.

Figures 3-17–3-19 exemplify three typical courtroom designs for federal courts. For each, the well of the court lies between the public seating area and the judge and staff; the well accommodates the lawyers, the parties, and the jury (in the trial court). The 2,400-square-foot standard trial courtroom shows a fairly common arrangement of the necessary elements, as do the representations of a smaller courtroom for a federal court of appeals and for an in banc court of appeals, accommodating (in this case, as shown) a bench of up to eleven judges.

In the trial court the court clerk serves at the pleasure of the judge and can be located in a variety of positions,

Acoustics can be a problem if waiting rooms are gathered around a central atrium without adequate concern for sound attenuation or distance between groups. This concern is even more evident in family courts or similar institutions that host playful children. Separate waiting areas are recommended for each party's privacy.

Courtroom types and compositions impact design in their distribution of the principals. Larger courthouses tend to place the first of several courtroom floors beginning on the second or third level. Often escalators are used as a means of moving people quickly to their court appearance location. Generally, in large courthouses, courtrooms are rarely located at grade, which is reserved for public spaces, jury assembly, and official transactions. An occasional exception is the arraignment court, in which many quick

96

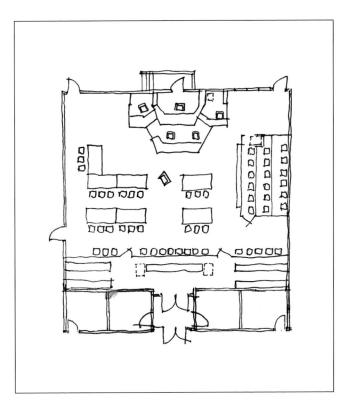

3-17. Standard United States district courtroom; 2,400 square feet, as typically arranged.

Below left:
3-18. A "panel" United States Court of Appeals courtroom, for a standard three-judge panel, 1,800 square feet.

Below right:
3-19. An "in banc" court of appeals courtroom of 3,000 square feet, accommodating eleven judges at the bench.

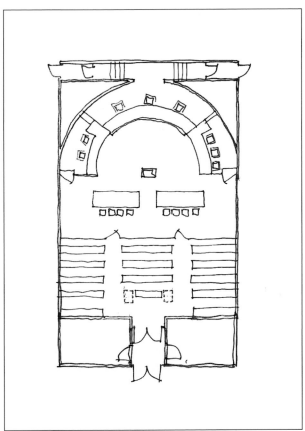

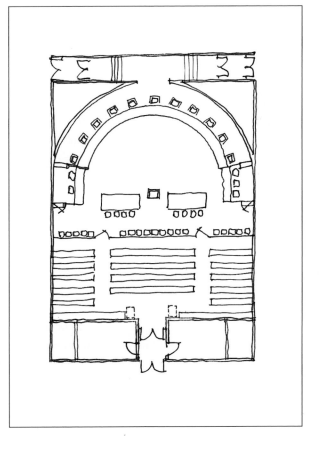

depending on judicial preference. Common arrangements include location adjacent to the bench on the side opposite the witness stand, or in front of, or to the side of, the judge's bench.

The witness box can be located directly to the side of the judge so that the judge, jurors, prosecuting (or plaintiff) and defending attorneys, and the court stenographer can view the witness without obstruction. In the corner bench arrangement the witness is usually at a 45-degree angle to the judge's bench. Also common is a freestanding witness box that can be moved to an isolated position opposite the jury. Witnesses must be able to view the evidence display areas.

The jury box commonly contains two or three rows and is set at right angles to the judge's bench. It is positioned for clear view of the witness and the litigants. Placing windows either behind the witness or behind the jury is not recommended, because it could cause glare and obscure the view of essential participants. Handicapped accessibility regulations generally require that ramps be provided for the jury.

The prosecutor's or plaintiff's table and the defense table are usually adjacent to each other, the same distance away from the judge's bench, and as close to the witness box and the jury box as possible. No appearance of favoritism may be evident in the layout. Cases with multiple defendants require additional tables and chairs and require a large courtroom well area to accommodate all participants.

Observers' seating within the courtroom is required in most courts. The observers' seating is separated from court proceedings by means of a rail with a low door. A center aisle provides witnesses, who may be in the audience, direct access into the well of the proceedings. Handicap areas are provided near the main courtroom entrance doors for ease of access.

The display of evidence is required in nearly every trial. With today's technology, cameras, computers, and monitors can be utilized. However, some evidence requires display of the actual material, such as a weapon. The placement of monitors and display tables is important, because all trial participants need to be able to view all evidence. Storage of all evidence is required near the courtroom and is always located in a secure room.

Evidence display and storage have changed with new technologies: much evidence can now be displayed as images. This type of display calls for large screens within the courtroom; additional personal screens can be provided when direct observation of larger screens is obscured. Individual screens at each juror's seat are not uncommon. Audiovisual equipment is stored outside of the courtroom, generally in an area between courtrooms, where evidence storage and detainee holding are located or in a central media room.

Handicap accessibility for public, staff, and judiciary areas has been mandated by the Americans with Disabilities Act (ADA). This legislation has had a major impact on courtroom geometry and design. With required elevation differences for judges, witnesses, and juries, ramps and lifts were introduced for individuals with physical disabilities. Sight and sound issues also require special attention to audio systems and the level of light necessary for viewing proceedings, including evidence displays.

Locating the jury deliberation room adjacent to the courtroom has obvious benefits: speedy access to and from the courtroom and enhanced security for all participants in the proceedings. Whether attached directly to the courtroom or located a short distance away, jury rooms are set on the restricted side of the facility but may need access from the public corridor for jurors' arrival, departure, and breaks when they are not sequestered. This intermediate position can cause layout problems when natural light into the jury deliberation room is desired and the courts are arranged in series.

Detainee access to the courtroom in a timely and secure manner is often a challenge when remodeling older courthouses. Pairing courtrooms with secure detainee holding cells between them is a successful solution. If holding areas are provided only in a group arrangement on the secure side of a courtroom floor, a security officer must escort detainees to and from the courtroom, an obvious disadvantage and a needless expense.

Space for noncontact attorney–detainee communications can be located between courtrooms adjacent to the holding rooms. The attorney can enter from the public corridor/waiting area.

Space must also be provided for seating of security personnel, including the bailiff (nomenclature may vary) who has overall responsibility for security within the courtroom and for escorting the detainee between the holding cell and the defense table. These personnel may also be also responsible for escorting jurors between the jury box and the jury room. The bailiff has a major responsibility to protect the judge and other courtroom participants and maintain order within the courtroom.

Judiciary Support Functions

Offices for public transactions with the clerk of courts are best placed on the first or lower floors of a courthouse to separate these functions from courtroom activities, which are generally located on upper floors. To limit high traffic to areas accessible to the entrance and for the convenience of citizens who may enter only to pay a traffic fine or check in for jury duty, these components are generally placed near the public lobby.

Courtroom docket and directional information should be readily available to the public. New technologies may provide graphic displays throughout the courthouse to announce the schedule for the day and other information relevant to court proceedings, such as jury room/hearing room/arbitration room locations.

The jury assembly and selection room is one of the more flexible architectural space challenges in a courthouse design. Most Americans know that waiting for court case selection can be a long and tedious proposition, so the environment should be brightly lit, spacious, and comfortable. Many courts provide large-screen television, music systems, or computer workstations and telephones to allow the waiting time to be well utilized.

The jury assembly room is often also used for school education in civics and after hours for community and bar activities. It therefore should be placed on the ground floor to permit public access while securing the other functions of the courthouse. A courtyard can provide outdoor space that is accessible only from the jury assembly room; landscaped terraces may also be an effective amenity.

A law library is a common element in courthouses. It may or may not be available to the public. Its position within the plan needs careful consideration. Libraries have been located on grade in the lower levels to provide easy public access, or on the rooftop where access may readily be limited.

Large courthouses offer food service in a cafeteria facility. This large room and its kitchen can be made available to the public for special events after hours. Generally the facility is closed to jurors, both prospective and those serving on a jury, to minimize the chance of overhearing a conversation that should remain private. Thus calculation of the number of people to be served should not include jurors unless it is known that they may use the food service area in conjunction with separate dining rooms.

If auxiliary agencies such as other branches of government are included in the program—elected officials' offices, post offices, or municipal functions—they may require separate entry.

Most courts prefer to separate prosecutors and public defenders by locating them in separate wings or buildings. When this is not possible, careful attention to their placement within the courthouse is required to avoid suggesting favoritism. To mitigate the problem, they may be placed on opposite sides of the courthouse or on different floors. Public defenders' offices must provide direct access from the public areas and convey the utmost appearance of judicial fairness. Probation offices may require separation and private access, notwithstanding the contrary requirement to

keep the number of entrances as few as possible for security and economy.

Architectural Solutions and Geometrical Form

Grouping the subdivisions of elements known as the courtset drives the overall form of a courthouse. The examples shown here focus on this major component and offer different courtroom floor plan solutions. Review of relevant guidelines is highly recommended for information regarding the placement of additional supporting elements.

The architect should examine the relative efficiencies between horizontal and vertical circulation patterns. The construction costs will differ: a vertical structure, including elevators and mechanical systems in tower designs, is more expensive than horizontally organized lower building layouts. The latter may have greater area for circulation but direct stair access for much of the population. How long it takes the three groups of users to reach a destination is an important consideration.

Plan options include *centralized, linear, radial,* and *clustered* approaches, the most often-used geometries of courthouse design. Each courthouse in the project examples that follow has been placed into one of these categories. Examples are drawn from federal, state, and county facilities.

Ceremonial public spaces are important factors in the design of a courthouse. Most designs focus on a central, vertical public space that serves as a point of orientation, assisting visitors in finding their way and providing access to particular functions. This space offers the architect an opportunity for an important aesthetic statement. Horizontal ceremonial spaces can also be aesthetically expressive way-finding devices for users. The comparison of alternate access via stair, escalator, and/or elevator to each function requires careful evaluation regarding function and cost.

Placement of elements vertically in section should be established before a courtroom plan is final. One should study and test the distribution of all elements with cross-sectional diagrams. Positioning heavily used public functions for quick and easy access can prove valuable in determining the final form of the design.

Courtrooms require higher ceiling heights than the support spaces that are generally adjacent to them. The courtroom ultimately projects the spirit of the judicial institution and therefore requires a specially designed volume. Support spaces are typically office like and do not require unusual height. The differences in heights provide many design opportunities: the extra space can be used for supply and distribution of mechanical and electrical systems to a courtroom; the introduction of natural and artificial light; greater three-dimensional ceiling expressions; more height for the elevated bench area for judges, witnesses, and juries. Double-decking of support spaces behind a higher courtroom is also possible and increases the efficiency of the whole but requires use of stairs or elevators for closely related parts. The St. Louis courthouse diagram shown here (fig. 3-20) utilizes a split-level, alternating floor layout to take advantage of the height difference between the courtroom and support spaces, and it reduces the overall volume of the building by minimizing the excess hung ceiling spaces.

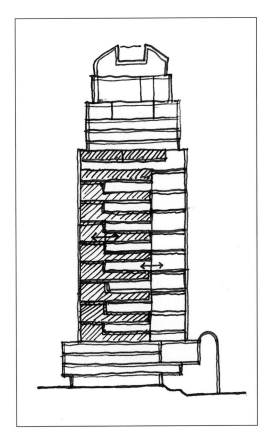

3-20. A split-level, alternating floor layout in the Thomas F. Eagleton United States Courthouse, St. Louis, Missouri, Hellmuth, Obata & Kassabaum, 2000.

The size of a courthouse—especially the number of courtrooms—is a key factor in the creation of the floor plan and the design of the overall building. A small number of courtrooms (approximately two to six) generally compels a low-rise design. Projects in this range present the architect with simple geometric options that require attention to achieve an expressive and functional solution. As with larger facilities, the same three circulation patterns are commonly required. Solutions where all the courtrooms are placed at a second level can leave the first floor free for all public and publicly accessible functions that involve high traffic, such as a jury assembly room, the clerk of courts, probation, and the library.

Medium-sized facilities (approximately six to twenty courtrooms), can be low-, mid-, or high-rise. The number of courtrooms per floor leads to a variety of options for building massing and expression. Both horizontal and vertical forms, or a combination of different height wings, should be explored. This number of courtrooms almost always requires pairing and stacking to limit the number of detainee holding areas and elevators.

Large facilities (twenty to sixty courtrooms) are generally high-rise structures or a large clustered arrangement that often results from grouping multiple court types and functions with different jurisdictions. This solution may call for separate wings, separate buildings, or separate vertical zones. A large number of courtrooms is challenging in that the movement through a large building requires greater attention to way-finding devices, either through architectural clarity of circulation space or clear graphics. Campuslike groups of separate buildings, or a mega-structure with many wings, may answer the same program.

The Centralized Courthouse

The four-courtroom layout is frequently used in small courthouses (figs. 3-21 and

3-22), where all the courtrooms are located on one floor, and in large courthouses where the floor-plate repetition takes the form of a tower. The four-courtroom tower is often used in cities where real estate is at a premium. Recent examples include the Thomas F. Eagleton United States Courthouse, St. Louis, Missouri (fig. 3-23), the Daniel Patrick Moynihan United States Courthouse in New York (fig. 3-24), and the new United States District Courthouse in Brooklyn (fig 3-25).

Because the tower geometry separates courtrooms from the building entry and support offices and fully relies upon elevator service, this solution tends to work more successfully for federal courthouses, which generally have lower traffic levels than state and county courthouses. These three federal courthouses address vertical circulation and the placement of courtroom support space through diverse and creative solutions. Centralizing all program components around an atrium accessible to the public may also reduce the gross area and provide rapid access to all parts of the courthouse while facilitating supervision.

In the St. Louis courthouse the split-

Right::
3-21. Centralized floor plan, Roman L. Hruska United States Courthouse, Omaha, Nebraska, Pei Cobb Freed & Partners.

Far right:
3-22. Floor plan, United States Courthouse, Hammond, Indiana, Pei Cobb Freed & Partners, Design Architect, Browning Day Mullins, Dierdorf, Inc., Architect of Record.

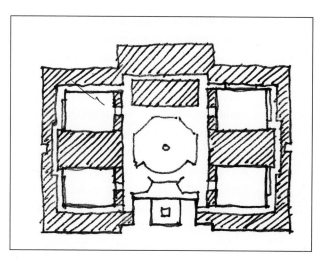

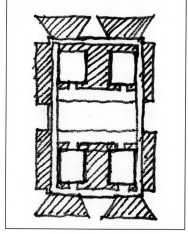

JORDAN GRUZEN

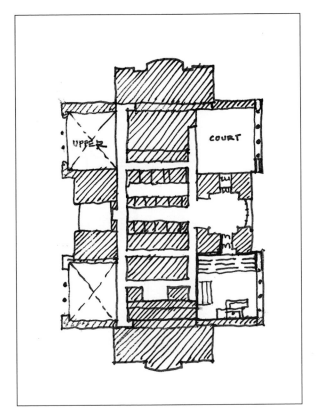

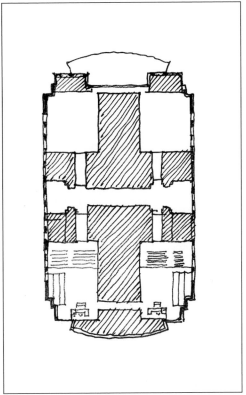

Far left:
3-23. A four-courtroom tower with alternating courtroom levels, Eagleton Courthouse, St. Louis, Missouri.

Left:
3-24. A centralized floor plan in the Daniel Patrick Moynihan United States Courthouse at Foley Square, New York, Kohn Pederson Fox, 1994.

level solution is quite simple. The courtrooms are placed at the four corners of the building to bring natural light directly into each. Judicial chambers are set at the ends of the plan. The plan is unique in the way it stacks court floors in an alternating arrangement, taking advantage of the generally unused space above the judicial chambers for support floors. The number of elevator banks is increased to provide timely access to each alternating court floor.

In the Manhattan courthouse (fig. 3-24) the small floor plate both locates each courtroom in a building corner position and provides an exterior location for the jury deliberation rooms. An abundance of natural light enters each of these areas as well as the public areas. To achieve this design solution in a very tall building on a small site, judicial

chambers were placed on every third floor, in a collegial arrangement that allows judges to move short distances vertically, either by stair or elevator (see fig. 3-14).

In the federal district courthouse in Brooklyn (fig. 3-25), the geometry of the typical courtroom floor provides a gentle curved shape for all of its elements: courtrooms, judicial suites, and jury deliberation rooms. The vertical access core, although centralized, bisects the floor and provides for an exterior lobby, placed at each end to provide visitors awaiting proceedings with natural light and views.

The Linear Courthouse

A linear courtroom arrangement solves numerous issues simply, has many benefits, and its form is adaptable to diverse

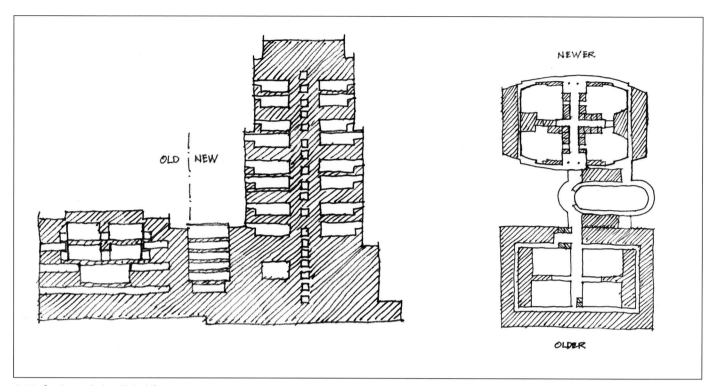

3-25. Section and plan, United States District Courthouse, Brooklyn, New York. Cesar Pelli & Associates/ HLW International, architects for new tower (2006); Gruzen Samton LLP, architects for renovation of existing courthouse.

architectural approaches. In the linear arrangement the public and the restricted circulation systems run parallel to each other and are easy to navigate. Natural light can be provided in both the public waiting areas and the rear-located judges' chambers. The linear solution lends itself to floor plates with many courtrooms and can be expanded by nature of its open-ended plan. The entry into the linear courtroom scheme can be placed in the middle to achieve a strong sense of center and cut long travel distances. Often the linear arrangement is manipulated into curved or L-shaped elements that contain an entry space.

Linear plans with long strings of courtrooms have other advantages. They do not concentrate all people in one area; they may allow increased waiting areas; and they provide acoustical and visual separation between groupings, resulting in a more relaxed environment.

In the Sandra Day O'Connor Federal Courthouse in Phoenix, Arizona, (fig. 3-26), the L-shaped plan creates a screen-covered atrium that captures natural light while filtering the harsh Arizona sun from the public on the court floors. Access to the lobby is through the atrium, which provides a means to see at a glance the various courtroom floors and thus helps in way finding. The judicial suites are located in a traditional manner behind the courtsets and are accessed through a private, secured corridor.

The D'Amato federal courthouse in Islip, New York has a double atrium layout to articulate the linear arrangement (fig. 3-27; see also figs. 2-17, 2-18, and 5-12). Richard Meier and colleagues created a solid "tepee" form as the entrance element that is distinct from, and in contrast to, the lighter appearance of the curtain-wall facade. The inner atrium, where vertical circulation takes place, separates the bankruptcy courts from the various district courts. The public corridor is slightly tapered in shape: its width is reduced as it leads to the courtrooms located furthest from the main entrance, in response to lower requirements.

The Radial Courthouse

The Scott M. Matheson courthouse in Salt Lake City, Utah (fig. 3-28) has a double L-shaped layout that creates two distinct and separate sides of the typical courtroom floor. It provides variety for visitors: one side of each ell has a continuous window wall that offers the waiting public a view of the mountains, and the internal waiting areas receive natural light from the end of the corridor. Judicial support and jury deliberation rooms have direct natural light resulting from their position on the exterior wall. A small circular atrium at the entrance is the element around which the courthouse plan is organized.

In the Kansas City, Missouri federal courthouse (fig. 3-29; see also fig. C-3) the courtsets are ordered about a semicircular atrium in a radial manner to provide compact way-finding through visibility from a single point at the main entrance. The radial form encircles most of the atrium, and the remaining opening offers an architecturally welcoming expression.

The Clustered Courthouse

Clustered plans provide separate building elements, each of which may contain various differing functions. The elements may be attached to one another by bridges or composed together to frame a space or a significant view. A campus plan often groups separate types of courts or jurisdictions in their own

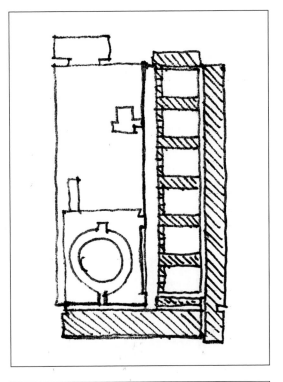

3-26. A linear plan: Sandra Day O'Connor United States Courthouse, Phoenix, Arizona, Richard Meier & Partners/Michael Schroeder Langdon Wilson.

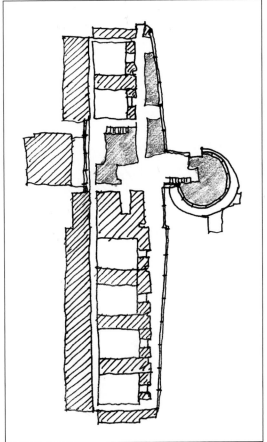

3-27. Alfonse D'Amato United States Courthouse, Islip, New York, Richard Meier & Partners/Spector Group, 2001.

buildings. This solution can provide opportunities for an enclosed garden courtyard or plans where all common elements are placed within the center of separated buildings.

In the Jefferson County, Colorado, courts building (fig. 3-30) a central atrium is the design link between two separate "bent" linear building forms; one for court functions, the other for other judicial activities. The atrium also clearly identifies the main entrance to this large facility, and moderates the architecture's long facades. This plan is effective with its abundance of views that look away from, and past, the opposite building element.

The proposed federal courthouse in Eugene, Oregon (fig. 3-31; see figs. C-12 and 4-17), is composed of three separate building blocks to create a defined outdoor space as well as to frame a view of the surrounding mountains. These blocks, each containing courts, are connected by bridges at various levels.

Recent Developments

Courthouse design has undergone major changes in the past decade as new courthouse construction and renovation projects have set new architectural precedents. The widespread state/county/ city desire for contemporary design and the federal General Services Administration's Design Excellence Program have supported a renewed commitment to high-quality courthouse design. Technological innovations, expressive engineering design, revised programmatic content, and heightened security concerns have encouraged architects to explore new forms of expression.

State court systems, in all their variety, are less constrained by any particular set of design guidelines. As a result, their architecture has been exceptionally varied. The sites are often suburban, and large site configurations are common.

The previous tradition of American courthouse design relied on a conventional imagery of justice and authority created over a span of two hundred years and based on historical precedent. Today the vocabularies of design that

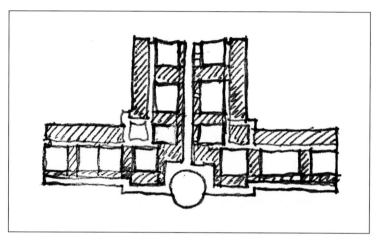

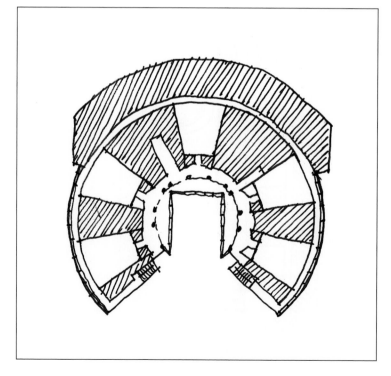

give expression to our modern society are unlimited in form and materials, and architects are experimenting with alternative massing of the plan elements, generally within the relevant guidelines, but sometimes none is applicable. Alternative building materials have given courts a different appearance. The extensive use of glass replacing opaque walls is expressive of the increased transparency of the judicial process, an aspiration for openness of our society's legal system. The pervasive and unavoidable conservatism of legal institutions has not inhibited the architect's ability to search for new forms to solve a functional problem, create a special environment, or to express an idea about the image of justice in our society.

The challenge of this search for form expressive of our intellectual and emotional values is illustrated by a list of often-used adjectives by the public and judiciary to describe the desired qualities of the courthouse. These include:

- Optimistic, formal, having probity
- Forward thinking, stable, solemn
- Inspirational, balanced, permanent
- Welcoming, clear, serious
- Respectful, restrained

Technologies have rapidly advanced the administration of court proceedings (see Chapter 9). One can envision the courthouse of the future relying more and more on developing tools. The tools themselves are calling into question the function of a courthouse and its relationship to more dispersed legal services locations within communities. Already there exists the virtual-reality courthouse environment, where the judge, jury, litigants, and defendants are all located in different

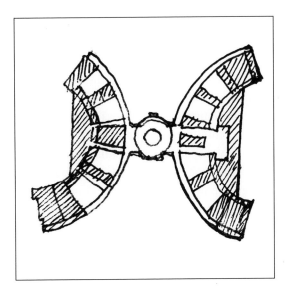

3-30. A central atrium with two bent linear forms: the Jefferson County Courthouse, Boulder, Colorado, C. W. Fentress, J. H. Bradburn.

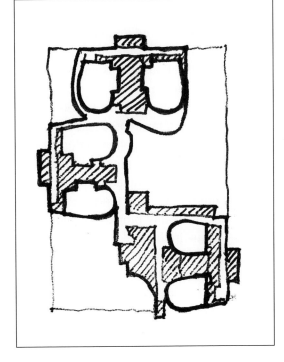

3-31. A clustered complex: the Wayne L. Morse federal courthouse at Eugene, Oregon, Thom Mayne, Morphosis.

places, linked by video technology to communicate in real time and in video view of one another. The future courthouse, like other public institutions, will search for the balance between personal presence and contact and the alternatives offered by technology. In the extreme the courthouse may resemble more of a symbolic temple of justice than the actual location where crucial judicial events take place. The architecture could merely identify the courts' position in the civic realm and the courthouse as the center for the management of highly sophisticated telecommunications activities linking widely dispersed participants.

It is probable that with the rapid development of technological options:

1. Communication devices will enhance audiovisual communications in the courtroom.

2. Personal TV monitors will increasingly be provided at every participant's position.

3. Increased technological development will ensure the intimate perception of each participant's features, mannerisms, and emotions that is necessary for human interactive judgments when participants are remote from each other.

4. Telecommunication of proceedings for both local participation and greater public access will be provided for those in remote areas, eliminating lengthy travel times to the courthouse.

5. Virtual-reality projections of matters at issue in the trial will be presented within the courtroom.

6. Dispersal of courthouse functions to locations more convenient for routine transactions via electronic communication will be provided.

7. Within the courtroom the trend will continue to increase use of portable computers for access to vast amounts of information quickly.

Security and protection have become a more urgent and heightened concern of the American people since September 11, 2001 and the attacks on American embassies abroad and U. S. federal office buildings. Courthouses have

increasingly become targets of terrorist threats. The traditional concern for the internal security of prisoners and the safety of staff and the visiting public has grown to include a realization that external threats need to be addressed with equal vigilance.

There is a belief among judges, court administrators, and architects that courthouses, with their public mission of openness and fairness in their administration of our laws, cannot become armed fortresses. To achieve security goals while preserving the openness of design solutions is a future challenge that architects are beginning to solve in a variety of ways.

Openness through site location and ease of public access has been increasing. Enhanced perimeter security and stand-off distances for building projects are being implemented in many courthouses. Unsightly concrete barriers—the immediate security response—are now being replaced with more decorative bollards, concealed pop-up barriers, and other noninvasive site treatments.

There is a continued desire to provide exterior glass facades to convey openness, bringing natural light into courthouse interiors and providing views from within. To facilitate this trend, new engineered blast-resistant technology is being employed. Engineering studies related to progressive building collapse and other building failure scenarios are increasingly employed in courthouse design projects. Architects and engineers have successfully provided highly sophisticated combinations of product and building assemblies to meet security criteria as well as many aesthetic and civic design goals.

A movement that challenges the

trends of design excellence, technological innovation, and greater security is the reuse and renovation of older courthouses. Courthouses that were turned over to private use, administrative offices of various governments, or left unoccupied are now being reconsidered for public court proceedings.

A prime reason for this trend is the expansion of court systems. The use of older criminal courthouses for civil proceedings is often an answer. The old D.C. courthouse from the 1830s is being renovated for the Washington, D.C., court of appeals. The Nix federal courthouse in Philadelphia has been renovated into a federal bankruptcy court and an old Brooklyn post office is under renovation for the same purpose.

Courthouses are built for decades of continued use and change. The union of the function of courthouse operations with the elements of light, air, circulation, well-planned technology, and security systems is the essence of courthouse planning.

New geometries will continue to fascinate architects and the public. We search for them with the realization that all well-designed courthouses contain a rational geometry that physically embodies the judicial process. We further see how courthouses reflect their time, and how their essential geometry responds to the goals and judgments of the many courthouse stakeholders. Courthouse relationships to the city or site, height, and distinctive features are often issues of public or political debate and are representative of the times in which the courthouses were built. These civic landmarks, most often major financial undertakings, cannot be separated from their political and social environments.

FOUR

Urban Design and the Courthouse: How Sites Shape Solutions

ANDREA P. LEERS

Of the many forces that influence the design of the modern courthouse, the site, its urban setting, and its particular limitations and opportunities have emerged as principal determinants. Internal functional relationships, which are now fairly well understood after considerable experience with the current generation of courthouses, have been found to be adaptable to a broad range of configurations (see Chapter 3). Consequently, external pressures on the courthouse from the city and site are frequently the most powerful factors in shaping the form of the courthouse.

The Courthouse in Its Historic Setting

Historically, as seen in Chapter 1, the American courthouse has commonly been located in a central position in the city or town, giving it prominence and a highly symbolic presence. The courthouse of the early republic defined the town square or town center together with its counterpart, the church, representing secular and sacred realms of public life. Courthouses such as the

Charlotte County Courthouse, Charlotte, Virginia (fig. 4-1) and the Fairfield County Courthouse in Winnsboro, South Carolina (Robert Mills, 1844) were small jewels set in a green landscape with a clearly visible approach and immediate legibility. The one-courtroom courthouse in a Greek temple form marked the center of the pastoral community with its simple and recognizable profile.

By the late nineteenth century and the completion of westward expansion, the program of the courthouse had grown to include several courtrooms, and sites became more urban. Courthouses occupied large sites, were seen in close proximity to other buildings, and began to define entire civic precincts. The paradigm of this period of courthouse building, the Allegheny County Courthouse in Pittsburgh, Pennsylvania (fig. 4-2), claimed a full city block at the heart of the city. This multicourtroom courthouse, in H. H. Richardson's distinctive interpretation of the Romanesque style, achieved its remarkable identity by introducing large-scale elements such as broad arches and deep porches to define entries and principal spaces, and a soaring tower to mark the courthouse on the city skyline.

In the prewar period of the early twentieth century a new model for courthouses emerged, moving away from the romantic rough-hewn Romanesque toward a Beaux-Arts neoclassical style. Because the new style was employed for federal courthouses, custom houses, and post offices, it became known as the federal style, but it was frequently employed for large state and county facilities as well. Courthouses of this era were urban palazzi, occupying a full city block, and, in dramatic contrast to the pastoral one-courtroom courthouses, were built continuously to the street edge. The courthouses of this era, such as federal courthouses in Portland, Maine (fig. 4-3), Providence, Rhode Island (1908; see fig. 6-15), San Francisco, California (1905; see fig. 8-4), San Diego, California (1913), and Laredo, Texas (1906, 1933), all overseen by Supervising Architect James Knox Taylor, were responsive to local conditions of geography and climate within a general neoclassical schema.

The courthouses of the early republic, of the years of westward expansion, and of the prewar federal style were all well-developed paradigms whose form and planning evolved continuously and consistently. Each type was built successfully in widely ranging locations and settings and adapted resourcefully to respond to climate, regionally available materials, and local conditions.

After World War II designers sought to set aside earlier paradigms and redefine the courthouse and its symbolic form in the urban setting. Two remark-

4-1. The paradigm for courthouses of the early republic: Charlotte County Courthouse, Charlotte, Virginia, Thomas Jefferson, 1823. (Photo: John O. Peters)

4-2. The quintessential courthouse of the age of westward expansion: Allegheny County Courthouse, Pittsburgh, Pennsylvania, H. H. Richardson, 1884–88.

Federal Court House, Portland, Me.

4-3. A federal-style courthouse: United States Courthouse, Portland, Maine, James Knox Taylor, Supervising Architect, 1905. (This postcard view predates a 1933 addition.)

able and distinctly divergent interpretations of the courthouse as civic center are worthy of note: Mies van der Rohe's Everett McKinley Dirksen Federal Center and United States Courthouse in Chicago, Illinois (see figs. PR-1, 3-2, and 6-7), which consists of two office towers and a low pavilion of meticulously proportioned and detailed steel and glass defining a public plaza as the new civic ideal; and Arthur Erickson's Robson Square and Law Courts Complex in Vancouver, British Columbia, Canada (fig. 4-4), a three-block complex that combines public plaza, stepped terraces, and the courts in a continuous structured urban park. Both Mies and Erickson chose to suppress the identity of the courthouse itself in the larger urban ensemble.

The Dominant Role of the Site

The loss of symbolic identity for the house of justice has prompted a renewed inquiry into the form of the courthouse (see Chapter 2), and that inquiry draws

important inspiration from the considerations of urban design and site-specific response. But it has been a struggle to find suitable sites for the new generation of courthouses. The most central, highly visible, and privileged sites have long since been built upon. The remaining available sites are more idiosyncratic. They are often tight infill sites, well-located but highly constrained, or they are peripheral to the main civic center and reach into residential or industrial areas. The new courthouses are typically bigger than buildings that surround them; they are often the largest public building in the city. Their design requires careful consideration of scale in massing and detail.

The courthouse is not only affected by the characteristics of the site but also can be a powerful force in transforming, restoring, and reinterpreting it—and, indeed, the entire sector of the city in which it is located. The courthouse can spur development and redevelopment, provide economic incentive to other investment, and generate a sense of vitality for the civic enterprise.

Each site and its place in the urban fabric creates demands as well as opportunities for the design of the courthouse. Some courthouses fulfill an important role in an urban ensemble; others must fit into highly constrained infill sites; some must respond to a unique edge or boundary condition; still others must negotiate a transition at the margins of the civic area. Each condition has a dramatic impact on the form of the courthouse, its approach, orientation, and overall configuration. Resourceful and imaginative responses to each of these conditions may be found in courts of every jurisdiction and type.

ANDREA P. LEERS

Creating or Completing an Ensemble

The challenge of unifying an unfinished precinct of cityscape was at the heart of the design for the Edward W. Brooke Courthouse in Boston, Massachusetts (see fig. C-2). The courthouse provides facilities for the expanded needs of the Suffolk County courts and is located in the Government Center area, steps away from Quincy Market, the city hall designed by the same firm in the 1960s, and two nearby historic courthouses scheduled for renovation. The site was a steeply sloping triangular parking lot originally intended for the completion of the State Services Center designed by Paul Rudolph in the 1970s (fig. 4-5). Surrounded on remaining sides by the refined early-nineteenth-century brick fabric of the Bulfinch Triangle and the rough concrete Government Center Parking Garage built in the 1960s, the new courthouse deftly negotiates the difficulties presented with an irregular courtyard building clad in limestone. The two wings containing the courtrooms define the two principal streets and complete the block. The principal entry to the courthouse is located at the juncture of the two wings. A third wing, with judges' chambers, contains a monumental ground-level arcade through the middle of the city block. The triangular interior atrium joining the three wings is the focus of the building. Although the courthouse derives inspiration from the model of the Allegheny County Courthouse, it adapts masterfully to its irregular site and creates a sense of satisfying

4-4. The civic center absorbs the courthouse: Robson Square and the Law Courts Complex, Vancouver, British Columbia, Canada, Arthur Erickson, Architects, 1980. (Photo: Ezra Stoller © Esto)

4-5. Government Center, Boston, Massachusetts, under construction c. 1969, showing Boston City Hall and Plaza at left (1), the government center garage at center (2), the future courthouse site at right (3), and State Services Center going up at right (4).

completion for a difficult urban ensemble.

In the federal court system, several new courthouses have been the catalyst for urban design initiatives. The Charles Evans Whittaker United States Courthouse in Kansas City, Missouri (see fig. C-3), and the new federal courthouse in Minneapolis, Minnesota (see fig. C-4) both face city and county offices and shape a new public plaza between the several civic buildings.

The design of the federal courthouse in Kansas City effected a major transformation and revitalization in the central business district. The courthouse was

sited on a Missouri River bluff, the highest ground in the downtown area, on a full block facing the city hall and on axis with the Heart of America Bridge into the city. Early in the planning process, community leaders saw the opportunity to create a new public space between the city hall and the new courthouse, then occupied by parking and other less effective uses. As the result of coordinated development, the new courthouse and the city hall face one another and frame the two ends of a new two-block civic mall, the focus of a larger six-block government area. The massing of the

ANDREA P. LEERS

city hall inspired the form of the court-house; the early-twentieth-century struc-ture has a prominent tower atop a broad base. The new courthouse has a tall crescent-shaped tower for the court-rooms and chambers and a lower rotun-da lobby for administrative functions that sits above a stepped podium. The inner glass facade of the tower and wel-coming rotunda embrace the planned Ilus W. Davis Civic Mall. The new court-house is a distinctive landmark on the city skyline, a significant contributor to a new urban ensemble, and a symbolic gateway to the city center.

The new Federal Building and United States Courthouse in Minneapolis is also specifically designed to complete an urban ensemble (fig. 4-6). At the center of the downtown civic district, the court-house site is a full block in front of the city hall. Immediately behind the city hall, the Hennepin County Government Center (John Carl Warnecke, 1971–75) occupies a comparable block. Conse-quently, the city hall becomes the cen-terpiece of an enlarged government ensemble. The design of the new court-house is significantly shaped by its role in the civic setting as well as by the architecture of the city hall, a late-nine-teenth-century Richardsonian structure with a prominent center tower rising out of the building base. Despite the large program required for the courthouse, the volume of the building pulls back from the city hall to create a generous public plaza between the two, reflecting a simi-lar space between the county facility and the city hall. The courthouse is com-posed of overlapping elements that frame the plaza—the tower of court-rooms and chambers, the lower adminis-trative block, and the lobby and

cafeteria—each with a concave curved facade embracing the city hall. Whereas the lower volumes mediate the scale at the pedestrian level of the plaza, the courtroom tower creates a vertical ele-ment complementary to the city hall tower. The flat curve of the courthouse facades on the plaza has its point of ori-gin at the center of the city hall block, with the result that the city hall becomes the legible center of a combined county, city, and federal complex.

The challenge of creating a successful

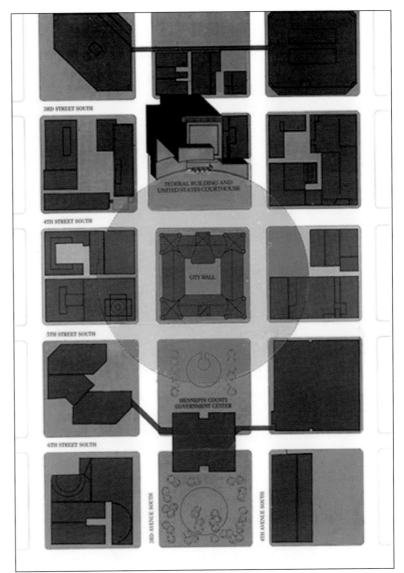

4-6. A new courthouse completes an existing urban ensemble. Site plan for United States Courthouse, Minneapolis, Minnesota, Kohn Pedersen Fox Associ-ates, Design Architect, and Architectur-al Alliance, Associate Architect, 1997.

dialogue between a very large courthouse and other buildings in a dense urban setting is considerable. At Foley Square in New York City, the Daniel Patrick Moynihan United States Courthouse (see fig. 2-21) combines a gracefully proportioned tower with carefully scaled lower elements to create a ground-level experience of considerable variety. Its relationship to nearby buildings by Cass Gilbert, Guy Lowell, and McKim, Mead & White creates an engaging ensemble of buildings in this extremely dense part of lower Manhattan. In Portland, Oregon, the Mark O. Hatfield United States Courthouse joins other significant public buildings, including Michael Graves's Portland Building (1982), which surrounds the three park blocks of government center (see fig. C-5). The new courthouse, at the corner of Lownsdale Square, is remarkably successful in achieving transitions to its surroundings. Its tower is slightly angled toward a focal point within the park and offers views of Mount Hood in the distance; the intermediate administrative block is offset from the tower and echoes the predominant height of its neighbors. The lower lobby is marked by an outdoor loggia that lines the park. Both the New York and Portland courthouses, despite their considerable size, contribute positively to the grouping of buildings and open spaces around them without dominating or diminishing their coherence.

The Courthouse as Urban Infill

In some instances the only available site in desirable proximity to the civic center is a small or fragmented infill parcel that presents enormous challenges for courthouse design. Two examples in dramati-

ANDREA P. LEERS

cally different settings illustrate a response to the issue of configuring a courthouse on a "residual" site. The Bronx housing court in New York City (see fig. C-6) is located in a dense urban environment of high-rise apartment blocks, commercial buildings, and public structures. It is embedded in a midblock site and surrounded by multistory buildings that occupy their sites from property line to street edge. An inventive and graceful solution accommodates the sizable program within the highly constrained site while maintaining the scale of adjacent structures. The lower half of the building, including the majority of courtrooms (fig. 4-7), is virtually blocked by the nearness of the adjacent building wall. To compensate for the inability to create windows, light wells and skylights introduce daylight at the sides of the building deep into the lower floors (fig. 4-8). Chambers and administrative spaces are housed in a slender tower rising above the adjacent building. The choice of materials—brick in three-color bands combined with large areas of glass—links the new courthouse to the adjacent building context without imitation.

In a contrasting small-city setting, the challenges of creating a courthouse on an infill site were equally demanding. Beckley, West Virginia is a regional center for the Appalachian coal country, which has experienced decline of its downtown as growth occurred on the edges of the community. The site for the new Robert C. Byrd United States Courthouse and Federal Building was selected at the center of town in an effort to reverse this trend (see fig. C-7). The available infill site was an L-shaped parcel bounded by buildings on its sides,

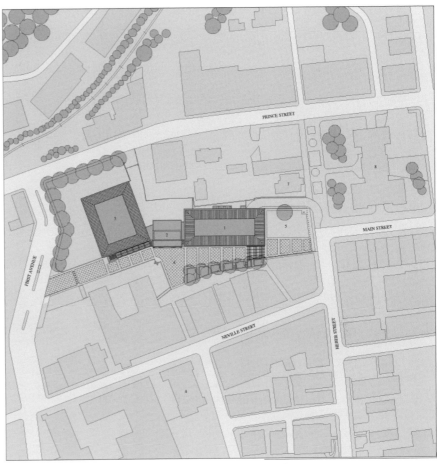

4-9. A complex site in a smaller city: site plan for Robert C. Byrd United States Courthouse and Federal Building, Beckley, West Virginia, Robert A. M. Stern Architects, Design Architect, SEM Partners, Inc., Local Architect, and Einhorn Yaffe Prescott, Architect of Record, 1999.

very narrow at its middle, and dramatically sloping down 30 feet from its Main Street side to First Avenue. It posed severe limitations on the optimal configuration of the building. The new courthouse is ingeniously woven into its difficult site by dividing its program into three distinct elements: the courthouse facing Main Street, the civic lobby and entry at midblock, and the Internal Revenue Service facility facing First Avenue (figs. 4-9–4-11). The three elements are joined by an arcade, stairway, and terraced garden on the south side of the building, creating an inviting passage through the block, despite the poor condition of the backs of the adjacent buildings. The subdivision of the program

4-10. Byrd Courthouse, Beckley, as seen from Main Street.
(Photo: Peter Aaron © Esto)

4-11. Byrd Courthouse entry at midblock, looking toward
Main Street. (Photo: Peter Aaron © Esto)

into component parts not only facilitated its adaptation to the site but also mediated the scale of this large public building in its small-scale environment. The courthouse facing Main Street is set back to create a grassy forecourt. As one approaches from Main Street, it becomes the centerpiece of a group of civic buildings, including the 1937 Raleigh County Courthouse and the post office.

Responding to a Dominant Site Feature

Courthouse sites that afford a direct relationship with the civic center are not always available. When sites are isolated from other public buildings or not clearly part of an urban grouping, then a prominent view or a unique site element may become the driving force in determining the courthouse design. A site at the water's edge is a powerful influence in shaping a courthouse for views and

ANDREA P. LEERS

SITE PLAN

4-12. A site at the edge of the historic canal offers opportunities for views and public visibility; site plan, Fenton Judicial Center, Lawrence, Massachusetts, Leers Weinzapfel Associates, 1998.

public visibility. Two notable examples illustrate a response to this opportunity. The Fenton Judicial Center in Lawrence, Massachusetts (see fig. C-8) is a large county courthouse in a former textile mill city. The new courthouse is the cornerstone of a downtown revitalization program and government center that includes the city hall and the superior court. The site has its long edge along the canal that brought waterpower to the mills and its short edge to the cross street that connected the mills with the downtown and the city green (fig. 4-12). The design of the courthouse creates a continuous exterior arcade and window wall along the canal and its newly developed linear park. The entry at the corner leads to an interior public lobby overlooking the canal. On the lower floor, administrative services line the lobby; on upper floors, courtrooms open on to generous waiting areas with views across the canal to the mills beyond. The city of Lawrence was built over a ten-year period in the late 1800s by Pacific Mills and has a remarkable consistency of material and building form. The new courthouse extends the context of simple forms with continuous roof lines, walls that meet the street, and predominant brick, while infusing the design with new elements in metal and glass, crisp modern detailing, and the proportions and scale appropriate to a civic, rather than an industrial, building.

4-13. A courthouse conceived to take advantage of an extraordinary site. John Joseph Moakley United States Courthouse and Harborpark, Boston, Massachusetts, Pei Cobb Freed & Partners, Jung Brannen Associates, 1998. (Photo: Steve Rosenthal)

4-14. A glass-wrapped atrium offers spectacular views of the harbor and the city, Moakley Courthouse. (Photo: Steve Rosenthal)

Sited spectacularly at the edge of Boston Harbor, the John Joseph Moakley United States Courthouse and Harborpark in Boston are configured to embrace the waterfront (see fig. C-9). The site is located on Fan Pier in the Fort Point Channel area of the city, once the locus of active shipping and warehousing, and currently a mix of low-density commercial, recreational, and industrial uses. The courthouse is the cornerstone of new development in the former industrial area, which is in close proximity to the downtown Financial District (figs. 4-13 and 4-14). The courthouse has two distinct sides that take advantage of its unique condition at the edge of the water. An L-shaped brick volume containing courtrooms and chambers lines the street sides of the site, with the entry and cylindrical rotunda at the corner. A glass-wrapped conical atrium on the water side, containing the public lobby, jury assembly area, and cafeteria, opens out to spectacular views of the harbor and the city. All the courtroom entries are visible through the curved glass atrium wall from the city, symbolically conveying the accessibility of justice to all citizens. The open space of the site on the harbor edge is a welcoming public park; at lunch time office workers and courthouse occupants enjoy sun and view; and on weekends residents and visitors find the park an extraordinary asset to the city. In both the Lawrence and Boston examples there is a dramatic difference between the open and closed sides of the courthouse in response to the condition of being at the water's edge.

Other unique site factors can be the dominant inspiration for the design of the courthouse. Retaining a significant

ANDREA P. LEERS

4-15. Mature trees contribute to a memorable exterior identity and define an important internal focus as well. United States Courthouse, Springfield, Massachusetts, model view, Moshe Safdie Associates, 2006. (Photo: John Horner)

group of very mature trees was the departure point for the new courthouse in Springfield, Massachusetts (fig. 4-15). The city, which was settled in the Revolutionary era, is located on the banks of the Connecticut River and is home to the Springfield Armory. The site for the new courthouse is on State Street, a broad avenue rising from the river and the downtown area. It is surrounded by the major cultural institutions of the city—Museum of Fine Arts, Springfield Public Library, Church of the Catholic Diocese—and set back from the street with generous lawns and trees. The courthouse site contained several very old and large trees valued by the city and the courts as much as the historic buildings in the area. Making the trees the centerpiece of the new courthouse was the key to the urban design of the building. The courthouse form is a spiraling crescent around three existing trees—a copper beech, a linden, and a black walnut, each two- to five-hundred years old. The curved pub-

lic arcade, gallery, and courtrooms embrace the trees, creating a memorable exterior identity and important internal focus for the building.

Marginal Sites

Increasingly, sites large enough to accommodate the new programs for the courthouse must be found in peripheral areas of the city that lack significant amenities, such as a compelling view of the water or a nearby park or significant landscape feature. Sites at the margins face the multiple challenges of creating civic identity within industrial areas, of adjusting the scale of a large building adjacent to residential areas, of mitigating the proximity of intrusive infrastructure such as major roads or train lines, and of compensating for the absence of pedestrian access and amenities. Such marginal sites, however, offer the extraordinary opportunity to generate new activity and development in neglected areas and to transform abandoned

4-16. The courthouse on a marginal site adjacent to an elevated highway reinforces the connection to the city center and creates a public park. Aerial view of site model, United States Courthouse, Orlando, Florida, Leers Weinzapfel Associates, HLM Design Joint Venture LLC, 2006. (Photo: Leers Weinzapfel Associates)

4-17. The courthouse as pioneer in an expanded downtown area. Site plan, Wayne L. Morse Federal Courthouse, Eugene, Oregon, Morphosis and DLR Group, 2006.

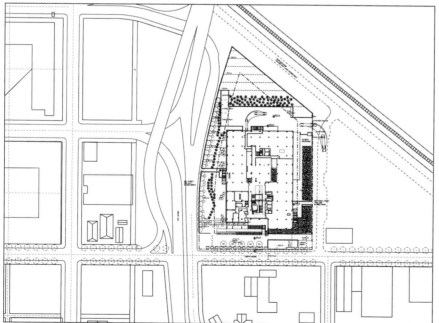

sites into a new public realm. The new federal courthouse in Orlando, Florida (see fig. C-11) and the Wayne L. Morse courthouse in Eugene, Oregon (see fig. C-12) are both located on sites separated from the center of the city by a formidable barrier of highways.

In Orlando, the courthouse site is located on one side of a highway and railway line that dramatically divide it from the center of the city. The site is a full city block, already occupied by the present Federal Building and bounded by a struggling residential neighborhood on one side and the elevated highway on the other. One edge of the block faces the principal east–west street, Central

ANDREA P. LEERS

4-18. A privileged site on the moat facing the Imperial Palace. Supreme Court of Japan, Tokyo, Shin'ichi Okada, 1969–74.

Boulevard (fig. 4-16). The design of the new courthouse is intended to bridge the divide between the two parts of the city. The courthouse, its public atrium, and a parking deck are aligned along Central Boulevard and set back from the street edge by a raised plaza shaded by a dense planting of live oak trees. A tower entry at the corner toward the neighborhood reinforces connections with the rest of the city. The new courthouse is linked to the existing building, and together the two structures define a generous city park facing the community.

In Eugene the site for the new courthouse is similarly challenged by its peripheral location in a largely industrial area along the Willamette River. A multi-lane through avenue divides the site from the center of the city. The design proposes a singular and memorable identity to connect the new courthouse to the city (fig. 4-17). A generous plaza and long, low porch draw visitors into the square building podium, which con-tains the entry and administrative functions. From this broad base the courtrooms and chambers rise in three curved sculptural forms clad in zinc panels, whose distinctive shape is visible on the skyline of this low-profile city. Inside, the public spaces at the upper level, which is the courtroom level, have views to the city, to the river, and to the mountains beyond. The courthouse is the first new construction in a part of the city designated to expand the downtown through significant redevelopment.

International Exemplars

Despite differences in judicial systems, modern courthouses around the world have much in common: their symbolic role in the community, their functional and secure planning, and, most relevant to this discussion, their response to challenging urban conditions. The Supreme Court of Japan in Tokyo (fig. 4-18) is sited in a highly privileged location: at the center of Tokyo, facing the Imperial

Palace across its private moat. Consequently, the design of this refined palace of justice is organized with its ceremonial entry court and most important judicial areas facing outward toward the Imperial Palace. The center hall and courtrooms, by contrast, are deeply embedded in the complex, focused inward, and lit mysteriously and dramatically from above.

More recently, the international competition for the Supreme Court of Israel in Jerusalem (fig. 4-19) resulted in a compelling design inspired by its dramatic hilltop site that is the locus of the government center. The Supreme Court is prominent when viewed from the dense residential neighborhoods below, and it faces east, as do many historic monuments of the city. Responding to the harsh desert climate, the courts complex is conceived as a series of stone masses carved into the hill, producing dramatic interior waiting halls and courtrooms, washed in light from above, and

oases of contemplation for the judges.

The Supreme Court of Iceland in Reykjavik (fig. 4-20), also the result of a competition, is designed to form an urban ensemble at the heart of the city, joining the National Theatre, the National Library, and the State Ministries buildings. The courthouse completes a sheltered courtyard and urban garden in this severe northern climate. The public promenade to the courtrooms passes along the garden edge behind a copper-sheathed wall that billows out to afford views of the landscape.

Dramatic demonstrations of the impact of site on courthouse design can be seen in several examples from the ambitious and highly innovative courthouse building program in France. As in the United States, France faces a recent dramatic increase in litigation and caseload coupled with an inventory of outdated facilities. An assessment of existing facilities indicated that very little had been built since the nineteenth century

ANDREA P. LEERS

and that the traditional courthouses had a shortage of both courtrooms and offices and were not operationally effective in terms of modern needs. Those few judicial centers (*cités judiciaires*) created in the 1970s and 1980s around Paris were deemed insufficiently symbolic and civic in stature. The Ministry of Justice, responsible for managing judicial facilities since the political reform of the 1980s, created an agency, led by civil engineers, charged with developing a multiyear building plan (Délégation Générale au Programme Pluriannuel d'Equipement du Ministère de la Justice; DGPPE). As of 2003, twenty major new and renovated courthouse projects have been completed and eighteen more are being studied. The new facilities are equal to nearly half the production of the last century.

In contrast to the U.S. approach, which began the courthouse building program by developing court design guidelines for planning, the French program began by defining the historic and symbolic function of judicial architecture, as expressed in a document entitled "Architectural Conception of Courthouses," given to every architect before design began. Seeking to reverse the drab design that characterized judicial centers in the 1970s and 1980s, which were little more than office buildings, the ministry proposed "a new monumentality, different from the traditional neoclassical type, and appropriate to a modern democratic society."[1]

A main goal of the French program was to put the courthouse back in the center of the city, despite the frequent conflicts with priorities related to historic preservation, so that justice would be seen as a fundamental part of its

4-20. The Supreme Court of Iceland draws together an urban ensemble, Reykjavik, Architect Studio Granda, 1996. (Photo: Dennis Gilbert)

democratic society and not an institution apart. The ministry wished to create courthouses whose presence was both monumental, reflecting the authority of the Civil Code, and transparent, reflecting the accessibility and mediation role of the judicial process. The overarching need was to inform and welcome citizens, and to render decisions in suitable conditions without unreasonable delay.

Architects for the courthouses are selected by design competition, as they are for nearly all public buildings in France. The focus on the importance of architecture in the public realm was given emphasis by President Giscard d'Estaing in 1977, when he officially declared that architectural creativity, quality

4-21. A courthouse embedded in an eighteenth-century district of the city. The High Court and Lower Court Building, Montpellier, France, Bernard Kohn, 1996.

Publiques; MIQCP). The commission introduced the practice of employing design competitions for public projects, and it acts as advisor to the competition process in selecting the jurors, which usually include magistrates, a project manager, and a well-known architect. The competition process invites diverse design responses and highly creative interpretations of the identity of the contemporary courthouse.

Two courthouses embedded in the historic fabric of their city demonstrate the distinctive way each takes part in the urban setting. Bernard Kohn's courthouse in Montpellier (see fig. C-13) is absorbed quietly into the dense residential matrix that surrounds it, whereas Richard Rogers's courthouse in Bordeaux (see fig. C-14) stands out as a highly identifiable new presence in the ensemble of existing justice facilities. At more marginal locations in the city, two courthouses draw on a clear and recognizable monumental image of the courthouse to anchor their civic purpose. The courthouse in Melun (see fig. C-15) and the courthouse in Nantes (see fig. C-16) both draw on the typology of the temple form, ceremonial porch, and symmetrical composition. Within this overall schema they are realized in different forms and materials.

A more challenging instance of urban infill than the courthouse in Montpellier can hardly be imagined. Located in the south of France, this Mediterranean city has strong connections to North Africa and has long been an education and research center. It enjoyed major growth in the seventeenth and eighteenth centuries, and street patterns and many buildings of the era remain today. The site for the courthouse is in one of the

of construction, harmonious insertion into context, and respect for the natural and urban landscape and historic building were all in the public interest. A commission was created to improve the practical, technical, and symbolic quality of architecture (Mission Interministérielle pour la Qualité des Constructions

ANDREA P. LEERS

4-22. An iconic monument in an ensemble of monuments. The High Court, Bordeaux, France, Richard Rogers Partnership, 1998. (Photo: Christian Richter)

oldest parts of the historic city (fig. 4-21). Two- and three-story housing surrounds the site, which lies at the foot of the Place Royale-du-Peyrou, an urban garden completed in 1774. A law of the eighteenth century, still in effect, prohibits any adjacent structure from blocking the horizon from the Place Royale, ensuring its place as a belvedere in the urban environment. The design response to these extraordinary constraints is a rich and low stone-clad carpet of spaces whose roof plane, seen from the Place Royale, becomes a fifth facade. Courtrooms are readily identified by their skylight roofs. A major entry courtyard and smaller private gardens are carved into the three-story block of the courthouse, offering relief for those using the building as well as breathing space for the narrow streets of the neighborhood. Both outside and in, the courthouse conveys a humane sense of justice and a careful balance between gravity and accessibility, between authority and restraint. The courthouse is a masterful effort of fitting a large civic structure into a delicate historic urban fabric with grace and imagination.

The courthouse in Bordeaux (fig. 4-22) responds to its place in the center of the city with a different strategy: it is an equal player among monuments. Near the southwest coast of France, Bordeaux is predominantly an eighteenth-century city that grew to prominence between 1720 and 1780, when it was France's major port along the Garonne River. Then, as now, wine led the exports in trade with India, northern Europe, and America. Beautiful boulevards, squares, and monuments characterize the city created during this period. The courthouse site is part of a judicial precinct located at the limit of the city as it existed in the early nineteenth century.

The new courthouse joins an exemplary nineteenth-century courthouse designed by Adophe Thiac, a law school of the 1970s designed by the Prix-de-Rome winner Guillaume Gillet, and two fifteenth-century towers that are vestiges of nearby fortresses protecting the entries to the city. The new structure is a simple rectangle divided in two parts and inserted into the ensemble of the block. The part facing the main boulevard and connected to the nineteenth-century courthouse contains the administrative functions and generally conforms to the urban fabric; it has a base of stone, bands of glass in the off-

4-23. The Bordeaux High Court from street level. (Photo: Andrea P. Leers)

4-24. Exterior view toward courtrooms of the Bordeaux High Court. (Photo: Vincent Monthiers)

128

ices above, and a canopied attic storey housing the library and conference rooms (fig. 4-23). The part facing inward and connected to the tower houses the public zone and is highly expressive of its symbolic function. The inner block is composed of a series of raised conical courtrooms wrapped in cedar, likened variously to wine casks, eggshells, or beehives, seen behind the sheer glass wall of the waiting space (fig. 4-24). Justice is dramatically on display. Between the two blocks an atrium, crossed by bridges and structural elements, brings light into the interior. A sinuous roof floats over the whole volume, pierced by the tops of the courtrooms. Many structural elements of the new courthouse are reminiscent of the architect's earlier design for the Centre Pompidou. The boldly theatrical Bordeaux courthouse maintains its own voice in the ensemble and is an extraordinary invention of unprecedented sculptural form.

When the site for the courthouse is on the margins of the city, giving the courthouse a clear civic identity becomes more important than responding to the immediate building context. In the city of Melun, whose history dates from the Roman period as a settlement along the Seine on the road to Paris, a site large enough to accommodate the new judicial facilities in the historic center was not available. Instead, the courthouse is located in a redevelopment area, the site of a former brewery, immediately adjacent to the Melun train station (fig. 4-25). In a setting largely defined by major roads, elevated train line, and high-volume traffic, the design for the courthouse resists integration into the context and instead claims its own identity and landmark role. Draw-

4-25. The courthouse is separated by an elevated train line from the historic center of the city, Melun, France, Jourda and Perraudin, 1997. (Photo: Jean Marie Monthiers)

ing broadly on a reinterpretation of the classical temple, the Melun courthouse is a serene structure, symmetrical and rectangular in form (see fig. C-15). The lower part of the volume, clad in etched glass, contains the waiting hall and courtrooms, and the upper part of the volume, defined by operable metal lou-

4-27. Riverfront plaza and great entry porch, the Nantes courthouse.

vers and windows, contains offices and meeting space. At the front of the courthouse a monumental porch, with gracefully branching steel columns and light glass roof, welcomes the public. Inside, the clarity of planning and the beautifully shaped and illuminated courtrooms reinforce the identity of the courthouse as a place of generous justice. The simple strength of the overall form, the highly refined and beautiful material palette, and the symbolic presence of the porch all contribute to its legibility as a courthouse in this marginal and adversely impacted site.

By contrast to the lightness of Melun, the new courthouse in Nantes is a

severe and powerful judicial presence, shaped by its role in the evolution of the city (see fig. C-16). It is the cornerstone of redevelopment in the city's former industrial area—the Ile de Sainte-Anne. Nantes, like Bordeaux, flourished as a maritime port in the eighteenth century. Located west of Paris on the Loire River, opening to the Atlantic, Nantes was an active shipping and industrial center. Today, new industries, including the famous Biscuits Nantais, have relocated, leaving a vast area largely abandoned. The choice of site for the new courthouse has important symbolic value; it is directly across from the center of the city (fig. 4-26). The courthouse establishes a new context for itself and for expansion of the city center across the river. As at Melun, the classical temple form is reinterpreted to give a strong symbolic legibility to the new building and its precinct. The courthouse is a symmetrically composed, horizontal pavilion with its face to the city. A deep steel-framed porch and inclined plaza reaching down to the river recall the steps and portico of the traditional courthouse (fig. 4-27). Beyond the porch, a large waiting hall with a full glass wall to the city leads to the courtrooms (fig. 4-28). A layer of gridded screens creates a waiting zone outside the courtroom entries. The courtrooms are independent cubes within the volume of the waiting hall. Administrative areas above, in alternating bands of offices and gardens, have a cafeteria and terrace overlooking the river and city center. The highly rational and functional planning is overlaid with a supercharged emotional quality. All exterior and interior materials—stone, steel, wood—in the public areas are black, possibly a reference to the color of local slate. Red-stained wood interiors of the courtrooms provide a dramatic foil to the dark tones of the porch and waiting hall. By day the north-facing courthouse is seen in silhouette against the sky; by night the effect is reversed and the illuminated interior is revealed through the glass wall. As the first demonstration of the potential of a new precinct, the courthouse has a somber beauty and conveys a powerful sense of judicial authority.

The Power of Place

Each of the courthouse examples presented here bears the unique vision of its designer; each responds to well-defined functional requirements; each meets growing security requirements. The defining differences, however, lie in each response to the nature of the place. In the most general sense, each courthouse is grounded in its physical region—its climate, history, and building fabric. A courthouse on a site in Jerusalem should differ significantly from one in Reykjavik, even if designed by the same architect with the same program. Beyond the regional response, the particular site and its characteristics will significantly affect the choices of form, material, and scale of the design. The size of the site, its location within the city, its adjacent conditions and structures all have enormous impact on the ultimate design of the courthouse. The choice of site is, therefore, a critical step in development of the courthouse. It will determine, in large part, the character of its design and present both opportunities and pitfalls.

The interaction of site and design is fundamental because the courthouse has a strong symbolic presence in the community and is a tangible connection to the democratic process. It represents a very significant economic investment in the city and in a neighborhood; the creation of a new courthouse is a stimulus to other development and investment. It is an unparalleled vehicle for creating or supporting a meaningful public realm. Courthouses will always belong to a place, and their design will always reflect this defining reality.

ANDREA P. LEERS

FIVE

Reading the Architecture of Today's Courthouse

PAUL SPENCER BYARD

Courthouse architecture can be read to understand contemporary public attitudes toward justice. Progressive attitudes toward justice tend to produce progressive designs; conservative attitudes, conservative ones. The match between courthouses and their times is quite precise. Architects work hard to express at once what they want to say, what their clients want to hear, and what will make their neighbors love what they build. Like litigants starting what ought to be a winning case, they harness every current favored thought about justice to argue for their building's basic proposition: "if you want a courthouse, this is the way to go." If they do it right, their courthouse—their argument—will be an instrument of leadership: its way will inspire. However they do it, their architecture will be a loud, public, and enduring revelation of the ideas about justice that seemed important to the participants at the time.

Reading today's courthouse architecture for today's view of justice is aided by a look first at a few courthouses from the past. A review of three earlier courthouses—two in the United States and one in Sweden—helps us understand not just the match with different times but how different the times were. It's hard for us to absorb how literal-minded the architects of the Gilded Age sometimes were, as the Allegheny County Courthouse exemplifies. It would be equally hard for them to absorb our sophistication. We're not dealing here with eternal verities but the verities of particular times and what they reveal about their times and, by contrast, about ours.

The Allegheny County Courthouse and Jail

Let's start our run-up to the present with a truly great American work of art, the 1888 Allegheny Courthouse and Jail in Pittsburgh, Pennsylvania (fig. 5-1). H. H. Richardson's masterwork no longer holds the heights of its city so clearly, enclosed as it is now by taller manifestations of still richer, later times. Nor does it emerge visually on its heights from time to time, as it must

5-1. H. H. Richardson's rugged Allegheny County Courthouse of 1888 for a rough, smoky Pittsburgh, Pennsylvania.

once have done in the thick, fast-passing plumes of Pittsburgh industry smoke.

Still, the Allegheny courthouse very well represents justice for the 1880s as the most solid of solid citizens, dressed in cleft stone like one of the big men of the Gilded Age, strong, frequently overweight, and, after the huge investment of the Civil War, richer than could previously have been imagined. Its main building—its main proposition about the place of justice—is strongly and almost conventionally symmetrical. The main entry is right in the middle of the short side of the courthouse block. Secondary entries are centered on each of the long sides. Above the main entrance, a slender square belfry tower comes straight down to mark the importance of the front door as the beginning of the building's discussion of justice. Inside, a mighty stair (fig. 5-2) leads to a perimeter of generous, single-loaded public corridors day-lit from a central court. The corridors give access to offices and a small number of ample courtrooms. The

5-2. The biggest ceremonial event—the mighty stair—inside the Allegheny courthouse.

PAUL SPENCER BYARD

volumes of the rooms are big, the varnished furnishings simple: public seating, a jury box, counsel tables, a wooden bench two steps up, all quite open and accessible. Through a big open oak door by the jury box the judge's desk and chambers are clearly visible; justice here is direct and homely. Rough-hewn as its stone and strong as its arches but with ample orderly windows, the courthouse's principal proposition about the law is something four-square and simple. Litigants come in, make "common" pleas to the local judicial power, and go out again.

With one crucial exception. Asymmetrically from the back of the courthouse, a small but significant bridge arches off and lands across the street in the wall of a remarkable fortified medieval town, the Allegheny County Jail (fig. 5-3). The bridge is not the principal outcome of the courthouse, but it is an important one. Some of the users of the courthouse do not go back out to business; they go to jail. When they do, they go by way of a close copy, in dark stone, of the celebrated Venetian Bridge of Sighs, which likewise took some beneficiaries of the doge's justice off to jail. The fortified town the arched bridge delivers them into is surely one of the wonders of American architecture (fig. 5-4). Its mighty wall wraps a sloping, irregular site penetrated by three of Richardson's characteristic heavy fanned arch openings. Behind the wall a heap of stone buildings culminates in the jail's peaked "keep," the central panopticon with the pinnacles and backs of the naves of the cell blocks radiating out below it. The manacled malefactor of the Gilded Age was delivered, presumably impressed and chastened, into Allegheny County's

5-3. One possible outcome, the walled medieval jail, inside the Allegheny courthouse.

5-4. Pittsburgh's own touch of Venice in the Allegheny courthouse.

5-5. H. H. Richardson at rest.

almost perfect evocation of a mythic penitentiary.

Taken together, the readable meanings of the courthouse and its pendant jail seem literal-minded. Consider the courthouse ventilation system. The twin thin secondary towers of the courthouse stretch up from the back of its courtyard, as if all that was needed to reach and drink clean air above the Pittsburgh smoke was a short pair of straws. In our sophistication, we enjoy the fact that the system seems wonderfully naive. But then we have to put aside our sophistication and realize that the design is not the least ironic, and that we are not to smile at it any more than we are supposed to smile at the literalness of the Bridge of Sighs as the best architectural expression for going to jail. Like the enormous Richardson himself, disarmed and pensive, relaxing in his monk's robe, the picturesque courthouse and jail are perfectly serious and unself-conscious, proclaiming in strong, literal terms both how mighty the United States was becoming after the Civil War and how simple and obvious it still seemed to us the business of justice was (fig. 5-5).

New York State Supreme Court Appellate Division, First Department

The little courthouse of the appellate division, first department, on Madison Square in New York shows vividly what happened next as the United States rejected the Gilded Age in the 1890s in an effort to lift itself to a new level of worldliness and sophistication (fig. 5-6).

Coming little more than a decade after the Allegheny courthouse, the appellate division is the first "white" building completed in New York after the World's Columbian Exposition of

1893 in Chicago (see fig. 1-23). There the assembled luminaries of American design had set about to establish a public architecture to fit a turn in the national direction. As the United States acknowledged the closing of its western frontier and turned eastward and outward to seek command of the world, architecture gave its assistance. Setting out to correct the burly riot of the Gilded Age—including the powerful poetry of the Allegheny courthouse—our public buildings should now be regular, classical, Beaux-Arts, and white. They would still be big, to match the country's needs and ambitions, but they would add a new level of command in their obvious order and symmetry. They would seek legitimacy for their command in the classical mantle of Imperial Rome, and they would adopt the discipline of contemporary European Beaux-Arts design to stiffen the American claim to a place by right in the great imperial fray. To top it off, the buildings would all be white. Unified in a dazzling polemic of correctness, purity, and right, the white architecture of the United States would project our new world power like our White Fleet.

At the World's Columbian Exposition, American architecture, moving fast, troweled on its new layer of self-consciousness and sophistication in plaster on wood. A few years later, at James Brown Lord's Appellate Division, the sophistication had become real marble and the World's Fair polemic had evolved into a serious presentation of an intelligent correctness. After a recent renovation, its white Vermont marble is dazzling, once again projecting strength, clarity, and order at its own appealing small scale.

The courthouse is at once small, rich,

Above left:
5-6. James Brown Lord brought New York the message of the World's Columbian Exposition in the Appellate Division, First Department, 1896.

Above right:
5-7. The gods and goddesses of justice spread the word atop the Appellate Division.

and unusually fine in its scrupulous Beaux-Arts classicism. The basic block of its regular symmetrical form is beautifully proportioned, the tall dark golden rectangles of its windows cutting sharply into its flat white walls. The pediments, columns, and pilasters add a play of light and shadow. Above its balustrade, the tall flamelike statues of juridical heroes add their flicker to the dazzle of its stone (fig. 5-7).

This is law and justice at their most well-dressed and elegant, like counsel in the possibly compulsory morning coats and silk hats for which provision can still be seen in the long brass racks of the lawyers' cloakroom. The decoration of the entry—the mosaic floor, the fine-grained marble paneling, the small bright figures of the high frieze, the crystal diffusers over the light bulbs of the chandeliers—begins to make clear that this consistent elegance is not just dressing. From the entry hall, a pair of dark wood doors opens into the building's single courtroom—possibly the most remarkable achievement of nineteenth-century American interior decoration (see fig. C-17). The doors open behind and beside the justices, allowing the person entering to see the order of the room and go to his or her place without disturbing the argument. In the middle of the same wall at the head of the room, the carved, curved dark wood bench for the justices is opposite three fine murals, one by Henry Oliver Walter depicting a large graceful central figure of descending Wisdom swathed in white. (The others in this triptych are The Justice of the Law, by Edward Emerson Simmons, and The Power of the Law, by Edwin Howland Blashfield.) Over the center of the room is a remarkable stained-glass dome that concentrates everything on the central exchange of words between counsel and the justices.

With its fine figured carpet, carved dark furniture, figured marble, crystal sconces, bright-colored friezes all around, all bathed in natural light diffused by the pale stained-glass dome and stained-glass windows, the room achieves a rare impact and unity at a scale that is very particular. In all this richness there is nothing gross, muscular, or over-blown. Its special nature is suggested by the names, exhortations, and other words that are made part of the decoration. The business of the room is appellate argument, the central intellectual effort of the law to come to understandings about the meanings of words. The fine decoration seems almost equally cerebral, expressing in detail as fine as words its support for the work of the court. Chapter 7 conveys how well this room achieves its central purpose to facilitate intellectual confrontation and exchange.

The Göteborg Courthouse

For a time so preoccupied with the use of decoration to impress, the "impression" of the Appellate Division is remarkably subtle, as if there were many valid choices in an architecture that so often seemed imperious. What was going on in the time between the Allegheny courthouse and the Appellate Division was a relatively peaceful if rapid cultural evolution in the United States, away from the rough vigor of the post-Civil War period to a new sophistication and worldliness at the turn of the century. What came next was very different, the result of catastrophe and revolution, though not in the United States. For Europe, the First World War called into question all the imperial certainties the United States had tried to adopt in its exposition architecture and loosed an aggressive search for alternatives. The best illustration of the next stage in interpretation of justice comes from the remarkable thirty-year history of Gunnar Asplund's proposed addition to the Göteborg Courthouse in Göteborg, Sweden. The design started before the war as a piece of Nordic Beaux-Arts architecture, a little more romantic but just as corrective and orderly as any other piece of architecture of the kind. By the time it was built in 1935, however, twentieth-century ideals of social reform had broken through in the architecture of Modernism.

The Göteborg Courthouse is a paradigm of the power of combinations of old and new architecture to illuminate the evolution of our view of the world— in its case our hopes for human justice —over the passage of time between the old and the new parts (fig. 5-8). The Göteborg Courthouse started as a fine

seventeenth-century court building by Nicodemus Tessin, as good an expression as any of Sweden's role as a major European power at the time. At the beginning of the twentieth century, after many intermediate interventions, the young Asplund won a competition to replace Tessin's courthouse. The Romantic replacement would have enclosed a standard axial Beaux-Arts progression from the relocated front door to a climax in the new big principal courtroom. After the competition the project stalled, Asplund returned to it several years later, now under pressure to save the old building, not demolish it, and to classicize his proposed addition. The project stalled for years more and then came back still more classical, with the Tessin facade intact and the new facilities in a wing more or less blended into the original "style." Had it been built in that form, it would have been an excellent expression of the notion that this far into the twentieth century, nothing much had changed in architecture or in justice.

In fact, nothing could have been further from the truth. Everything was changing. A huge struggle was being resolved, at least for purposes of this project's place and time, in favor of a progessive view of human possibility. In an abrupt switch just before construction began in 1934, Asplund proposed a Modern wing, novel in its simplicity, showing the unadorned order of the grid of its structure, filled in with lots of glass. The addition created a dialogue with Tessin about the purposes of the building across interesting differences of expression (fig. 5-9). The addition got more and more adventurous as it went into the ground, achieving its final fascinating complexity when Asplund, during construction, pushed his new windows off the center of the bays of his grid.

Asplund was a great artist, and he had been thinking about the problem of the courthouse and what it should represent for almost twenty-five years. Most importantly, he came back to it finally in 1934 after a political change that, with the accession to power of the Social Democrats, had brought Swedish justice itself into line with the highest ambitions of the Modern architecture Asplund had come to favor. This particular intersection of new architecture and new social policy produced a combined work of rare clarity and importance to illuminate its times.

In the final scheme, the front door—the way in to justice—still belongs to the old building—to Tessin and to a familar expression of a classical order and authority. Immediately behind the arches of the old building, however, comes a right turn through a glass wall into a superb, tall atrium obliquely lit from the top with a cascade of natural light. Off the court are floors of simple, plain, courtrooms loosely planned with judges benches just inches above the floor. Outside the courtrooms are tables and chairs, inviting conference. On the other side of the atrium are long open passages with armchairs looking into the court between the old and new buildings. At the start of the connection between old and new is an ingenious glass elevator and a long, straight stair which by design can only be climbed slowly (fig. 5-10). Like the new notion of justice, everything in the architecture conveys calm, thought, light, and a fundamental optimism about human possibility and the resolution of conflict. As a young prosecutor said, crossing the atrium, "If you have to prosecute, this is a wonderful place to do it."

A part of the pleasure in seeing Göteborg today is the chance to reflect on its novelty—its ethical freshness and fertility. The Göteborg embodies the argument fundamental to the very best innovative architecture: that if we try this different way forward, everything will be better. The facade of the old building offers the best of conventional ideas about established civic order. The addition, however, is now literally abstracted from the old, pulled out from under the old convention to reveal what is really going on behind it. The exposed structural grid reads like a tool for organizing rational decision making, the glass like a commitment to the admission of light.

PAUL SPENCER BYARD

5-9. The Göteborg courthouse brings out the reason inside the rule.

5-10. The steady rise in the light in the Göteborg court-house.

Asplund's novel facade beautifully sets off, and is set off by, Tessin's gently authoritarian old one. Asplund's final design gesture establishes the meaning of the combination, putting his windows off center, as if to defer to the symmetry of the old, letting the new be new but setting it in combination with a proper respect for the past.

In contrast to the freshness of Göteborg, America's highest idea of justice was embodied in the very same year in the derivative majesty of the United States Supreme Court, where the conservative Cass Gilbert, working with an ancient William Howard Taft, tried to put Modernism in its place, as if the pre-war Beaux-Arts status quo could be updated and restored to power (see figs. C-1, FW-1, and FW-2). Notwithstanding Gilbert, what would go on thereafter in the United States was a sustained engagement with the Modern project Asplund so beautifully illustrated in Europe. The engagement continued through the New Deal and World War II, at least until the next catastrophic turn of events, the upheaval of the late 1960s and early 1970s. Then came the gradual abandonment of the Modern project and the turn against the progressive ideal that brought us where we are today.

The Contemporary Courthouse

Contemporary courthouse design makes clear that where we are is in a bind. The bind comes from a dominant postmodern political emphasis on criminalization, prohibition, and retribution as proper responses to socially undesirable behavior. This emphasis produces for the architect an almost insuperable programmatic overload in the quantities of space for courtrooms and related func-tions—duplicated and even trebled by requirements for segregation and security—to accommodate all the required adjudication and punishment. The bind is exacerbated by the lack of fresh ideas about how to justify and lift the load, when the only apparent answer to the "why?" of the current state of justice is "because I say so. . . ." The current political emphasis thus offers the designer very little to celebrate except the authority that generates all the trials and penalties. The design exercise is reduced to an effort to bury very large volumes of space in symbols that will lend them some legitimacy.

Federal Building and United States Courthouse, Islip

Borrowing to lend authority and legitimacy is particularly ironic when the imagery is, in fact, the imagery of progressive Modernism, as at Islip, the most striking and strictly beautiful of all contemporary courthouses. Richard Meier's mastery of the imagery of the high Modern tradition is authoritative. Beautiful original forms shape the progress through its hierarchy from the distant view to the remarkable white central atrium to the doors of the courtrooms (fig. 5-11). The surprise, from the Southern State Parkway, of his flawless white courthouse on its flawless green Long Island ground plane is breathtaking. The progress he organizes to and into the functions of his building is awe-inspiring. The enormous programmatic demands of the courthouse and contemporary justice give Meier plenty to control and shape. In his assembly of all the necessary parts, he delivers an extraordinary experience.

The problem in all of it is that Meier

5-11. Alfonse D'Amato United States Courthouse, Islip, New York, 2000, Richard Meier & Partners.

has nothing new to reveal to us or explore on our behalf with all the power of what used to be an adventurous architecture. Forms that once were strange and illuminating are now a stock-in-trade. Some of the most influential and challenging ideas of twentieth-century architecture are now reduced to monuments, as if monumentality were the best we could hope for under the intellectual and political circumstances of our times. Islip is the ultimate *"jeu savant des formes sous la lumière"* (the studied play of forms and light) of Meier's master, Le Corbusier, but assembled strictly for effect. Meier's perfect white building on the perfect green plane evokes Le Corbusier's heroic Secretariat at Chandigarh—part of the astonishing capital that fifty years ago represented the beginning of a whole

new life for India—but with all the mission, valor, and struggle drained out of it. In all its sharp whiteness, it has nothing to say. The heroic object on the heroic ground plane of Modernism is there strictly to lend its authority. Behind the forms, at the heart of the Islip courthouse, is literally and figuratively a monumental white void.

The Brooklyn Courthouse Projects

The consequence of this lack of mission —other than to express authority—is particularly vivid in the Brooklyn courthouse projects (fig. 5-12). There a succession of additions offers a wonderful opportunity to use the past, not just to illuminate our times but to help us advance with its help, as the best architectural additions do. The first and richest piece of the combination is the original

5-12. The Brooklyn federal courthouses, one hundred years of United States justice in architecture, with not necessarily the best for the last.

courthouse from 1892, a picturesque Richardsonian wonder with courtrooms and corridors wrapped around an ornate, enclosed and skylit central court. The old courtroom volumes are almost preposterously big—again, like the men of their times—put together with a kind of genial insouciance that means the connecting corridor around the light court at one point has to bump out into the void of the court simply to get past. The building is designed to fit a dense intersection of small streets, now long since disappeared. The courthouse's peaked bell tower at the corner still announces it to Brooklyn's City Hall some blocks down the street and pins it in place at the top of a slope.

In 1933 the old courthouse got a very large annex that almost tripled its size and updated it into a post office/courthouse/office combination typical of federal buildings of the time. The U-shaped

addition was abruptly and unapologetically bigger than the original, giving the combination a kind of intriguing whaleback, dressed in granite and terra cotta intended to look like granite. Inside, the courthouse light court became the post office sorting room with the daylight made truly useful as a vantage point for postal inspectors trying to keep postal sorters from sorting valuables into their pockets. Despite the classicism of most federal buildings of the time, the regularized annex stayed perceptibly Romanesque, like the original.

Urban renewal in the 1960s then changed its setting dramatically, taking away the street walls around it and leaving it broadside to a swath of formless urban open space called Cadman Plaza. By the end of the twentieth century the old courthouse remained a curious and interesting anomaly, underused and directionless in a fairly grim assembly of dirty Modern civic buildings, of which one is a faintly Modern 1960s exercise now outgrown by the federal district court.

The Brooklyn courthouse projects sought to give the old building a future as part of a courthouse expansion vast enough to meet the huge programmatic demands of the Eastern District of New York. Rejecting schemes that would have added a tower over the 1930s addition, the project made the old building the lead piece of a three-part combined composition to culminate in a large new office building. The redevelopment of the original building undertook scrupulously to restore the best decorative features of the old interior, notably its skylit light court and its vast courtrooms, assigning them to the bankruptcy court's relatively leisurely supervision of busi-

ness failure. The post office was relocated to a position that addressed Cadman Plaza, where the architect's graceful new steps (fig. 5-13) and the annex's new multiple entries help make sense of both the annex and the urban open space across the street. Above the post office are offices for the U.S. attorney, with the space of the annex now elegantly expanded in very restrained glass and metal office floors angled gently into the U-shaped court.

The emerging result of the project is intensely sad in many ways. The new third piece of the composition, the large new office building, is so mediocre as to represent a kind of achievement in its own right—yes, we can still do it!—a huge and costly compromise that handles the bulk of the business of one of the nation's most important federal dis-

5-13. Justice made readily accessible: United States Post Office and Courthouse, Brooklyn, New York, R. M. Kliment & Frances Halsband Architects, 2005.

5-14. A costly contemporary compromise; United States District Court, Brooklyn, New York, Cesar Pelli & Associates, 2006.

Sad, too, is the loss of the potential of this third piece to lift the combined work into something truly powerful for our times, starting with the little original tower, stepping up to the annex, then taking off in the courthouse we need now. Height here—with all its implications of confidence and hope—could have been put to good use. Its absence says a great deal about our own state of mind.

Equally interesting and important lessons come from the old building. Here one feels the impact of the power achieved in our conservative times by historic preservation. On the good side, the scrupulous restoration will be full of pleasing wonders—bringing back, making public, and enhancing the experience of the colorful original, adding at least the usefulness of its service to the Bankruptcy Court. But on the sad side is the degree to which, even so, the project makes so very little of its potential. Old architecture, in fact, lives most and best not fossilized in restoration but at work in combination with new architecture meeting human needs. Here the old will entertain us—indeed fill us with self-satisfaction for having been so kind and generous to this old building—but it will not be put to work, as it was at Göteborg, to help illuminate our differences and give energy, by its contrast, to solutions we are actively exploring for problems of our times.

The valiant architects, Robert Kliment and Frances Halsband, make clear the limit of the scope offered them—and our frustration—in the very handsome new public gallery they create outside the new bankruptcy courtrooms in the annex parallel to the old light court. The prospect from their new glass wall is the

tricts without lifting a single spirit (fig. 5-14). The building looks stumpy—and it is. In a cost-saving move, the building was substantially shortened, losing whatever grace height would have added, and it still cost just as much.

146   PAUL SPENCER BYARD

length of the long gray granite back wall of the old building some thirty feet away (fig. 5-15)—handsome, yes, but nothing like what openings could have revealed about what is going on inside. Under construction, lights shine from the old light court through the old wall: what it might have done to break through it and make the light court the climax of a powerful new assembly of spaces, with the dramatic old decorated volume reinterpreted and back at work at the head of the hierarchy of an exploration of justice for our times!

The problem of the building is, once again, the problem of justice in our times: the huge weight of a system bent toward retribution, trying, at its best, not to do wrong. At the head of the architectural hierarchy of the Brooklyn projects is the bankruptcy court, at the cutting edge of justice only if you acknowledge that justice is finally about business and personal financial failure. We are vividly careful of the old building, we do it no harm—in fact, we have fun with it— while we herd our newly innumerable "perps" through the back door into the new grim building beyond.

Scranton

The addition to Scranton, Pensylvania's United States courthouse lacks the same poignancy but illustrates the same shortcoming. Here the starting point is a pleasant, well-executed 1930s classical courthouse/post office combination in gray stone that is an architectural high point of Scranton's downtown square (fig. 5-16). The tan stone addition is almost the original's equal in size, joined to it by a large dark recessive glass

5-16. Bohlin Cywinski Jackson elevates the 1930s Scranton, Pennsylvania courthouse and post office, 1998.

joint—a little like Venturi's historic gooey soft-joint addition to Cass Gilbert's Allen Art Museum at Oberlin, Ohio—that covers the new public space and connects the old and the new. The facade of the addition is carefully composed and beautifully executed, with strong references to Asplund's great paradigm in Göteborg, starting with the deference of its asymmetry to the old building. The new entry here is also oblique: one enters through the new door and then makes a right turn into what is, also as in Göteborg, the abundantly top-lit public space. In the new space powerful steel stairs and flying passages knit the old and the new together, leading to serene side-lit courtrooms of great dignity.

The public space—now only marginally public, alas, as all such spaces must be in an age tyrannized by metal detectors—is the showpiece of the composition, satisfying in its animation but disturbing in its message. The powerful tall legs of the skylight structure, the long stairs, and the bridging passageways are impressive as they cross the space. They have a power you might conceivably connect with the lofty passages of Piranesi's *prigione*. Consistent details, multiples of elements that would be structure if they were not ornament, also talk about power and strength. On the whole, though, the effect of all the straight and bent steel is simply overwrought—too heavy to be Asplund on enlightenment and change and too light to be Piranesi on incarceration and chains. The architecture takes its task seriously and makes the most of what it understands about, for example, the virtues of public access. It talks about intelligence and strength and dignity and monumentality, but beyond that, looking for direction, it is as baffled as we all seem to be.

Boston Federal Courthouse

The one courthouse project that most successfully comes to terms with the limitations of our times is Pei Cobb Freed's federal courthouse in Boston (fig. 5-17; see also figs. C-9, C-10, 2-5, 2-6, 4-13, and 4-14). The site overlooking Boston Harbor is turned to great advantage, made a prospect to be embraced and combined with the composition not just for its animation and occasional beauty but also for what it contributes to the meaning of the courthouse. The courthouse embraces the harbor with two brick wings set in a 90-degree V. Between the wings, addressing the harbor, is a curving glass wall that has to be a homage to one of America's great "lost" architectural ideas: Aldo Giurgola's winning entry in the AIA (American Institute of Architects) headquarters competition some forty years ago, that similarly embraced a historic object and brought its meaning into combination with an addition. The falling curve is much heavier than Giurgola's and less clearly a segment of a sphere but retains some of the implica-

5-17. Pei Cobb Freed's calm, strong federal courthouse anchored on the edge of Boston Harbor, 1998.

5-18. The courtrooms in the Boston courthouse take their cue from Wiscasset, Maine. (Photo: Steve Rosenthal)

tion that it is embracing the globe itself. Now the specific object of its embrace is Boston Harbor, the great historic port vividly attached to the American pursuit of justice by its famous tea party, and still the home of the most glorious warship of the nascent republic, the *Constitution*. Looking out over the harbor through a cascade of glass are the single-loaded arms of corridors, off which open the courtroom doors.

On the city side away from the harbor, the two wings are stately presentations of brick-windowed rectangles that meet at a recessed tall central cylindrical hinge at the point of the V. The approach to the building is along the western wing past a series of arches whose flat brick is imprinted with law-related quotations. A single larger flat arch is set in an abstract

flat brick panel to mark the entry, reminiscent of a great Louis Sullivan midwestern bank. The entry leads to the cylinder of the hinge, which serves as the distributor of the building's circulation. The top-lit cylinder is hung with large abstract works of art and has no view of the harbor. The bank of elevators in the cylinder leading to the courtrooms faces away from the harbor, and the cars open at each floor with no obvious clue which way to turn. The harbor then comes as a revelation. The building opens out to the drama, reassurance, and meaning of the view and to the beautiful walk the courthouse offers past it to the courtrooms.

The courtrooms themselves make a similar connection with history. Over each courtroom door is a concave quarter-sphere "beehive," (see fig. C-10) borrowed from a lovely eighteenth-century courthouse in Wiscasset, Maine; this image connects us with Thomas Jefferson at the University of Virginia and with all the traditional associations of bees and beehives—industry and enlightenment, and so on. The wainscoted courtrooms are organized around flat arches, like the entry sequence, and stenciled above the wainscot and the arches in early American fashion. The open-back "banker's" wooden spectator benches could have been made for H. H. Richardson (fig. 5-18).

Embracing the historic harbor with all these supporting references to history, the whole building is a meditation on justice as a human undertaking rooted in some of the best, most important, and most honorable excerpts of our history. The meditation reflects the evocations of history that have dominated the postmodern age of historic preservation, making history the "context" for its design in a time when the new and the future have been discredited. At the same time, in the freedom of its form, in its exploitation of possibilities of abstraction, the courthouse is a true child of the twentieth century. As a sophisticated combined work, the Boston courthouse makes the most of history as a way to dignify, support, and explain what the courthouse is doing today. In the best of contemporary courthouse architecture, the Boston courthouse uses the past to exhort us to do at least as well as we once did.

This emphasis on the past, though, returns us to the same disquiet about contemporary justice as expressed in architecture. Throughout the United States, courthouse architecture suggests few possibilities for the improvement of our condition. Even the most nearly adventurous of federal court architecture seems to use its novelty only as an enhancement of its monumentality—a device to make courthouses more impressive with a touch of the unexpected. Like our times, contemporary court architecture is about effect, not substance; about reassurance, not inspiration; about how great we have been, not how great we might become. For our next new direction—for an architecture of leadership that will help us move toward what we need next—we still have to wait.

PART THREE

The Courthouse,
Its Publics
and Its Users

SIX

Drawing Meaning from the Heart of the Courthouse

DOUGLAS P. WOODLOCK

Any meaningful architecture for courthouses must be drawn from the building's distinctive feature: the courtroom. The courtroom is the space that makes the courthouse different from many other buildings in which decisions—even very important civic decisions—are reached. Without explicit recognition of the centrality of the courtroom as the heart of the courthouse, any courthouse design is doomed to lose the meaning of the structure.

The high purposes of the courtroom were captured in a memorial tribute to Frank J. Murray, the judge for whom I served as a law clerk when I started down my own path in the law. Speaking at a portrait presentation ceremony for the oil painting that now hangs in my own courtroom in the new Boston federal courthouse, Edward B. Hanify, senior partner of the Boston law firm of Ropes & Gray, encapsulated Judge Murray's then forty-four years on the state and federal trial benches by observing that

To Judge Murray, the Court room, State or Federal, is the Law's citadel of civilized honor. The manner and conduct of its proceedings are both exemplary and educational for lawyer or lay person. It is the seat of Justice where no man or woman, lawyer, litigant, prosecutor, defendant, juror or court attaché may enter or depart without respect for the honorable Rule of Law; where the formalities and decorum worthy of the rational resolution of controversies must be punctiliously observed; where undue sympathy does not warp judgment, or prejudice or predilection bias decision, where government is not all powerful, and the humblest and the greatest citizen can be heard with equal balanced consideration of their merits . . .[1]

It is not surprising that Mr. Hanify began his description of the paradigmatic courtroom by noting its "exemplary and educational" role. The concept of an open courtroom, where the public has the opportunity to observe formal pro-

6-1. Hanover County Court House, Hanover, Virginia, c. 1735. Architect unknown. (Photo: Richard Pare, Seagram's Courthouse Project, Library of Congress)

6-1. Hanover County Court House, Hanover, Virginia, c. 1735. Architect unknown. (Photo: Richard Pare, Seagram's Courthouse Project, Library of Congress)

ceedings for the resolution of its legal disputes, is at the core of this nation's cultural and constitutional values of democratic transparency. Successful courthouses also discharge their didactic responsibilities through programs of murals and inscriptions; but it is in the courtroom where what the courthouse has to teach comes alive.

The familiar courthouses of our early history, although housing "citadels of civilized honor," were not ostentatious, flamboyant, or overbearing structures. They were open and accessible buildings in which the community's concerns were directly focused on the courtrooms where our history was written. The pattern is evident in the earliest structures, such as the early-eighteenth-century Hanover County Courthouse, still standing in Virginia just outside Richmond

(fig. 6-1). It is a simple, warm, and inviting building where the community periodically came together to affirm its values and decide its future. This purpose is well captured in an oil painting of Patrick Henry in that building delivering his 1763 argument in the *Parson's Cause*, a precursor to the demands for religious freedom later embodied in the United States Constitution (fig. 6-2). Through the open courtroom door, just across the green, is a tavern where the community would retire for a more extended, and no doubt less orderly, discussion of the case's implications. In short, this was a building whose central feature was firmly embedded in the larger life of its community.

A more elegant example, as the nation grew in size and sophistication, was the mid-nineteenth-century St. Louis

DOUGLAS P. WOODLOCK

County Courthouse (see fig. 1-11). Yet the St. Louis building and virtually all the familiar courthouses of the American antebellum Eden can be read in a provocative way. At their core, if unacknowledged, is an abiding insult to the guiding principle of American jurisprudence: equal justice under law. The decision making in their courtrooms was exclusive: African Americans were not merely absent as decision makers; they were treated as difficult pieces of property, when treated at all in the buildings.

The old courthouse in St. Louis is now most remembered as the site for the trial of the *Dred Scott* case, litigation that was concluded by a Supreme Court opinion in which the chief justice of the United States held that a black person had no rights a white person was obligated to respect.[2] In thinking about our nation's historic courtrooms, we must leaven our recollections with the recog-

nition that not everything about that history commands unalloyed appreciation from all members of our society. Those courtrooms bear the stain of the great American racial dilemma. Comfort with their familiar architectural language and iconography is not necessarily shared throughout our increasingly multicultural community. That tragic dimension to their memory provides the first principal condition of contemporary courthouse design and provokes a critical question: How can we properly transmit our nation's highest aspirations through structures whose history bears witness to occasions in which we did not live up to them?

It is not only in the painful history of the Old St. Louis Courthouse that we find a cautionary condition for contemporary courthouse design. A second condition is found in the program itself. In St. Louis we can see the beginning of

6-2. Patrick Henry arguing *Parson's Cause* in the Hanover County Court House, 1763, depicted in a painting attributed to George Cooke (c. 1830). (Virginia Historical Society, Richmond, Virginia)

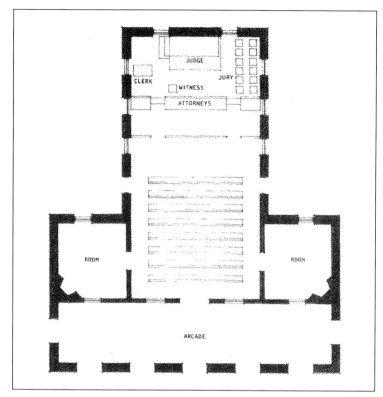

6-3. The courtroom as the exclusive focus: plan, Hanover County Court House.

6-4. The individual courtroom begins to be devalued: plan, "Dred Scott" Courthouse, St. Louis, 1839–1861.

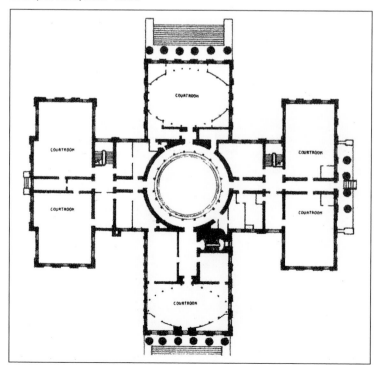

the proliferation of courtrooms within the courthouse. In many of our early historic courthouses the courtroom is the pearl within the shell; it is the single ceremonial space. The plan of the Hanover County Court House illustrates the point (fig. 6-3). But with the growth of the country in its urban areas, the numbers of courtrooms in courthouses began to multiply, as shown in the Old St. Louis Court House plan (fig. 6-4). At the same time, the support spaces for those multiple ceremonial spaces began to enlarge, with a parallel devaluing of the individual courtroom.

That second principal condition provokes a second critical question for modern courthouse design: How can we properly celebrate a ceremonial destination for the program when the numbers of those destinations have proliferated and the surrounding bureaucratic space has begun to flood the building?

I find the response of the federal courthouses in Chicago instructive. When I was growing up in the Chicago suburbs, the old Chicago federal courthouse designed by Henry Ives Cobb "stood out sharply in the midst of the dense corridors of commercial buildings."[3] Its full dimensions were disclosed when one emerged from the urban canyon. The building was, to be sure, essentially a Renaissance palazzo on steroids, with a Roman temple dome planted at the top to signal that the courtrooms were reached through a multistory open rotunda (fig. 6-5). That is one way to accommodate, and deploy the community to, the growing number of courtrooms. And, in doing so, the Cobb building called itself out as a courthouse for which courtrooms were the ultimate destination. It is not difficult to

DOUGLAS P. WOODLOCK

imagine Judge Kennesaw Mountain Landis presiding there in the United States District Court, as he did before he became the commissioner of baseball (fig. 6-6). It was a building which, despite its antiquarian conceits, somehow embodied the accurate and eloquent definition of a courthouse provided by former Chief Justice Edward Hennessey, of the Massachusetts Supreme Judicial Court; it was a building which tangibly "evoke[d] the memory of historical events and of the aspirations, frustrations and fears of the many people—the learned, the dedicated, the articulate, the oppressed and despised, the avaricious and the brutal—whom the law has summoned to exercise their skills or to account for their actions."[4]

The Chicago federal courthouse I

6-7. A courtroom in the Mies van der Rohe "filing cabinet," the Everett McKinley Dirksen Federal Building and Courthouse, Chicago, 1966.

knew when I was growing up during the early 1960s was replaced in the middle of that decade by a work of a modern master: Mies van der Rohe. One of the saddest images of modern architectural photography (see fig. PR-1) shows the Mies courthouse rising about a block from where the demolition of the Cobb courthouse was simultaneously taking place. The new courthouse is a straightforward example of his International Style: It is a rigorous, orderly, elegant filing cabinet for human functions. It does not present itself as a courthouse, although there are over twenty courtrooms filed inside. This was not inadvertent. Phyllis Lambert notes that when confronted with a "program [that] called for large, two-story-high court rooms," Mies adhered to "the principle of a universal rather than a specific solution . . . asserting [his] desire to develop a common language rather than 'particular, individual ideas.' 'I have no great admi-

ration for special programs,' he said. Thus, the facade of the Courthouse Building veils its program."[5]

I worked in the Mies courthouse as a newspaper reporter in the late 1960s and early 1970s, sporadically covering aspects of the trial of the Chicago Seven before Judge Julius Hoffman, among other proceedings. Yet, I think I have a better feeling for what it is like to be in a courtroom I never saw presided over by Judge Landis, whom I never met, than I do for the austere, indeed lobotomizing, courtroom spaces Mies van der Rohe designed for Judge Hoffman and his colleagues, where I was a fully engaged observer (fig. 6-7).

The program of a courthouse, even when veiled in the office building form the Mies building adopted, carries with it an intense, almost liturgical significance. The courtroom is the sanctuary for that liturgy. No space of such programmatic significance exists for the

DOUGLAS P. WOODLOCK

office building. Vincent Scully was accurate when he said that "office buildings are intrinsically less interesting and lively than almost any other kind of building."[6] And in the latter half of the twentieth century, that is what our nation was mostly building. "Never before in human history," as Scully observed, "have cities been dominated by forms growing out of a program so fundamentally inane."[7] By putting on the empty raiment of an office building, a courthouse formally repudiates the distinctive features of its program.

As different as the designs of the two federal courthouses in Chicago are in form, they both underscore the third principal condition of modern courthouse design: courthouses are potentially dangerous places because of what goes on in courtrooms. The challenge is to answer a third critical question: How can we create a secure environment without burying the courthouse's important civic program in a bunker? Courthouses can be targets from the outside, as when the IWW (Industrial Workers of the World) claimed credit for the 1920 bombing that killed a mail carrier outside the entrance to the old Chicago federal courthouse. Or they can be threatened from within, as in 1992 when a prisoner attempting an escape from the new Chicago courthouse killed two security personnel before turning his weapon on himself. In all events, courthouse design demands careful attention to both external and internal security concerns. And it is in the courtroom that the concerns are focused, because that is the only space in which the three necessary but distinct circulation paths within the modern courthouse —those for the public, the backstage for the court staff and jurors, and the custo-dial for prisoners—must intersect.

The challenges that confront courthouse designers, then, are three: first, to cleanse, enhance, and transform the ambiguous memory of the American courtroom; second, to present the heart of the activity of a courthouse, the work of the courtroom, in a fashion that does not subordinate the importance of each individual case resolved in that room to the growing bureaucracy and multiplication of courtrooms required by modern urban life; and third, to do all this in a secure setting that does not disguise, but rather celebrates, the building's program.

The proper conceptual approach to those challenges is, I think, found in the architecture of approach: the processional. At its highest level of generality, the processional for a courthouse can be conceived as the movement from the disordered world of the street to the highly ordered precinct of the courtroom. Successful marriages of memory and invention, which are the essence of great architecture, are well illustrated in the ways different architects in different centuries have solved the problem of the courthouse processional. This can be seen quite dramatically in the gathering and deployment of the community from the world of the street through the courthouse to courtroom destinations provided by the different processionals developed in James Gandon's late-eighteenth-century classical Four Courts for Georgian Dublin (fig. 6-8) and Richard Rogers' late-twentieth-century European Court of Human Rights in Strasbourg (fig. 6-9). The buildings seem to share only river-front sites. But, looking closely at their respective use of an organizing rotunda with decidedly different materiality—each capped by a com-

6-8. James Gandon's Four Courts, Dublin, 1791, as seen from across the River Liffey. (Photo: Jacqueline O'Brien)

6-9. The European Court of Human Rights, Strasbourg, Richard Rogers, 1984. (Photo: Katsuhisa Kida)

manding dome—one sees them speaking differently about the same thing for their different times (figs. 6-10–6-13).

In their processionals, courthouses must speak for their times with authoritative craftsmanship and concern for the way in which the materiality of the building can serve the larger purposes of conveying meaning. At no point is this more important than at the penultimate station of the courthouse processional: the entrance to the courtroom. For the late-twentieth-century Israeli Supreme Court in Jerusalem (fig. 6-14), Ada and Ram Karmi made use of Jerusalem stone to create that sense of craft. The invitation provided by the craft of a courthouse entrance in creating the sense that behind it is something significant (the courtroom) was among the elements prompting Paul Goldberger to describe the Israeli Supreme Court building as "less a piece of knock-your-eye-out razzle-dazzle architecture than a series

DOUGLAS P. WOODLOCK

6-10. Continuing the processional: the central rotunda, Gandon's Four Courts, Dublin. (Photo: Jacqueline O'Brien)

6-11. Central rotunda, Rogers's European Court of Human Rights, Strasbourg. (Photo: Christian Richter)

6-12. Rotunda ceiling, Gandon's Four Courts, Dublin. (Photo: Jacqueline O'Brien)

6-13. Rotunda ceiling, Roger's European Court of Human Rights, Strasbourg. (Photo: Christian Richter)

of wise and knowing gestures pulled off with consummate sensitivity and intelligence."[8] And, Goldberger explained, "that stance is itself a kind of moral lesson in what public architecture can be. With the completion of the Supreme Court...Israel produced a building that can stand as an example to the world of the potential of public works to reflect a culture's highest aspirations."[9] In the new Boston federal courthouse, the intensity of craftsmanship involved in the execution of the brick elliptical half-vault entrances chosen for each of the twenty-seven courtrooms, including my own, reflects a similar effort to convey meaning and high aspiration through the processional (see fig. C-10).

6-14. The penultimate station of the processional: the entrance to the courtroom. Supreme Court of Israel, Jerusalem, Ada Karmi-Melamede and Ram Karmi, 1993. (Photo: Richard Bryant/arcaid.co.uk)

The sense of a legible and intriguing processional executed with the craft of a dignified but inviting entrance ultimately brings us to the heart and soul of the courthouse—the courtroom itself. However ambiguous our memories about the past of our courthouses, this room must never be treated as a drawer of a filing cabinet. There has not been a better statement of what happens in a courtroom and why it is exceptionally important that we refine its craft to ensure that it is an appropriately detailed and developed space than observations given in 1991 to Harry Cobb, the architect for the new federal courthouse in Boston, by Stephen Breyer, then the chief judge of the court of appeals resident there. Justice Breyer told Cobb:

> [A] Court, unlike any other government agency, concerns itself not with the public en masse, but with the individual citizen who appears before it. It devotes as much time and attention to the particular individual's specific problem as the problem requires. In this modern age when people need extensive government, but fear dehumanizing bureaucratic tendencies, it is particularly important to emphasize that the judicial branch of government treats each citizen before it not as a member of a group, but as a separate individual, a separate human being with a right to call upon the court's considerable resources properly to resolve his or her specific dispute almost irrespective of how much time it takes to do that.

The courtroom is where that takes place most visibly. How we create and preserve such places tells us a good deal about the value we attach to justice. If you bring a person into an undistinguished room to resolve a dispute, you have told a story before the case even starts: that justice doesn't really count very much; that it is just another one of those things bureaucracy dispenses. A courthouse building must convey a different story. Every effort must be made to ensure that every public space within

DOUGLAS P. WOODLOCK

a courthouse—and particularly the courtroom—is properly constructed with the greatest craft we can provide to lift the spirits of the participants—parties, witnesses, jurors, spectators, and judicial personnel—so that they can perform their critically important task of seeing that justice is done.

The detailing of the courtroom need not—indeed, should not—be woodenly formal. The goal is a warm, humane space of tangible dignity expressing what Andrea Leers has called "a grand order with a human scale." An important model for expressing that sensibility in the courtrooms in the new Boston federal courthouse is the nineteenth-century Barnstable County Courthouse courtroom (see fig. 1-10), perhaps the favorite courtroom among Massachusetts trial lawyers. By responding to such models, courtroom architecture can approximate Vincent Scully's description of "what urban architecture really is: a creation of interior and exterior spaces,

and most of all, a continuing dialogue between generations which creates an environment developing across time."[10] That description implies an important responsibility to keep up each generation's part in the conversation.

Andrea Leers demonstrated how this responsibility can be met in her designs for courtrooms in the Worcester, Massachusetts and Portland, Maine federal courthouses. In Worcester, she renovated the building's old, well-loved courtroom from the 1930s (see fig. C-20) and then provided a subtle and elegant new interpretation of courtroom space in the same building (see fig. C-21). In Portland, she drew inspiration from the elegant Beaux-Arts Providence, Rhode Island, federal courtroom (fig. 6-15) to create a new courtroom with a contemporary aesthetic (see fig. C-22). These courtrooms seek to maintain the conversation between generations not merely to secure continuity between past and present and to consummate marriages of

6-16. Courtroom of the United States Court of Appeals, Second Circuit, New York, Cass Gilbert, 1935, as seen from the spectators seating area. (Photo: Jordan Gruzen)

memory and invention, but more fundamentally to embody both the stability of the law through its reliance upon past precedent and the adaptiveness and dynamic quality of the law in addressing new problems.

The sensibility that flows from such efforts is found in one of my favorite courtrooms and one of the finest public rooms in Manhattan: the courtroom of the United States Court of Appeals of the Second Circuit panel in Cass Gilbert's Foley Square courthouse. Whether seen from the spectators' view of the bench (fig. 6-16) or the judge's view from the bench (fig. 6-17), it is not an ostentatious room by any but the most parsimonious of standards. But it is a room that, I think, gave a judge such as Learned

6-17. Second Circuit courtroom, as seen from behind the bench. (Photo: Jordan Gruzen)

DOUGLAS P. WOODLOCK

Hand the inspiration to describe what it was he did virtually all of his working life. At the ceremony to mark his fiftieth anniversary on the bench, Hand, who was then 88 years old, reflected on what it is to be a judge. "Why isn't it in the nature of an art?" he asked. "It's a bit of craftsmanship, isn't it? It's what a poet does. It's what a sculptor does. [And, he might have added, it's what an architect does.] He has some vague purposes and he has an indefinite number of what you might call frames of preference among which he may choose, for choose he has to do and he does."[11]

The demands of shaping those "frames of preference" with all the artfulness a judge can muster was the fundamental craft challenge for Hand throughout his career. In 1927, delivering the commencement address at Bryn Mawr College, he used a rich but homey metaphor to describe his vocation with reference to a judge's "bench, where, like any other workman, he must do his work."[12] And in his last major public addresses, the Holmes Lectures in 1958, he returned to the theme by summing up a lifetime of reflection on the role of the judge with the conclusion that "it is as craftsmen that we get our satisfactions and our pay."[13]

That is the shared responsibility of architecture and judging: to frame the issues and shape them with all the craft we can muster: to accomplish, in the structure and work of our civic institutions, Paul Goldberger's paradigm: "a series of wise and knowing gestures pulled off with consummate sensitivity and intelligence."[14]

During a memorial service that was given to honor Justice Joseph Story, the greatest Supreme Court justice from Massachusetts during the nineteenth century, Daniel Webster, speaking for the Massachusetts bar, observed: "Justice is the great interest of man on earth." And then he continued with a metaphor that accurately describes what it is that all those involved in courtrooms are doing: "Whoever labors on this edifice with usefulness and distinction, whoever clears its foundations, strengthens its pillars, adorns its entablatures or contributes to raise its August dome . . . connects . . . with that which is and must be as durable as the frame of human history."[15]

We are not creating universal space when designing courthouses. We are creating buildings with distinctive destinations that are meant to be as durable as human history. In doing so, the heart and soul of the courthouse—the courtroom—must be expressed to reflect its animating spirit, its commitment to craft, and its connection to the highest aspirations of our civic life.

SEVEN

The Lawyer's Perspective

GEORGE A. DAVIDSON

The courthouse is the lawyer's workplace, episodically or continuously depending on the nature of the lawyer's practice. That many of the design elements most important to lawyers respond to their practical, quotidian concerns does not mean that lawyers are unconcerned with majesty: the atmosphere of dignity, seriousness of purpose, and impartiality of the law created by a well-designed courtroom is treasured by lawyers at least as much as by litigants, witnesses, visitors, and court personnel.

As the preceding chapter makes clear, the courtroom is the heart of the matter, for lawyers and for everyone else. Lawyers may be in court all day. Families of litigants, reporters and similar representatives of the media, and other observers may also be in court for hours and days on end. Seating is a paramount concern: chairs should be comfortable and provide lumbar support. The pew-style spectator seating common in prewar courtrooms is too uncomfortable to sit on for any extended period. Chairs at counsel table are at least as important,

as are chairs for the judges. It is not uncommon to see judges in courthouses equipped with high-backed throne-style chairs replace them with ergonomically comfortable chairs, often something that looks like what a typist or court reporter would sit on. Courtrooms are more than ceremonial settings; furnishings should reflect functional needs at least as much as office furnishings do.

Sightlines often are not adequately addressed. Generally, witness stands are positioned to give the jury a good view of the witness; often this comes at the expense of the judge's view. Trial practice expert James W. McElhaney has suggested that witness stands be movable so that in a judge-trial case, the witness can be positioned facing the judge.

In the age of television, trial lawyers rely increasingly on visual aids in presenting evidence. In the standard courtroom configuration it is not easy to place an exhibit so that everyone can see it. If counsel facing the bench are looking, say, north, then the judge and the witness typically look south and the jury west, with the witness between the judge and jury. Thus a chart placed at a 45-degree angle (northeast), to be accessible to the judge, jury, and witness, may not be visible to opposing counsel.

Even worse than this standard arrangement is the placement of counsel tables one behind the other rather than side by side, common in many smaller courtrooms and a few large ones. This placement handicaps counsel at both tables: counsel at the rear table can see only the back of what is shown to judge and jury, whereas counsel at the front table cannot see what their adversaries are up to.

In the Isabella County courthouse in Mt. Pleasant, Michigan, an unusual courtroom arrangement poses additional sightline difficulties. In this rather large courtroom, the counsel are facing north and the jury is in the usual position looking west, the witness box is in the center of the courtroom facing south, and the bench is at a 45-degree angle in the northwest corner facing southeast. Here it is very difficult for counsel to address the judge and the jury at the same time.

Providing clear lines of sight is not enough: distance introduces further difficulties. Some courts require counsel to stand behind a podium when questioning witnesses rather than stride about the courtroom. This practice introduces at least two design considerations. First, it should be possible to raise or lower the podium. Otherwise, short counsel will disappear behind it, and tall counsel will find his or her notes too far away to be read. Second, the podium must not be placed too far from the witness. People are comfortable conversing within a limited range of distance from one

another. Standing too close is intimidating to a witness; standing too far away from one dissipates the rhythm of natural verbal interaction. Even if voices are amplified, distance destroys the intimacy on which civil exchange depends. Podiums in Manhattan's Moynihan Courthouse often are placed too far from the witness box; although the podiums appear fixed, they are in fact moveable, and counsel may be able discreetly to reposition them.

Determining the right distance between the elements of a courtroom depends on what takes place in the court. One of the courtrooms in the federal courthouse in Hartford, Connecticut, intended to accommodate a magistrate judge, was designed by shrinking the plans for a district judge courtroom. When expansion required that this room be reassigned to a district judge, it proved impossible to conduct criminal jury trials there. The witness box was so close to the jury that jurors felt menaced and the judge himself not terribly secure.

Size plays a role in creating majesty, ceiling height being perhaps most important. As a young lawyer, my first trial was against a pro se (self-represented) litigant in New York City's Civil Court. The assigned courtroom, in blond wood, was very small and narrow with only three rows of spectator seating. A small American flag on a wooden dowel hung on the wall, and a tiny rail separated spectators from tiny counsel tables and a tiny bench with a tiny door behind it. When the door opened and a tiny judge emerged, I felt much like Alice after she went down the rabbit hole.

Courtrooms should be designed to permit unobtrusive entrances and exits, to avoid distractions to court, jury, and counsel. Doors in the rear of the room are thus preferable to doors on the side. And the doors themselves should be designed to open and close noiselessly.

Courtrooms should have windows, even if the windows are so high on the wall that only sky is visible. Lawyers involved in lengthy trials put lack of windows at the top of their list of complaints, finding it dispiriting to not even be able to tell whether it is day or night.

The choreography of movement in and out of a courtroom is complex. There are individuals and groups that should be kept separate from one another, and courtrooms therefore usually are designed with several doors for entry and exit. Think of a French bedroom farce played very quietly and very slowly. Whereas civil litigants, lawyers, and witnesses may mingle, the jury should be able to move from the courtroom to the jury room without encountering others, incarcerated defendants must be escorted to detention facilities, and judges should be able to access at least a robing room and perhaps their chambers without passing through a public hallway.

Courthouses in general have too few signs, but the Herkimer County Courthouse in Oneida, New York, perhaps takes signage too far. The door behind the bench to the judge's robing room has a frosted glass panel through which those in the courtroom can make out the words To Bench Designers who are content to leave the ordinary citizen to stumble unguided through the courthouse might have had more confidence in the judges, who are there every day.

It is essential to provide some accommodation for the occasional big case. Most courtrooms were designed for a world in which every case had two parties and each party had one or perhaps two lawyers. In today's world of class actions and multi-defendant asbestos conspiracy cases, numerous parties and dozens of lawyers may be present in court for conferences, oral argument, or trial. Although it would be wasteful to design every courtroom to accommodate extraordinary cases, special temporary courtrooms can be created, as was done for the massive asbestos insurance coverage litigation in California and the DuPont Plaza fire litigation in Puerto Rico. At least one or two courtrooms in every courthouse should be designed to accommodate cases involving a dozen or more lawyers.

Courtrooms for specialized proceedings present special problems. The best appellate arguments are those that become discussions between the judges and counsel, and a well-designed courtroom will create an environment conducive to such discussions. At the same time, the design must reinforce the dignity and sense of security of the judges on the bench by horizontal and vertical separations between counsel and the judges, reinforced by physical barriers. The challenge for the architect is to create both a sense of intimacy and a sense of separation at the same time.

Cass Gilbert's United States Supreme Court very successfully reconciles these somewhat conflicting goals (see fig. FW-1). Its high ceilings, rich ornamentation, and liberal use of dark wood confer an atmosphere of dignity, whereas intimacy is achieved by positioning counsel close (but not too close) to the bench. As shown, the original bench has been

GEORGE A. DAVIDSON

replaced with one that has a gentle arc, thereby permitting the Justices to better see and hear one another during the course of the arguments. New York's highest court, the Court of Appeals in Albany, also successfully achieves both of these objectives, although the bench might better have been placed at a higher elevation in this large courtroom.

Another magnificent appellate courtroom is the rather prosaically named Courtroom No. 1 of the United States Court of Appeals for the Ninth Circuit in San Francisco (see fig. C-23). Constructed in 1905 by Italian craftsmen, the courtroom has white Pavonazzo marble walls, mosaic murals, skylights, and an ornamental plaster ceiling. A riot of decoration, it resembles a Roman bath converted to courtroom use with the addition of rich red drapery and generous use of warm woodwork. The room is literally irreplaceable; to its eternal credit the federal government restored the courthouse, at great expense, following heavy damage in a 1989 earthquake. Most appellate courtrooms have a more muted feel, relying primarily on substantial use of dark wood. The courtroom in the Mosk Courthouse in Sacramento, used both by the California Supreme Court and the regional court of appeal, employs wood extensively to create an atmosphere of dignity and seriousness while preserving a sense of warmth. Cass Gilbert's Second Circuit courtroom on the seventeenth floor of New York's Foley Square Courthouse does likewise but is less assertive, leaving the focus on judges and lawyers (fig. 7-2).

Appellate courtrooms built more recently seek to achieve dignity through the use of space rather than rich materials and ornamentation. This approach

7-1. Cass Gilbert's 1934 courtroom for the United States Supreme Court in Washington, D.C., combines dignity with intimacy. (Photo: courtesy of Office of the Curator, United States Supreme Court)

sacrifices intimacy; the cavernous surroundings and substantial distances from the bench make effective dialogue more difficult to achieve. The courtrooms of the supreme courts of Kansas and New Jersey are examples. In contrast, the Michigan Supreme Court's courtroom, at the 2002 Hall of Justice in Lansing (fig. 7-3), has a round courtroom that evokes the sentencing circles of the Chippewa, Ottawa, and Potowatomic tribes native to Michigan. The wall of the courtroom is paneled in richly grained dark wood. High windows just under the domed ceiling provide glimpses of sky, softening the effect of the dark wood. The result seems fully satisfying to appellate advocates: the architects have successfully recaptured traditional virtues within the limits imposed by contemporary restraints, aided considerably by the Michigan legislature's willingness to invest in materials of the quality required to create a lasting monument.

7-2. Cass Gilbert's unassertive Second Circuit courtroom in New York, 1934, allows a focus upon the judges and the lawyers. NB Jantzen/USSC

7-3. A rare success among recent appellate courtrooms: the Michigan Supreme Court, Hall of Justice, Lansing, Michigan, Albert Kahn Associates and Spillis Candella & Partners, 2002. (Photo: Justin Maconochie)

Modern appellate courtrooms, apparently for aesthetic reasons, also place the podium, from which arguing counsel addresses the court, in the center of the courtroom, a considerable distance from the counsel tables at which counsel and assistants sit while not actually arguing. In older courtrooms, counsel tables immediately flank the podium, sometimes as part of a single piece of furniture. Here again, the older style is more serviceable because arguing counsel is physically close to supporting materials and in a position to read notes passed by colleagues.

Courthouses in urban environments often have courtrooms devoted to arraignments and other pretrial proceedings in criminal cases. Detention facilities for defendants in custody are typically adjacent or nearby. Most criminal cases are disposed of after arraign-

GEORGE A. DAVIDSON

ment or other pretrial proceedings. It is thus critical that there be interview rooms in these detention facilities, in which defendants can consult privately with their lawyers. It is helpful also to have a private conference room nearby, for conferences at which a proposed disposition can be worked out.

Courtrooms dedicated to arraignments or other pretrial criminal proceedings are bustling places, with lawyers, family members, and court personnel coming in and out. Acoustics are frequently a problem. Where appropriate, amplification devices should be employed so that family members and other spectators can hear what is being said.

Ancillary facilities supporting the courtroom present distinct design issues. Robing rooms should be planned for the range of functions they must perform. Many robing rooms are designed as if their only purpose were to provide a private refuge for the judge, convenient to the courtroom for use during recesses. However, robing rooms frequently serve as places for the judge to confer privately with counsel for all the parties about legal or administrative issues. Room for a conference table and adequate seating should be provided.

Witnesses who have not yet testified at a trial typically are not permitted to sit in the courtroom but must remain nearby so as to be available when called. Few courthouses have suitable facilities. A witness lounge—or, ideally, two of them—equipped with a television set and reading material and connected to the courtroom by an intercom, through which witnesses can be summoned, would make the process of waiting far more comfortable.

Few courtrooms today have adequate storage facilities for the use of counsel. In trials of complex cases, the day begins and ends with a caravan of porters delivering or removing brief bags, client file boxes, tapes, and supplies. Courtrooms in which multiday trials are likely to be scheduled should have large, lockable closets for overnight storage of these materials.

Many courthouses have cafeterias for courthouse personnel, litigants, witnesses, jurors, visitors, and the bar. Many of these groups require privacy in their lunchtime conversations. Seating arrangements should be designed to permit groups to sit together out of earshot of other groups.

The courthouse must be designed in a fashion that reflects well-considered plans for security. Courthouses designed to welcome the public in recent years have had their entranceways marred with ugly and temporary-looking metal detectors and other security apparatus. It seems safe to assume that security screening will be with us for a long time to come, so security should be planned for, and integrated harmoniously with, the overall design.

Courthouses should be designed with the possibility of expansion in mind. Too many courthouses have accommodated expansion by awkward conversions of space—even closets—into makeshift courtrooms that have numerous deficiencies in function and appearance.

Design must allow for efficient maintenance. Courthouses are, of course, public buildings and are dependent on tax revenues for their upkeep. It may be expected that over the life of a courthouse there will be periods of straitened resources. Trial lawyers in urban areas are all too familiar with courtrooms whose motto has deteriorated to OD WE RUST, the ventilation system has failed, and the clock has not worked for years. Courthouses should be designed for easy, low-cost maintenance.

Judgment must be exercised in locating other facilities in courthouses. For many years, while federal jurisdiction was limited, it was very common for federal court functions to be located on the second floor of a post office building. Although the overall architecture of these buildings was typically dignified and even monumental, there is something about being a flight up from the parcel post window that seems not quite appropriate for a federal court. Federal courts today are typically freestanding facilities that sometimes, as in the case of the courthouse in New Haven, Connecticut, expand courthouse uses into the portion of the building formerly occupied by the post office.

Many state or county or municipal courthouses are part of mixed-use government buildings. Some of these other uses are more compatible with a courthouse use than others. A litigant searching for a hearing room in the Chester County Courthouse in West Chester, Pennsylvania may encounter a sign for a room devoted to Dog and Doe Licenses. The courthouse is a place of serious business, where virtually every case seeks to compel change in human relations, putting at stake personal liberty, family relations, personal or real property, or money in amounts great or small. The well-designed courthouse conveys a sense of history, of the continuity of the law, of principles and values transcending individual concerns—and in a realm quite apart from dog and doe licenses.

A golden age of building these secular temples ended about seventy years ago. The combination of design elements, favorable construction environments, and a growing nation that came together in the late nineteenth and early twentieth centuries produced magnificent courthouses throughout the country, culminating in Cass Gilbert's United States Supreme Court building in Washington, D.C. and his federal courthouse in New York City, both completed shortly after his death in 1934 (discussed elsewhere in this book; see, e.g. the Foreword and Chapter 6). But far more numerous than the federal examples are state courthouses in county seats across America.

The Marquette County Courthouse in Marquette, Michigan, a red sandstone neoclassical revival structure built in 1904 was the site of a libel suit brought by President Theodore Roosevelt and later served as the site for filming *Anatomy of a Murder* (fig. 7-4). A central section flanked by two wings is fronted by a two-story portico and topped with a large dome. As one Michigan lawyer

7-4. Marquette County Courthouse, Marquette, Michigan, Dimetrious F. Charlton and R. William Gilbert, 1904. (Photo: Calvin Beale)

GEORGE A. DAVIDSON

remarked, if you don't feel like a lawyer when you walk into that building, you sure do by the time you come out. Other outstanding county seat courthouses include the 1911 Beaux-Arts Brown County Courthouse in Brown County, Wisconsin, the 1882 Tippecanoe County Courthouse in Lafayette, Indiana, the 1905 neoclassical Bourbon County Courthouse in Paris, Kentucky, the 1890 Second Empire limestone Hood County Courthouse in Granbury, Texas, the 1898 Adair County Courthouse in Kirksville, Missouri, and the 1909 Madison County Courthouse in Wampsville, New York. Some of these courthouses have become tourist attractions, and books containing photographs of state courthouses have been published.[1]

From the perspective of courthouse architecture, there is much to be said for the county seat remaining a backwater. Not much has happened in Wampsville in the last century or more, so the courthouse remains its magnificent self. In venues where rising populations have substantially increased court business, contemporary architects have faced the difficult task of expanding buildings that were never designed for expansion, that reflect the styles of earlier days, and that contain detailing and workmanship impossible to replicate under today's economic conditions. Sometimes this expansion has been accomplished successfully, other times not.

The Victorian era also gives the lie to Mae West's dictum that too much of a good thing is wonderful. To the modern eye the profusion of design elements can give a space a crowded, claustrophobic feel. The appellate division building on Madison Square in New York City comes close to going over the top, but somehow remains a successful space today (see fig. C-17). The 1909 James Brown Lord building in the Palladio style is full of statuary, marble, carved wood, murals, and stained glass. The impressive carved wooden bench is backed by a carved wooden screen, over which are colorful murals, and the decorative ceiling is topped with a huge stained-glass skylight. The richness of the room suggests a debt to graft of a prior generation, but the project came in at more than 10 percent under its admittedly substantial budget.

In the Victorian era, the popular styles could be found pretty much anywhere in the country. Later, designers began to reflect a sense of place. The 1933 federal courthouse in Miami, for example, is in the Spanish Mediterranean revival style, whereas the Santa Barbara, California, courthouse (see figure 1-29) is in the Spanish Moorish style. In Miami, caseloads have exploded far beyond the capacity of the original structure; the solution has been to leave the original courthouse intact and build a new courthouse on adjacent land to absorb the caseload increase.

Despite considerable variety in architectural styles, all of these courthouses share one thing in common: they make a lawyer feel like a lawyer. Most of the time, that's good for everybody involved.

EIGHT

Creating a Courthouse That Works for Diverse Constituencies and Constituent Parts

STEVEN FLANDERS

The starting point in designing and realizing a successful courthouse is to believe Gilbert and Sullivan when they tell us that "things are seldom what they seem." It is essential for all design team participants to get good advice about every part of the projected building, not least because any given project is likely to be more or less unique. Effective communication is the essential first step, because so delicate a program cannot be realized without good advice. Yet good advice may be in short supply—and bad advice plentiful.

Commonly the nominal client is a government agency that is not a user, may have little contact with the courts, and may even have internal interests that are inconsistent with achieving an excellent design. For example, the client may be a board of county commissioners, say, or a statewide or nationwide agency for construction or building management that has only sporadic contact with the courts and related agencies, and its representatives may put keeping costs to a minimum ahead of design considerations.

Efforts to get sound advice by going beyond the nominal client to courts and users may be risky. The nominal client, who holds essential power as to how funding is obtained and money is spent, may be alienated by any effort to communicate with others.

Even if suitable communication with court users is established, information gleaned from the courts may be less than useful or usable. It has been said that every judge knows with certainty exactly how a courtroom or a courthouse should be designed; unfortunately, this knowledge differs from one judge to the next. Multiple and conflicting views that all sound authoritative may confront a design team. Deciding which are actually useful or authoritative, and which may safely be disregarded as idiosyncratic or marginal, requires an exercise in judgment that will test the diplomatic as well as professional smarts of any design team.

If discerning a user's perspective is difficult, gathering a perspective of the broader public is exceptionally so. Few among the general public have more than very occasional contact with the courts. And would anyone desire that such repeat players as repeat offenders or chronic litigants have a special role in informing design? Occasionally, a committee representing the public may be available to the design team, but participants are unlikely to have extensive or comprehensive workaday experience with court needs or facilities. Their individual views may be governed by their particular axes to grind. Ideally, an informed and experienced architect is the public's best representative.

Another difficulty is that institutional names may well conceal more than they reveal. A little knowledge or experience with court projects in another jurisdiction may actually be more misleading than helpful. For example, in New York State the supreme court is the trial court of general jurisdiction; unlike the United States Supreme Court or the supreme courts of most states, its judges are locally elected and are subject to two levels of appellate review. The space requirements of a general jurisdiction trial court, including the supreme court in New York State, with its confusing name that is much older than that of the U.S. Supreme Court and most others, could hardly be more different from those of any top appellate court, state or federal.

Because any courthouse project, even the simplest and most straightforward, involves multiple constituencies that often are in conflict with one another, an architect and design team must be alert to possible turf battles. All participants must be able to accommodate changes when the unexpected arises and some new player wins at the expense of an existing player that seemed dominant, or

at least seemed in control of its particular stake in the project. In most courthouse jobs, no one is truly in charge, at least not for long.

As numerous contributors to this book make clear, security issues present extreme difficulties as design teams try, in the post-9/11 environment, to reconcile the conflicting concerns of safety versus openness. Creating a court space that is truly inviting to the public has become very problematic, as architects confront security requirements that may place an exclusive value on safety. How is any designer to argue that safety should be secondary to any other priority, especially to aesthetic ones that hardly are matters of life and death? As Chapter 10 demonstrates, doing so is especially difficult on behalf of priorities as uncertain as public amenities in public spaces or the imagery appropriate to the courthouse.

None of these problems admit of easy resolution. The best advice is for the design team to keep listening and looking, seeking the widest possible variety of sources of advice backed by sound and proven experience. Nearly all design teams on large projects, and many on smaller ones, include a firm with specific courthouse experience. Whatever the ultimate composition of the design team, all members must try to exercise effective judgment about everything that is seen and heard as the program unfolds, while continuing to ask probing questions. When a formal and authoritative program provides answers to some of the questions just raised, much is gained, but even then it remains useful to continue to look and listen and ask questions.

If no defined program exists, it may

be helpful to import one. The National Center for State Courts' *Planning and Design Guide for Court Facilities* or the federal design guide or state guides may be helpful.[1] California, Connecticut, Massachusetts, and Michigan are among the states that have published volumes that some architects have found useful, outside the state in question as well as within it. Regarding the specific problem of courtroom layout, in refining a large project it is very helpful to undertake a life-sized courtroom mock-up if funds are sufficient. A variety of judicial and support personnel, and lawyers, should actually sit in the spaces assigned to their tasks and briefly play their roles in a mock proceeding. Such factors as handicap access and technology requirements must be addressed in exacting detail, and often no program or design guide addresses adequately the specific problems a new design raises. It is best to identify and correct any anomalies well before construction.

A brief survey of judicial organizations and the spaces they require reveals a bewildering variety of names, functions, and roles. Nomenclature, in particular, varies greatly both within the United States and especially among different countries. Yet patterns are not impossible to define at a useful level of generality, even though similar institutions often have different names, and similar names apply to different institutions in different places. What follows is an attempt to discern a useful level of generality regarding American court systems, in all their bewildering variety throughout fifty states, the federal government, the territories, and the District of Columbia. This overview draws upon the useful manuals on *State Court Organization* published irregularly by the U.S. Department of Justice, Office of Justice Programs, based upon a joint effort of the Conference of State Court Administrators and the National Center for State Courts. The most recent manual refers to court organization in 1998 and was published in 2000, but it remains reasonably current at the time of writing.

At the appellate apex, and often administratively as well, is a court of last resort, often known as the supreme court of its state or other jurisdiction. The federal judiciary and all but a few of the smaller states have intermediate appellate courts as well. There are eleven regional circuits in the federal system, each with its regional court of appeals located in one or several cities within its states, plus two courts of appeals located in the District of Columbia. Many states have a single intermediate appellate court located in the state capital that hears all appeals there, but the largest states have several appellate courts that are located in the regions they serve (e.g., California has six), and others have one statewide court that occasionally travels to one or more locations outside the capital. Below this appellate structure are a variety of trial courts, many of them specialized and requiring specific combinations of facilities, and many that hear many or all kinds of cases.

Courts of last resort and intermediate appellate courts are a good place to start in sketching the distinctive requirements of courts of different types, because their program is the simplest and yet the most particular to a court setting. An appellate court's program is simple because the focus is on the courtroom (often there is only one); traffic patterns are relatively simple because there are no prisoners and often few spectators; security arrangements, although essential, are straightforward because traffic of non-employees is light and patterns uncomplicated; and office space requirements are not exceptionally specialized. The justices or judges must have a suitable work space that reflects the nature of the judicial institution, and support staff require office space of a fairly conventional sort as defined by what normally is a fairly exact program. Partly because appellate courts are closest to the courts' governing structure, their needs are often better defined than are those of less exalted judicial institutions (treated later in this chapter), which nevertheless have more exacting design requirements.

But courts of last resort, especially, require facilities in which the expressive requirements of a court program are strong, even dominant or paramount. It is no accident that there are many books of a coffee-table style that portray the physical facilities of courts of last resort, possibly more than for those of all other types of courts combined.[2] Paul Byard, author of Chapter 5, traces the evolution of Cass Gilbert's thinking about his United States Supreme Court building (in another publication) in a sequence that can assist many architects confronting the problem of presenting a monumental judicial institution upon a monumental site, notwithstanding a program that intrinsically is quite modest (see fig. C-1). Gilbert had a monumental Washington site opposite the Capitol and adjacent to the Library of Congress upon which to define one of the three branches of the national government, yet "the Supreme Court building did not have to

be very big to function. Its program was tiny, to house nine individuals engaged in the most cerebral of tasks, big in stature but still small in actuality. . . . For Gilbert, this absence of a necessity for much size was a real difficulty. He needed size to permit the exercise of the power of this kind of architecture, big enough to permit the flexing of its particular stylistic muscle to confer on the Court the authority and sense of right Gilbert felt he should be giving it. And he needed a way to differentiate it from the Library of Congress."[3]

There are many solutions in a great variety of styles and settings, to this sort of problem. A well-known and distinguished example is the Supreme Court of Israel (see fig. 4-19). In the grandest, such as the U.S. Supreme Court, the working program may amount to a relatively small portion of the total space. An effective search for the relevant symbolism and an appropriate stylistic vocabulary may begin with a close relationship—ideally, a friendship—between architect and chief justice or other relevant judicial official. This kind of collaboration occurred in the case of Gilbert and Chief Justice William Howard Taft—Professor Byard describes their work as the ideal committee, of two—though Taft died before the building was far along, and Gilbert died before it opened.

One solution—too rarely employed—is to make use of an old courthouse of distinguished or at least effective design that is essentially obsolete for trial court purposes. It is often impractical to retrofit for trial service an old courthouse that is both small and lacking in the complex circulation paths generally required of any structure that is to be used for criminal trials today. But the

8-1. Former Bronx Borough Courthouse, Michael J. Garvin, 1905–15. (Photo: Steven Flanders)

monumental spaces, distinctive materials, and striking locations of courts built a century or more ago may be excellently suited to appellate use. The old Bronx County Courthouse (fig. 8-1), now derelict and the subject of considerable community agitation as to appropriate reuse, is an example both of the possibilities and the obstacles. Although there has been considerable recent court construction nearby, adaptive reuse as a courthouse has never been proposed. Certainly this is a sensible position with regard to trial court use, because Michael J. Garvin's 1905 derelict is small and inflexible. It is pleasing to indulge the fantasy that this monument—to municipal corruption, among other things—might one day serve as a court again, this time for appellate arguments. But in this particular instance, as in some others, such a proposal may be pure fantasy. Though James Brown Lord's appellate division courthouse on lower Madison Avenue in Manhattan

(see figs. C-18, 5-6, and 5-7) is much in need of expansion room, it is far away. Moreover, the distinguished appellate court it houses is hardly likely to seek expansion room in a problematic, even if recovering, commercial area in the South Bronx. Within cities, as in less populated places, an old courthouse is often poorly located for appellate use. The once-bustling neighborhood of law offices of the Garvin courthouse will be populated only by ghosts of its past, well represented by a "Law Building" now occupied by a car service, an auto parts shop, and other miscellaneous tenants (fig. 8-2).

Two examples of successful adaptations are the headquarters of the United States Courts of Appeals for the Fifth and Ninth Circuits in New Orleans and San Francisco, respectively (figs. 8-3 and 8-4; see also figure C-23). Both were constructed nearly one hundred years ago, when James Knox Taylor, then the supervising architect of the treasury, established a particularly grand federal

STEVEN FLANDERS

presence in these and several other cities. Both served originally as general federal buildings and housed both trial and appellate courts. Both served also as the central post office in town and housed the regional headquarters of numerous executive branch agencies. They have been suitably and excellently restored, notwithstanding the unavoidably expensive problems of providing adequate power, HVAC (heating, ventilation, air conditioning), handicap access, earthquake resistance, and other modernization; both serve today as positively sumptuous headquarters for regional federal appellate courts. Notably, the grand spaces that originally served the post office serve well today's expressive needs of court use, in these and many other restorations. Neither is used for trials, which would have required massive reconstruction that would have been both destructive and prohibitively expensive.

Beyond courtrooms and judicial chambers, appellate court facilities present few special problems. A substantial clerical staff must have standard office space and suitable computer access. Most appellate courts today have a substantial central legal staff as well; in most federal courts of appeals and somewhat under half of the state courts of last resort and intermediate courts of appeals, these include a corps of pre-argument attorneys who require significant conference facilities, including video capability. Other service offices needed by most appellate courts are for security staff and facilities, a computer staff, a mail room, and a press room.

Another big space requirement, but sometimes housed in another building, is for the staff of the offices that provide

judicial administration support to the region served. In the federal system nationally, this is the Administrative Office of the United States Courts, an important body to any design team seeking federal work because its Space and Facilities Division plays a pivotal role in new construction, working with the General Services Administration in the executive branch. The regional counterpart is the judicial council of each circuit, which also holds important power in any federal court construction. (It is a bit ironic to note that the national Administrative Office was created in 1939, only a few years after Cass Gilbert's Supreme Court building went up; had this office existed a few years earlier, Gilbert might have had the massive program that would truly have filled his massive shell.) Most states have an administrative office that reports to the court of last resort or directly to the chief justice or chief judge. Apart from conference and training facilities that may be specified, these agencies do not have space requirements that differ

8-2. A commercial "Law Building" abandoned by its courthouse neighbor, Bronx, New York. (Photo: Steven Flanders)

8-3. James Gamble Rogers's New Orleans Federal Building of 1909, now the headquarters of the United States Court of Appeals for the Fifth Circuit. (Photo: courtesy of the Fifth Circuit)

8-4. James Knox Taylor's sumptuous United States Post Office and Courthouse in San Francisco of 1905, now the headquarters of the United States Court of Appeals for the Ninth Circuit. (Photo: courtesy of the Ninth Circuit)

STEVEN FLANDERS

noticeably from ordinary office space.

The design of trial courts is more complex and more engaging in operational terms. In the United States it is now common, or close to universal, that new facilities for general jurisdiction trial courts (those with no upper limit to their jurisdiction) are required to have three separate circulation patterns (except sometimes in small locations where no criminal matters are heard): private circulation for judges and some staff, also serving jurors; prisoner circulation; and circulation for the public. Achieving an efficient and effective solution to this puzzle can present knotty problems; solutions are explored in Chapter 3.

The trial court also presents the problem, in especially acute relief, of balancing public access with security for public and court personnel. Only the United States Supreme Court and a handful of especially prominent appellate courts are public places in anything like the degree that is typical of the general jurisdiction trial court in any large- or medium-sized city. Yet more than any other, the trial court necessarily draws in highly dangerous visitors, by no means all of whom are in custody. And it may present an inviting target for violent as well as peaceful demonstrations, and even for terrorists, just as a prominent appellate court may. Achieving a proper and effective balance that is specific to the site offered and to specified security requirements may be the most demanding problem faced by a design team.

When civil and criminal proceedings are physically separate, even if the same judges preside at both (while on different assignments), there can be considerable savings, and design problems can be mitigated. For a courtroom used only in civil proceedings, two circulation systems or even a single one may suffice, lockup facilities are not needed, and security concerns may be less than elsewhere. It is worth noting, however, that security remains an issue outside the criminal context. Judges are as vulnerable to threats, and even their realization, as much in civil matters as criminal, perhaps more so.[4]

Little known and less understood (except by persons with in-depth experience in courts) are the distinctive design issues presented by courts that handle family disputes and juvenile crime, indeed, these court venues may present the most volatile security problems of any category of court proceedings, serious criminal trials *not* excepted. Nomenclature varies greatly from one jurisdiction to another, as do the relevant administrative arrangements. Separate family court facilities, sometimes staffed by judges on short- or long-term assignment from other trial courts of general or limited jurisdiction, present opportunities to address the problems of these proceedings in a specific and appropriate fashion. For example, many proceedings that address custody or child support matters, or juvenile crime, are confidential. Because the public is not permitted, courtrooms can be smaller than otherwise. On the other hand, ancillary facilities must be carefully planned and thoughtfully executed. Many families arrive together, often in high-conflict circumstances that call for separation. Witnesses and victims often bring whole families, including a number of children, because no other option is available. Any urban court that hears proceedings addressing juvenile crime has as much need for three circulation systems as any general jurisdiction trial court (though jurors are rarely, if ever, used), yet many courthouses do not provide for even minimal separation.

Family courts thus require a unique number and variety of facilities, yet funds are rarely available to offer any but the most minimal opportunities for the architect to express the character and importance of the institution. The range of services typical of family courts is wide and varied. One effort to address the particular design issues involved noted that "they begin to take on the appearance of a corporate conglomerate. . . . It will probably administer family conciliation, mediation, and some adult probation, plus services usually administered by juvenile courts. If it is a specialized juvenile court, it will administer juvenile probation to include intake, investigation, and probation supervision . . . secure and non-secure detention, group homes, shelter facilities. . . ."[5] The organization, placement within the judiciary, and services provided by these courts under their various names vary so widely that design teams can do no more than be alert to the issues these courts present and thoroughly investigate the program for any omissions. The central message is that a sensitive design will well accommodate the opposing imperatives of safety and civilized treatment of the public, including in this case many who are confronting possibly the most conflicted moment in highly conflicted lives.[6]

For other specialized trial courts— probate courts, municipal courts, traffic courts, magistrates courts, small claims courts, tribal courts, and (in the federal judiciary) bankruptcy courts—it is impossible here to offer definitive guid- ance as to space requirements or special problems, because organization and placement in the administrative and physical structure of court systems vary too widely. Sometimes these functions are physically and administratively separate; sometimes they are separate physically but are staffed by judges and support staff on temporary assignment; sometimes there is little separation or none.

Lower-level trial courts employ a larger staff in relation to the judicial size of a court than do their appellate counterparts or even the general jurisdiction trial courts, because more of the work is of an administrative character. A municipal or traffic court may resemble a large branch bank more than a grand judicial institution. Its internal traffic may be very high. In addition to a clerk's office, substantial staff offices of trial courts may include probation (sometimes separately housed, sometimes administratively separate), mediation and conciliation staffs, investigative staffs to determine if an arrested defendant may be eligible for pretrial release (in the federal judiciary these are known as pretrial services agencies), and a court security staff. Closely related but administratively separate agencies that may be housed in a new or updated court facility include the prosecutor, a public defender (preferably *not* housed with the court, so as to preserve a sense that a defendant's appointed lawyer is independent), and (in the federal bankruptcy system) the United States Trustee. Many courts provide work space for non-employees who spend much or most of their professional lives in the courthouse; these may include public or private attorneys, social workers, guardians, police officers, and investigators, among others.

We now reach the question of how big the courthouse or justice center should be, not in terms of simple physical size but as a matter of what it embraces or includes, and how its constituent parts relate to one another and can be expressed in its physical form. There has always been a very wide range of possibilities. Only recently did it become common for a "courthouse" to include courts only. Traditional county courthouses included most local and county functions, as was noted in Chapter 1, and many federal courthouses constructed through the 1930s were general federal buildings that included the central post office for their city. But those structures began life in a different era in at least two crucial respects. No one questioned the word *courthouse* in their names, even if it might be coupled with something else, as in "Post Office and Courthouse." And it was never doubted that their design, whatever the style, would identify them with something formal and monumental, of which the rule of law was a significant, usually exclusive, component. Location helped also. A courthouse on the town square, surrounded by lawyers' offices as well as a concentration of office and retail facilities, helped define the courts and their place in the community as something close to the essence of what made it a community at all.

We can appreciate the significance of the shift when we contemplate the Justice Center that is "conveniently" located on the town's periphery, near malls and freeways, or in a suburban location that is not specifically associated with any one town or legal community (see fig. 5-11 for a distinguished solution). In a small city or county seat the police facilities may still be quite substantial, as are the associated lockup facilities, probably overwhelming a rather modest court program that is, for the judiciary, a small outpost that is served only intermittently. A Justice Center thus may present an insuperable design challenge: it may be impossible to forestall the impression that a person who enters the court—to respond, say, to a contract suit filed in connection with some local dispute—is entering the police station. And the juror summoned to such a Justice Center may believe, understandably, that he or she is discharging a police-related function.

This misapprehension is all the more likely and difficult to forestall in the larger structures that also house related but noncourt functions, such as investigative agencies, administrative agencies that frequently file in court, city, town, or county clerk and records functions, and sheriff's or marshal's offices. Perhaps it was all very much simpler in the days when the court/courthouse was the starting point, and it was natural for citizens with business in the building to speak of going to "the courthouse" to transact even business unrelated to courts: motor vehicle registration, paying local taxes and fees, licensing pets, or attending meetings of local legislative bodies such as a town council or county legislature.

Given these complex issues, a design team must listen, and listen well and critically, to as many sources of guidance and experience as possible in addressing the problems specific to a particular project. And architects, in turn, must also educate judges and other stakeholders to participate usefully in helping to create a successful courthouse.

PART FOUR

The Future
of the Courthouse

NINE

The Courtroom in the Age of Technology

FREDRIC L. LEDERER

The courtroom is the inner sanctum in the temple of justice. Here asserted facts mix with raw emotion as human beings strive, some willingly and many unwillingly, for the closest approximation of justice available in our society. The very existence of the courtroom and the possibility of trial within it drives much of our legal system's dispute resolution apparatus. Until recently, courtrooms were almost immune to the technological revolution that has swept our nation and culture. That is no longer true.

The origins of today's high technology courtrooms are unclear. Although there were earlier developments, the modern age of courtroom technology may have begun in the 1980s when United States District Judge Carl Rubin presided over a complex tort trial in which counsel installed computers in an Ohio courtroom to present evidence. During this decade United States District Judge Roger Strand likely created the nation's first ongoing integrated high-technology courtroom in Phoenix, Arizona, achieving significant gains in trial

efficiency. The widely televised high-technology murder trial of O. J. Simpson in Los Angeles was the first to capture the public's imagination. The Simpson case led many people to believe, erroneously, that such technology-augmented trials are more commonplace than, in fact, they are. However, the reality is rapidly catching up to the perception.

As of 2003 it appeared that of 1,366 U. S. district court courtrooms, approximately one-quarter was substantially augmented by technology.[1] There are no accurate statistics for state courtrooms. However, there are clearly a substantial number of them, with many more now under construction (fig. 9-1). Clearly we are in the midst of a major change in the nature of courtrooms in the United States. Other nations are also developing similar facilities. High-technology courtrooms have been established in Australia, Canada, England, Israel, Hong Kong, Mexico, Northern Ireland, Scotland, Serbia, Singapore, and in the International Criminal Tribunal for the former Yugoslavia in The Hague. Probably there are others as well. The potential extent of

9-1. Roger Barker Courtroom, Courtroom 23, of the Ninth Judicial Circuit, Orlando, Florida.

the revolution can be seen in Michigan, which, in 2002, created by statute the world's first "cybercourt."[2] Modeled on the William & Mary School of Law McGlothlin Courtroom (fig. 9-2),[3] home of the Courtroom 21 Project, the cybercourt, a nonjury business court, will be predominantly virtual, with participants other than the judge appearing by video conferencing; evidence and other submissions will be presented by Internet or other technology.

The impact of technology on courtrooms and courthouses is, and will be, multifaceted. Technology is being installed not only by courts of general jurisdiction but in many other types as well, including family courts (fig. 9-3),

9-2. McGlothlin Courtroom at William & Mary Law School, home of the Courtroom 21 Project.

FREDRIC L. LEDERER

traffic courts, and administrative tribunals. A proper understanding of its effects on courtroom and courthouse design requires a review of contemporary courtroom technology.

Courtroom technologies can be divided somewhat artificially into the categories of administration, interpretation, court record, counsel communications, remote appearances, information/evidence presentation, jury room deliberations, assistive technologies, and infrastructure.

The Trial Courtroom

Administration

As information technology has become commonplace in courthouses, judges and clerk administrators have required data access in the courtroom. Courtroom access to the electronic docket, electronically filed court documents, case management data, and other fundamental court information, including access to individual and institutional information, is increasingly mandated. At the same time, because most electronic legal materials are now available primarily or entirely by Internet, judges (and often counsel) wish access to electronic legal materials and the Internet. Access to this information requires network/Internet connectivity and, usually, a computer with monitor at the bench and a similar installation at the deputy clerk's location.

Interpretation

Language interpretation is a significant requirement in many proceedings. As the number of languages spoken by residents has increased sharply, the ability of the courts to easily obtain competent interpreters has become problematical.

9-3. Rendering of Bexar County (San Antonio, Texas) Children's Courtroom.

Technology provides two options. Coupling remote interpretation services (such as LanguageLine) with speaker telephones provides consecutive interpretation. More sophisticated services, such as that offered by Rausch Industries, use two telephone lines to provide simultaneous interpretation but require that special arrangements be made ahead of time with an appropriate interpreter. The year 2003 saw the advent of commercial interpretation by two-way videoconferencing, an innovation that permits remote American Sign Language (ASL) interpretation for those who cannot hear.

Although jurisdictions in the United States rarely require multiple language interpretation as a general matter, New Mexico requires that both English and Spanish be made available to jurors. Interpretation for multiple persons may best be provided by using infrared headsets with the emitter linked to the interpreter.

9-4. Diane Gray, real-time stenographic court reporter in the McGlothlin Courtroom.

Court Record

A number of different court record technologies are now available. They can be divided into those that make primarily only a record of what is said and those designed to produce a contemporaneous real-time record.

Analog recording permits the recording, on analog tape, of everything said incident to the proceedings. Digital methods record audio (and, increasingly, video) signals in the form of computerized digital data, usually with optional copying to CD-ROMs. Videorecording customarily uses multiple courtroom cameras. Coupled with voice-switching technology, those cameras can be used either to switch the image to a full-screen picture of whomever is talking or to create a multi-image (multiple picture-in-picture type) master image, usually with the speaker in the largest window. None of these systems provides a contemporaneous text transcript, and effective access to the court record requires

"log notes"—text notes prepared by a monitor or reporter indicating who is speaking and, often, additional clarifying information. Ordinarily the person making these notes is within the courtroom, although there are a number of multiple courtroom recording systems in which a single person monitors more than one courtroom from a central location. Court recording systems may be operated or supervised by court reporters, by other court personnel, or left in a stand-alone mode, with the system turned on and basically left running unattended.

Stenographic court reporters are an integral feature of many courtrooms. Most stenographic reporters are machine writers who use a machine to convert their key presses (using the stenotype conventions) to symbols on paper tape or to internal computer storage. The tape is later transcribed by the reporter. Voice-writers (formerly Stenomask reporters), especially common in the Southeast, traditionally have used tape recorders, repeating everything said in the proceedings into muffled microphones for later transcription. Now they increasingly use speech-recognition computers.

Real-time court reporters use their technology to create immediate rough-draft text transcript that may be sent electronically to computers used by judge and counsel. This service permits judge and counsel not only to read the transcript but also to retain electronic copies and to make private notes on the individual copies. Most real-time reporters have been stenographic reporters (fig. 9-4). However, some voicewriters now use speech-recognition technology to produce real-time draft transcripts; they speak into "silencers"—rubber-type masks that muffle the voice—and a computer con-

FREDRIC L. LEDERER

verts the speech to first-draft text.

Court record requirements have direct implications for courtroom design. Court reporter–based systems require that courtrooms be designed to accommodate the presence of the reporters. Experience suggests that too many courtrooms were designed with little thought for reporter seating and whether available locations were both functional and comfortable; designers should consult local court reporters in the design stage. Good acoustics should be a basic requirement for all courtrooms; court record technologies will fail without adequate acoustics. Similarly, video systems require unobscured sightlines. Nearly all recording systems require courtroom wiring; real-time systems must distribute the real-time "feed" to the bench and counsel tables, usually by an electronic connection known as a "serial connection" (although alternative forms of electronic connections are now being introduced).

The type of courtroom record that we are likely to see in the future is shown by Courtroom 21 Project's annual "laboratory trial," a high-technology experimental case conducted to determine the pragmatic, legal, and human consequences of high technology use. The project customarily combines the real-time transcript with digital audio and video and computer images of the evidence to publish a live contemporaneous court record available on the Web (fig. 9-5).

Counsel Communications

Counsel communications is a relatively new technology. Utilizing notebook computers and connections to the Internet, counsel can now communicate instantly with supporting colleagues, experts, legal assistants, or nearly anyone anywhere in the world. When combined with a contemporaneous court record available on the Web, this technology can substantially bolster trial counsel's in-court capabilities. Because many courts are especially concerned about the security of their computer and communications networks, the developing tendency was to restrict counsel communications to dial-up connections using telephone lines. More recently, courts have been entering into arrangements with Courtroom Connect, a private vendor that installs wireless computer connectivity in the courthouses, concentrating on courtrooms and, increasingly, jury assembly areas in return for the right to charge counsel usage fees during trial.

Remote Appearances

Modern video communications make it possible for trials to include remote judges, witnesses, and counsel. At present, the most common use of remote video occurs in the numerous state

9-5. Courtroom 21 multimedia court record.

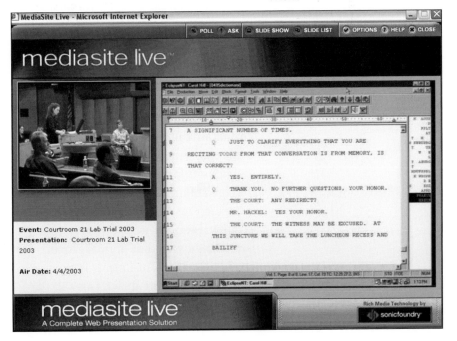

9-6. Remote witness testifying from London.

ding provisions has been legally rocky regarding federal criminal cases. An attempt to permit it via amendment to the Federal Rules of Criminal Procedure was blocked in 2003, when the Supreme Court refused to transmit the proposed amended rule to Congress, with Justice Scalia expressing grave constitutional concerns. As of 2005 the issue was being considered in banc by the United States Court of Appeals for the Eleventh Circuit.[4]

Remote appearances necessarily raise numerous questions.[5] Even when legal concerns are satisfied, basic practice questions persist. Controlled scientific experiments conducted by William & Mary's psychology department in conjunction with the Courtroom 21 Project have shown no significant difference in result whether key expert witnesses testified remotely or in person, in the courtroom.[6] However, that result took place when the witness testified life-sized on a TV screen located immediately to the rear of the witness stand. As a result, the Courtroom 21 practice is to recommend that courtroom designers use large flat-panel monitors placed behind the witness stand when planning to implement remote witness testimony. This approach rejects the practice of using an integrated "roll-about" in the center of the courtroom.

Remote counsel and judge appearances are also possible. In the 2001 Courtroom 21 Experimental Laboratory Trial, for example, one counsel appeared remotely from Leeds in England and examined a witness appearing remotely from Canberra, Australia (fig. 9-7). Remote judge appearances are still quite rare, although a number of federal appeals proceedings have included one

courts that use the technology for remote first appearances and arraignments in criminal cases. The image and testimony of the accused originate from the detention facility via a two-way audio and video connection with the judge, usually in the courtroom. This procedure has now been authorized on a voluntary basis for federal criminal cases as well.

Remote witness testimony is a growing practice in state and federal courts (fig. 9-6). A distant or ill witness's inability to travel to trial or the expense and inconvenience of obtaining personal testimony can impel counsel to use videoconferencing. This procedure is being used increasingly for witnesses in foreign countries and has great potential for expert testimony in cases where the testifying experts would be very expensive if removed from normal pursuits for extended periods of time. It is expressly authorized in federal civil cases in the Federal Rules of Civil Procedure on a good-cause basis. Adoption of correspon-

FREDRIC L. LEDERER

or more remote judges joining the appellate panel. The potential for remote appearances was demonstrated in the 2003 Courtroom 21 Laboratory Trial, a simulated al Qaeda financing prosecution, judges in the United Kingdom and Australia appeared remotely in the Williamsburg, Virginia, courtroom, along with the sitting U. S. district court judge, so that all three judges could rule seriatim on the attorney–client privilege claim of an Australian lawyer in Australia claiming the privilege under Australian, English, and U. S. law (fig. 9-8). After all three judges reached the conclusion that the lawyer was not protected by the privilege, the Australian judge ordered the lawyer to testify, and he did so via videoconference.

In April 2005 the Courtroom 21 Project tried *In re Blossom & Blossom*, an experimental parental child-abduction case in which the Mexican wife had returned to Mexico with one child, leaving the American father in the United States with the other. Courts in both Mexico and the United States had jurisdiction to determine custody of the children; neither had the effective power to do so successfully. In the experiment, both courts convened at the same time in their own nations, took evidence from each other via videoconference, heard arguments from counsel in the other court, and then resolved the case after the two judges conferred privately via videoconference.

As *In re Blossom & Blossom* demonstrates, ultimately we are likely to have to determine, as a matter of policy, what constitutes a "trial" and what we mean by a "courtroom." The Michigan cybercourt, once constructed, has the poten-

tial to consist only of a room with perhaps a judge and a member of the court staff, and any interested citizens. All other persons may appear remotely.

Information/Evidence Presentation

Lawyers use technology to assist them during opening statements, presentation of evidence, and closing arguments. Modern technology-augmented litigation customarily emphasizes the use by counsel of document cameras (a TV camera aimed downward at a document or exhibit), high-technology white boards (a vertical white surface on which computer images can be displayed and annotated), and notebook computers. Counsel may use a variety of software applications to display images of documents, photographs, or computer slides. Touch-sensitive screens even permit witnesses to use their fingers to annotate exhibits. Courtroom 21 designs customarily use a single large flat moni-

9-7. Courtroom 21 Experimental Laboratory Trial 2001: remote counsel in Leeds, England, examines witness testifying from Canberra, Australia.

9-8. Courtroom 21 Lab Trial, 2003: three courts on three continents meet concurrently via video-conferencing.

9-9. Witness uses a Smartboard overlay on a Pioneer plasma display to annotate evidence.

tor (with electronic overlays that permit annotation of the images displayed on them) for this purpose, placed behind the witness (fig. 9-9). Counsel may use whiteboards installed elsewhere in the courtroom to make especially dramatic interactive closing arguments to the jury.

Counsel most often present their evidence either from a central podium (fig. 9-10) or lectern or from counsel table, although in some courts counsel are required to submit exhibits to a member of the court staff for presentation.

Counsel's images traditionally have been displayed on television or monitor screens, but many other options are now available. These include a single large screen on which a ceiling-mounted projector displays the images that the trial lawyer is showing, small flat-screen monitors (usually one monitor for every one or two jurors [fig. 9-11]), and large flat (plasma or LCD) screens or large rear-projection monitors (fig. 9-12).

In most cases, the judge, counsel, and witness see images on small computer monitors. Originally CRT, these are now nearly always flat-screen monitors.

The defining element of a high-technology courtroom is an evidence display system. We can expect them to become commonplace in our courtrooms.

Jury Room Deliberations

In their deliberations, jurors often review evidentiary exhibits admitted at trial. State Justice Institute–funded Courtroom 21 experimental work has shown that deliberations can be enriched by allowing jurors to collectively view projected exhibit images during deliberations. This usage also permits jurors to emphasize matters of perceived importance for one another via various forms of annotation,

FREDRIC L. LEDERER

even in nontechnology trials. This suggests that jury rooms should be designed with some form of large-image display capability (fig. 9-13). A basic system includes a document camera and a display means; a more elaborate system for a technology-augmented trial requires a computer system as well. Experimental work shows no difficulty in juror operation of such systems if they are properly designed.

Assistive Technologies

Courtroom technology can provide substantial assistance to trial participants who have special needs. Judges, lawyers, court staff, jurors, and witnesses, as well as observing members of the public, sometimes find full participation in a hearing made problematic by individual difficulties they may have in hearing, seeing, moving, and the like. Just as courtroom design should comply with both the letter and the spirit of the Americans with Disabilities Act and similar statutes and rules, courtroom technologists must work to make the courtroom effectively accessible to all. Infrared headsets linked to the courtroom's audio reinforcement system can be used to provide hearing assistance. (The same system is used to assist court reporters hampered by poor courtroom acoustics.) Real-time transcription supplied by court reporters is often used to provide a running text version of proceedings for those who cannot hear. Braille devices linked to scanners and notebook computers can permit the blind to read documents and testify concerning them. Assistive technology podia for counsel in wheelchair have been constructed by the Courtroom 21 Project. Technology offers great potential to

9-10. Counsel presents case from the Courtroom 21 litigators podium in the McGlothlin Courtroom.

9-11. McGlothlin Courtroom jury box.

9-12. SMART Technologies SmartBoard 3000i.

9-13. High-technology jury deliberation room.

systems, and significant amounts of hardware, all of which will need maintenance. Further, use of courtroom technology almost always means planning for equipment upgrades and new technology, some of which may not yet even exist. In short, the high-technology courtroom must be designed and constructed so that both maintenance and future improvements can be accomplished quickly and economically. "Infrastructure" concerns are critical.

The "category 5" cabling now in use is being replaced by fiber-optic cable, which is thinner and more capable; indeed, the Courtroom 21 Project's McGlothlin Courtroom was the first in the world to be based entirely on a fiber backbone. Wireless applications offer new possibilities as the technology is improved. Early 2004 brought developments that now make it possible to connect display devices to the courtroom video distribution system wirelessly. Although of great potential importance, especially regarding renovation of historic courtrooms, this technology, although encrypted, likely will trouble judges and court managers deeply: concerns about data security will be exacerbated.

Control systems now usually take the form of touch-screen control panels that allow one or more persons to control what is being shown to judge and jury and where it is shown (fig. 9-14). In sophisticated systems, different monitors may display different images. The jury, for example, may see the image of a remote witness behind the witness stand while viewing documents about which the witness is testifying on the jury monitors. Many high-technology courtrooms use three such panels: one for the

make the courtroom accessible to all in a meaningful fashion.

Wiring, Switching, and Other Infrastructure

Traditionally, courtroom design focused primarily on basic issues of where the participants should be located, sightlines, traffic flow, and acoustics. Technology has complicated courtroom design; it calls for special wiring, control

FREDRIC L. LEDERER

judge, one for the deputy clerk, and a smaller one for counsel. All of these panels take up surface space and must be planned for.

The need to maximize flexibility and accommodate later technology modifications reinforces the need for raised floor systems that permit easy installation of cable under the floor. In some cases the floor can function as a complete cabling solution. Although such systems can increase the initial construction cost, they make maintenance and modification easy. Courtroom 21's Powerflor (fig. 9-15) was recut and relaid easily and quickly, for example, when the courtroom well was completely redesigned some years ago.

Security systems, video court record systems, and videoconferencing technology require installation of television cameras in the courtroom, and thus require a design that does not visually block the cameras. The placement of computer monitors and other forms of display technology affects millwork and furniture design because the displays must be easily visible but not block visual sightlines. Audio technology influences design too. For example, high ceilings and hard wall surfaces are bad choices for courtrooms designed for remote appearances or an electronic record of the proceedings. At the same time, the increasing use of high-tech hardware requires convenient and accessible storage locations. Designers and technology consultants must communicate their needs. Although tomorrow's courtrooms should look very much like today's, the increasing amount of technology to be installed in those courtrooms will further limit architectural options.

9-14. AMX courtroom control panel.

9-15. Martin Gruen, codesigner of the McGlothlin Courtroom, shows Courtroom 21 PowerFlor.

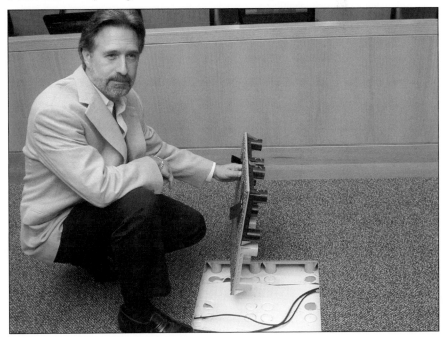

The Appellate Courtroom

Although courtroom technology is spreading rapidly in the trial courtrooms of the United States, the same cannot be said of appellate courtrooms. Some appellate courts use hypertext CD-ROM appellate briefs, which permit the judge to retrieve legal authorities and the court record electronically by clicking on citations in counsel's electronic briefs, just as is done on the Web. Most appellate courtroom technology, however, is limited to remote appearances by judges (e.g., the United States Courts of Appeals for the Second and Tenth Circuits and the United States Court of Appeals for the Armed Forces) and, in the Second Circuit, for remote counsel participation at locations available to lawyers. Because appellate proceedings are based on the trial record, it is rare for counsel to wish to show the judges documents or other images, although Courtroom 21 experimental work has shown the utility of doing so (fig. 9-16).

Although appellate adoption of court-room technology is proceeding slowly, the potential impact of trial courtroom technology cannot be overstated. As trials increasingly use copious technology and create high-technology multimedia court records, appellate courts will need to cope with what is happening "below." One of the likely consequences of the explosion in trial courtroom technology will be the need to install courtroom technology in the appellate courtroom for proper consideration of the trial record during oral argument.

The Future

How will today's courtroom technological innovations impact the nature of dispute resolution in the future, and how in turn that will affect courthouse design? The core characteristic of modern technology is its ability to eliminate distance. At its heart, dispute resolution presents an information management question. At trial, lawyers present and question information. The fact finder—judge or jury[7]—applies the law (which is also information) to the facts as determined, to reach a result. In theory, we could eliminate the entire courtroom and substitute a virtual environment. Contemporary experiments with immersive virtual reality would allow us to do just that if we were not concerned with the quality, and perhaps cost, of the experience (fig. 9-17).

Fundamental American notions of fairness probably will prevent a large-scale move to virtual courtrooms, although it would be wise not to rush to such a conclusion. The Michigan cyber-court is largely to be a virtual courtroom, although it will actually be housed in a physical space. The cyber-court will be a nonjury forum, a commercial dispute resolution mechanism

9-16. Courtroom 21 high-tech appeal demonstration.

FREDRIC L. LEDERER

that might be considered acceptable to most citizens, and a far cry from the most problematic settings, such as a virtual capital criminal trial. The enhanced speed and efficiency of technology-augmented hearings impel the use of technology, especially in times of limited court budgets

Although people may be troubled by virtual *trials*, they are less likely to be concerned about alternative dispute resolution (ADR) mechanisms such as mediation and arbitration. Accordingly, it will not be surprising if we find an increasing use of technology in ADR proceedings, initially in commercial proceedings,[8] and discover that, as a result, the type and number of trials in courthouses are affected. Indeed, it may be that courthouse architects will decrease the number of courtrooms in new courthouses while increasing the number of facilities that foster settlement and other types of ADR proceedings. Ironically, public acceptance of virtual ADR could increase public willingness to participate in virtual trials.

Finally, we must ask if the public would accept the elimination of physical courtrooms. Teenagers are used to instant and text messaging. University students in class surf the Web, E-mail, and instant-message from their notebook computers and hand-held devices. As our new generations become used to those forms of technology and to instant video communications, they may have a

9-17. Courtroom 21 immersive virtual reality.

radically different notion of "normality" than we do. Virtual courtrooms may no longer seem so strange.

Although the long-term implications of courtroom technology for courtroom and courthouse design are unclear, what *is* clear is that today's designs must take technology into account, not as an afterthought but as an essential element. The courtroom is not now a stable and unchanging environment. The ability to adapt the current design to whatever the future brings will be increasingly critical. We must continue to do justice, but where and how we shall do so is in flux. Change comes to all of us, and it has finally come to the courtroom itself.

TEN

Courthouse Design at a Crossroads

TODD S. PHILLIPS

It is anyone's guess how courthouse design will continue to evolve in coming years. The challenges to the development of successful courthouse projects are greater now than they have ever been. From the substandard conditions in many existing facilities to the mounting pressures to resort to one unsuitable expedient or another in new ones, courthouse design has come to a crossroads. Ultimately at stake is nothing less than the independence of the third branch and the capacity of its architecture to engender public trust and confidence. This chapter addresses some of the challenges, arguing for renewed conceptual clarity about what a courthouse should be and for the primacy of the citizen's experience and of public space.

We begin with the quiet crisis: the poor physical condition of existing courts. A great deal of justice in America is being administered in buildings that fall short of the mark. The complete inventory of courthouses throughout the country represents a strikingly mixed assortment of old and new, good and bad. A panoramic look across all levels of courts, from federal to state to the 3,000-plus counties, reveals too many facilities that are both dysfunctional and dispiriting.

The dysfunctional ones fail in at least one of the major elements of any courthouse: adjudication space, work-processing space, building-support space, and citizen service space. The circulation systems that tie the elements together tend to be substandard as well. Often the problems extend to all parts of the facility, and it is deficient as a whole.

The space allocated for adjudication—for example, courtrooms, hearing rooms, chambers, judicial support areas, small conference and jury deliberation rooms —is frequently too limited to handle the court's work smoothly. Many courtrooms are remodeled spaces with low ceilings, acoustical tile, and fluorescent lighting overhead, and it is not uncommon to see an awkwardly located structural column that obstructs sightlines. Many judges' chambers are cramped and windowless rooms that are accessed via the same back corridor used for the movement of defendants in custody.

Clerical work-processing space for handling case files and records is often undersized and windowless. Before the growing appreciation for high-quality office design in the last several years, these areas tended to be treated as architectural afterthoughts. The result is clerks' offices where the work stations are crowded and file storage is inadequate.

Support space for prisoner handling often involves holding cells that are too small and too few in number. Providing proper separation by gender, age, condition, or offense is problematic or impossible. The work flow of the court is slowed by the need to shuffle different classifications of defendants through poor holding areas. A shortage of attorney-client interview booths can add to the bottlenecks. Jury assembly space in the courthouse may even be lacking. Some facilities have no room for this function at all.

Citizen service space—from entrance lobbies to waiting areas and counters where the citizen can interact with court staff—is the most seriously compromised part of many courthouses. Some corridors are congested to the point of being dangerous. There may not be enough room for queuing. Public information resources, especially for self-represented litigants and the non-English-speaking, are often inadequate.

Finally, these major functional areas are generally linked together in older

10-1. Middlesex County Courthouse, Cambridge, Massachusetts, Edward J. Tedesco, 1974. (Photo: Keller & Post Associates)

facilities by circulation systems that fail to provide separate movement paths for the public, the judges and court staff, and persons in custody. Many older buildings, and almost any one-story building of any vintage, have undesirable cross-circulation. The worst see defendants walked, in shackles, through public corridors in the presence of other citizens who may be there merely to pay a traffic ticket.

How did this happen? What explains the many dysfunctional facilities? The answers begin with time and the degradation of space that can take place over the course of many years. Some facilities were poorly designed in the first place. Others began as something else—an office building or a bowling alley—before conversion to court use. Still others involve court operations housed in commercial leased spaces or even double-wide trailers in parking lots. But the wear and tear of time and the changes that inevitably take place in the volume and complexity of court work are most to blame.

Many older courthouses are asked to do far more today than they were designed to handle. Building spaces and systems are strained to capacity and beyond. The number of people entering a fifty-year-old courthouse now may be four or five times greater than the number its planners and designers anticipated. The nature of a court's operations, like the demographics of the population it serves, may have changed substantially. New processes and programs may have been added, and manpower levels—for judicial positions, court staff, and allied professionals—may have increased in ways that exceed the capacity of the building to accommodate them adequately.

Remodeling and retrofit work are ongoing facts of life in many courthouses. Most of the older ones, however, were designed for a comparatively static situation in simpler times. Floor-to-floor heights, structural column spacing, and vertical circulation systems were not conceived at the outset with flexibility for growth as a key priority. Even when growth was anticipated, it was difficult to project more than ten years ahead. Thus few older facilities have had the capacity to adapt to changing circumstances over the long term.

Successive rounds of remodeling have seen various court operations shoehorned into woefully insufficient space. And the overall clarity of a facility's initial layout becomes obscured by ad hoc modifications in later years. Whatever rational organization of space there was in the beginning has broken down, time and time again, into barnacle-like and make-do assemblages.

Sadly, the problems go beyond functionality. Too many court facilities are also dispiriting as a matter of design, at the level of how they look and feel. In the last sixty years numerous courthouses were constructed quickly and cheaply, with no attempt to fashion a distinctive judicial image. The "more-or-less modernist" architecture of post–World War II America in the 1950s and 1960s was neutral as to specific building type or special function. A judicial identity was downplayed in favor of a flat, planar, International Style sameness (fig. 10-1).

At their best, these modernist buildings have a pristine elegance and clarity. They also reflect the sea change that took place in American sensibilities when the isolationist politics and regionalist aesthetics of the prewar period were replaced by a new consciousness of global power and, with it, the new design and construction capabilities associated with wartime mass production.

It is a complicated story that is perhaps too easy to misconstrue. The phenomenon of midcentury Modernism had many causes and forms and significant benefits. But much of its legacy now is

TODD S. PHILLIPS

unfortunate. The tendency in the post-war period to treat everything from courts to car washes in the same architectural vocabulary, combined with the fact that many of the buildings were never robustly constructed and have not aged well, has left a body of work that largely fails to convey the dignity and importance of the judicial process. The problem is especially visible in smaller low-rise, flat-roof courts that sprang up in postwar suburban areas.

More monolithic and even forbidding versions of Modernism also appeared at the same time. Gray, blocklike halls of justice hug urban sidewalks across America like bunkers. Today they are period pieces, stuffed with asbestos, recalling the mood of the cold war and the deadpan authority of the 1950s television show *Dragnet*. Entering these buildings and moving through their windowless, double-loaded corridors can be a numbing experience.

Almost nothing improved in the 1970s. The cross-currents of architectural fashion included the influences of some 1960s projects as disparate as MLTW's Sea Ranch and Le Corbusier's La Tourette, with more concrete and reflective glass and more of the blandly nondescript, until postmodernism took hold by the 1980s. Spurred partly by the growing awareness of historic properties and preservation and by the writings of Robert Venturi, postmodernism threw open the doors to a variety of forms from popular culture and earlier times.

The loose, free-style classicism that characterized much postmodernist work reintroduced architectural elements that had been associated with courthouse design many decades before. Columns, domes, pediments, base–middle–top

hierarchies, and symmetry reappeared—sometimes as grotesque cartoons—with all kinds of buildings. Using them in some courthouse designs was essentially an exercise in styling that had become ubiquitous, from small branch banks to corporate office buildings, rather than a search for forms specific to justice.

More recent court design, invigorated by the federal courts construction program that began in the 1990s, continues a pattern now half a century old in one ironic respect. Implicit in the Design Excellence Program that governs the federal work is the assumption that the freshest and most innovative architecture-as-architecture is automatically the most appropriate style for justice. This assumption is arguable. It is not yet clear how many new courthouses will emerge that are less dispiriting in the long run than the buildings from fifty years ago that are still in use today.

These functional and aesthetic short-comings are acute at the state and local levels, where they may worsen. Severe budget shortfalls in most states exacerbate the familiar problems of deferred maintenance and the upgrading of existing buildings. Many courthouses are old, manpower levels are down, public coffers are empty, and a generation of senior staff leadership is approaching retirement without having had the time and resources to mentor its successors. The people who have managed to keep some facilities going beyond their useful life will soon be gone.

Even more disturbing, this bleak overall situation increases the pressure upon courts systems to do more with less in the future. It makes them vulnerable to "lean and mean" operational and architectural solutions. It adds to the risks of wrongheaded decisionmaking that plague courthouse design at all times and under the best of circumstances.

New Challenges for Courthouse Design

Substandard conditions with the existing infrastructure are the sobering and generally overlooked backdrop to other challenges that have burst on the scene in the last ten years. As if the problems with existing conditions were not enough, several sets of new dynamics have appeared, almost overnight, to make the task of designing courthouses more complicated than ever before. As a planning and design problem, the courthouse is much harder to solve successfully than it was even a decade ago. There is more to think about now.

Electronics-based technologies, heightened security and accessibility issues, and an array of building performance considerations that include sustainability and green design are hitting all at once. Some of these are entering through the front door; others are coming from out of the blue. After decades of relatively predictable conditions, the new forces are challenging traditional design strategies and points of view, and they are piling on numerous new requirements that courthouse design decision makers must address.

The most aggressive new dynamics are security and information technologies. These have the potential to redefine our sense of what a courthouse should be and to drive its design in troubling directions.

Security has become an exceedingly complex and ugly issue. Since the bombing of the federal building in Oklahoma City in April, 1995, the awareness of new weapons, new targets, and new motivations for violence has grown considerably. To knives, handguns, and explosive devices have been added biochemical threats and cyberterrorism. Targets now include groups of innocent people, whole buildings, building systems, and other critical assets. And politically and religiously motivated violence, as distinct from spontaneous outbreaks by individuals, has become an even more urgent concern in the aftermath of the attacks on September 11, 2001.

Fortunately, the planning and design responses to the security issue have themselves become more varied and sophisticated. Passive, active, and operations-based systems feature the integration of such components as static physical barriers and setbacks with advanced surveillance/detection devices and highly trained security personnel. But a climate of fear weighs heavily and poses a risk that it may lead to an architecture of fear. The late Senator Daniel Patrick Moynihan argued that our public buildings should not be designed as fortresses and should remain open, inviting, transparent. His persuasive argument for courts, that we should not "harden" overtly a system that many citizens already perceive as remote, may become more and more difficult to sustain, however. As security concerns intensify, the costs in dollars for any degree of literal transparency will soar.

Windows and walls that are designed to be as secure as Wedge One, the portion of the Pentagon that was struck on September 11, 2001, are ten times more expensive than conventional construction. If the courthouse of tomorrow is required to provide a Wedge One level of protection, budget considerations alone will guarantee that its walls are largely

TODD S. PHILLIPS

blank. Meanwhile, the costs of other security measures will continue to consume portions of the project budget that would have otherwise been spent on other things.

The fortress scenario and its associated mindset will be a central issue in courthouse design for the foreseeable future. Keeping the issue in perspective will be difficult because security can trump other considerations and overwhelm a design process.

At the same time, subtler and potentially sweeping challenges to courthouse design are being posed by emerging information technologies. They have been gathering momentum for several years.

The impact of technology first grabbed the attention of courthouse designers in relation to the courtroom. It became apparent by the mid-1990s that display technologies for the presentation of evidence and argument were making their way into the litigation space. Computer monitors, document imaging devices, and projection screens began to appear. They stirred questions about the layout of basic courtroom elements, the degree of obtrusiveness the technology should or could be allowed, and the best ways to support it with something other than cabling held down on the floor with duct tape.

Courtroom geometry involving the judge's bench, the jury and witness boxes, the attorneys' tables, and spectator seating has always required a careful balance of sightlines and distances. The introduction of display technologies raised new questions about how to arrange courtroom components in a way that enabled everyone to see and hear the same thing at the same time. Discus-

sion about how to keep the gadgetry from becoming an interloper followed. There was early and resounding consensus among some federal judges, at least, that the dignified character of the courtroom should remain something that Thomas Jefferson himself would recognize. The space should not resemble a video arcade.

Attention to the impact of court technologies expanded by the late 1990s to include the "back of the house" administrative and support spaces. These portions of the courthouse formerly supported telephones and typewriters only. But the rapid proliferation of desktop technology for automated systems has changed that, and new issues about office layout and individual workstation design have become priorities. How much surface area does a clerk working on a computer require? How relocatable do workstations have to be to handle future change on a "plug and play" basis? How can the environmental conditions of heat, light, air, and acoustics be controlled to minimize discomfort and maximize amenity?

As the impact of technology has spread to all major functional areas in the facility, a new emphasis on "whole building" design has emerged. This more complete and performance-driven approach gives added weight to building infrastructure and systems integration questions. The building envelope or shell, for example, is no longer simple cladding only; it is a dynamic system that is integral to the building services delivery strategy. Similarly, the infrastructure to support data and telecommunications systems requires more engineering and specialized expertise than ever before.

Help with meeting the new planning and design challenges has been developed in the form of updated guidelines as well as from lessons learned on a trial-and-error basis in the field. Still, the people who are creating new courthouses are trying to catch up. The courthouse continues to be conceived and constructed to last fifty to eighty years or more; some of the technologies inside it are changing every eighteen months. A building that takes five to seven years to complete may be functionally obsolete by the time it opens its doors. Lag times and asynchronous processes are serious problems.

The first generation of challenges posed by emerging technologies turned on questions about how to accommodate them within the framework of otherwise familiar forms. Metaphorically, the initial task has been to figure out how to pull more wire through traditional floor plans.

But that initial task is almost the least of it now. A second generation of technology-driven challenges is starting to appear as potentially far more transforming. Having gotten inside the door, the technologies now threaten to knock the door down: they are altering the ways that courts manage their business and, correspondingly, the physical environments within which the business takes place. Space requirements, physical adjacencies, staffing levels—all are being thrown back to the drawing board to be reexamined from the ground up.

Several changes are occurring at the same time. The business of the court is becoming increasingly dependent upon information technologies for the handling of both routine cases and new, more complex ones that may involve many parties and cut across jurisdictional lines. Courts increasingly are becoming linked via technology to other entities inside and outside the justice system. Some "integrated justice" initiatives are laying the groundwork for closer informational ties with others across the spectrum from law enforcement to corrections. At the least, the engineering and hardware required to support these linkages exceed anything that courts designers have dealt with before.

Traditional physical adjacencies are also being called into question. Trends away from paper-based files that move from space to space as a case is handled from beginning to end mean that those spaces no longer have to be next to each other. Nor do they have to be the same size as before. The technologies are opening up the possibility that major elements of the courthouse—its records storage and clerical case processing areas, for example—may be significantly revamped. They may be located elsewhere in consolidated centers off site that serve numerous buildings.

Opportunities and Dangers

Viewed optimistically, the alternative possible configurations of space may be an opportunity to develop networks of streamlined, smaller-scale facilities in which the designer stands a better chance of achieving an architecturally satisfying solution. It is conceivable that some information technologies can have a restorative, not subversive, effect in this way. Some "unbundling" scenarios may make it possible to find again something akin in scale and feeling to the iconic nineteenth-century county courthouse.

There are new dangers, too. The alternative configurations include possibili-

TODD S. PHILLIPS

ties for even bigger and more mixed agglomerations of functions in which the architectural legibility of the judicial process is further obscured. Great heaps of multipurpose buildings are possible. Somewhere inside them, the face of justice may be reduced to little more than a 21-inch computer screen. This outcome would satisfy the proponents of a radically "virtualized" judicial process. For them the traditional courthouse is an anachronism anyway; for them, the hard materiality of the brick and mortar building has already vaporized.

In short, new sources of confusion have entered the picture. The pervasive technologies have ceased to be merely pieces of equipment to be inserted into familiar space. They are acting now as destabilizing forces that challenge our sense of what the space should be in the first place.

The deeper they go, the more they intersect with the core values of the system. For example, courtroom design for criminal trial proceedings is organized around the constitutional right of the accused to confront the accuser in the same physical space. If remote video technology becomes as magical as its manufacturers and friends say it will—if "total immersive telepresence" makes old-fashioned reality less important— debates about the immutability of that constitutional cornerstone will intensify.

Back to Basics: Conceptual Clarity and Public Space

A recognition of the substandard conditions in many existing facilities and an awareness of the added challenges posed by new security and technology-based dynamics reveal a need to rethink courthouse design at a deep level. The

rethinking should aim for at least two goals: recasting conceptual clarity about what a courthouse should be in the first place and reaffirming basic considerations about the primacy of the citizen's experience and public space.

One conception of the courthouse would have us envision it as an essentially single-purpose facility that embodies and affirms judicial independence. Other conceptions open the door to multipurpose functioning in which an array of occupants from different sectors may be present. There is no consensus; confusion abounds.

To be sure, absolute clarity about what a courthouse can or should be is not possible or even necessary. The system and the situation are too complicated. Much new construction will continue to take place within the immediate context of justice facilities that are already in place. Ad hoc assemblages of buildings are inevitable. Conceptions of the ideal courthouse will therefore always be enshrouded in the kind of ambiguity that stems from the mix-and-match nature of the new and old, both architecturally and operationally. But where there are opportunities to plan and design afresh, it is critical that the decision makers engage in careful—not fast-tracked—thought about what kind of facility best addresses the interests of the third branch of government.

Traditional ideas about courthouse design are most intact in the federal courts system, where they are perhaps most likely to withstand pressures for radical change in coming years. State and local courts are a different, and often far more complicated, story; they can make the federal situation look like child's play. The program for a juvenile and family justice facility in a large urban setting, for example, can severely test traditional conceptions of what a courthouse should be as soon as one begins to reckon with the issue of allied professionals and community services that need to be housed somewhere.

One new emphasis in public sector building that risks undermining any vision of the courthouse as a discrete, stand-alone embodiment of judicial independence is the idea of "one-stop shopping." A variety of government services is provided beneath one roof. Lower cost and more convenience are often cited in support of this approach: the "Government Building" in which court operations are subsumed and where, increasingly, private sector tenants may also occupy space. These buildings are not, in fact, necessarily cheaper to construct and operate. Nor are they always more convenient for everybody. They are now commonplace in many communities, however, often in the form of bland boxlike structures or essays in architectural schizophrenia.

Whether or not the appeal of "one-stop shopping" survives the heightened concerns for security that have now blanketed public buildings is an open question. One effect of the concern for security may be a turning away from all-purpose buildings that serve more users than can be readily screened and monitored. But arguments about cost and convenience will persist in an era that is likely to see more and more reliance upon public–private partnerships, as well as profit motives in public services. The issues will continue to underscore the need for second thoughts about what kinds of entities and interests can be combined appropriately beneath the same roof.

The concept of public safety buildings, in which a range of justice and emergency response operations, supported increasingly by sophisticated technology, are co-located, may be even more challenging. Some combinations of courts, police, and holding cells are familiar and may be traced back to earlier periods when the local jail, the sheriff, and the judge were in the same building. The mayor, town council, and tax assessor may have been there, too.

But those were smaller buildings and simpler times. The dominant image and character of otherwise multipurpose buildings a century ago was generally defined by the court. The other functions were ancillary.

Dramatic increases today in building scale and shifts in the relative proportions of different operations—in which the law enforcement, detention, or other components eclipse the courts—produce an altogether different kind of facility. Its explicit purpose may be to ensure public safety. The problem is that public safety and justice are not necessarily the same thing; the courts may appear an adjunct to police-related functions.

Along with renewed clarity about what a courthouse should be, we need to reaffirm the importance of those whom it serves. The tendency in discussions about courthouse design is to concentrate on how best to satisfy the functional requirements of the justice system professionals—judges and staff— who go to work in the building every day. These are the people whose input is included in the design decision-making process. The owners and professional

TODD S. PHILLIPS

users have a place at the table when design questions are raised and resolved.

The missing party, not present at the table, is the citizen. There is no formally designated champion of the citizen's interest throughout the process. Unless public meetings can be held in which design alternatives are presented for review and comment, and unless the others engaged in the process step forward to champion citizens' needs, a new courthouse project can end up out of balance and off the mark. Its design may satisfy professional users but leave the citizenry shortchanged in amount and quality of space. The importance of ensuring the best design response to the interests and needs of the citizen is difficult to overstate, however. It is a priority that has become more urgent than ever before.

The last decade or two have seen a growing emphasis upon accessibility, as well as the steady broadening of the concept itself. The Americans with Disabilities Act (ADA) highlighted the importance of accommodating the physically disabled. Ramps, lifts, and various assistance systems have been developed and provided for the mobility-, hearing-, and vision-impaired. The concept has enlarged in recent years to include the geriatric, the economically disadvantaged, the non-English-speaking, and others among the citizenry in general.

The number of self-represented or pro se litigants has increased greatly, especially in urban areas where there are growing populations of first-generation immigrants and others who cannot afford attorneys' fees. In some jurisdictions over 50 percent of the cases handled by the courts involve the self-represented, many

of whom require the assistance of court-certified interpreters. These cases place heavy demands upon all the available resources.

The public space of the courthouse mediates the interaction of the citizen with the justice system; it enables and informs. It is a continuum that links spaces to each other through a series of steps, a procession. These steps can be distinguished as the initial approach to

10-2. An exemplary courthouse site and ground-floor plan. The entry plaza includes varied paving patterns with integral signage, level changes, a water feature, and trees in a comprehensive design that extends seamlessly into the enclosed lobby areas. United States Courthouse, Seattle, Washington, NBBJ Architects, 2004, Peter Walker Landscape Architecture.

10-3. Rendering of pedestrian approach to the main public entrance, United States Courthouse, Seattle, Washington, NBBJ Architects, 2004. (Delineator: William Hook)

10-4. Rendering of entry lobby featuring generous high-volume space and transparency, United States Courthouse, Seattle, Washington, NBBJ Architects, 2004. (Delineator: William Hook)

TODD S. PHILLIPS

the entrance, the checkpoint, the decision point, the circulation routes, the waiting areas, and the destinations. The space begins with an entry sequence that leads to a main lobby or gathering point, followed by horizontal and/or vertical movement that, in turn, leads to waiting areas, counters, and rooms. Restrooms, pay phones, vending machines and, occasionally, a library and cafeteria round out the allotment of square footage that the citizen may enter and use.

Ironically, these areas, so essential to the success of the citizen's encounter with the system, are vulnerable to last minute cost cutting, and compromise in general. The structure of the design process itself can also work against them insofar as it classifies a considerable amount of square footage for the public as "nonprogrammed" space that is in the category of building support. It is space that is not assigned to any of the main functional components involving adjudication or clerical case processing; it does not have a name. Instead, it is factored in with loading docks, mechanical system shafts, wall thickness calculations, and so on.

Although some court design guidelines specify sizes for some waiting areas and lobbies, corridors and the rest are left as largely undefined space to be provided as necessary. All of it together—public corridors and loading docks—is bundled up in a total amount for building support that must not exceed a certain percentage of the facility's gross square footage if an acceptable level of "efficiency" is to be achieved.

This emphasis upon efficiency can be unfortunate in the extreme when it sweeps the big issue of public space

10-5. View at dusk of public plaza and luminous entry pavilion, United States Courthouse, Denver, Colorado, Hellmuth Obata & Kassabaum and Anderson Mason Dale, 2003. (Photo: Greg Hursley)

under the rug of mere arithmetic. The entire approach risks turning into an invitation to go in the wrong direction. One of the clear lessons learned from the substandard conditions in numerous older courthouses is that good public space is vital. One should err on the side of more of it, not less, in anticipation of growing crowds and caseload over time.

The pursuit of efficiency in design, combined with intense pressure to satisfy the requirements of so many other portions of the courthouse that are sub-

ject to highly specific guidelines, can exhaust design energies and drain project budgets. Public space becomes the slack to be taken up, if necessary, in the course of making sure that everything else is worked out. If something has to be scaled back at the last minute to reduce project costs, the cut is more likely to take place in the public corridor than in other functional areas.

And yet the portions of the building that the citizen passes through are arguably the most subtle and important design problem of all. This continuum of space has to do many things: provide information, guide people to their destinations, and enable users to reach a destination comfortably and safely (figs. 10-2, 10-3, and 10-5).

The path of movement proceeds through the series of steps and variously proportioned volumes; they must be linked together in a comprehensible,

10-6. Lobby interior where security screening takes place, United States Courthouse, Denver, Colorado, Hellmuth Obata & Kassabaum and Anderson Mason Dale Architects, 2003. (Photo: Maguire Photographics)

10-7. Entrance lobby, new Queens Civil Court, New York City, Perkins Eastman Architects, 1997. (Photo: Chuck Choi)

TODD S. PHILLIPS

10-8. Modestly sized but clear, easy-to-navigate lobby with good signage and subtle handling of materials and details, Seattle Justice Center, Seattle, Washington, NBBJ Architects, 2002. (Photo: Christian Richter)

Below left:
10-9. Public information desk, Seattle Justice Center, Seattle, WA. NBBJ Architects, 2002. (Photo: Christian Richter)

Below right:
10-10. Customer service counter. Note generous spaces for public queuing and between lines for privacy at the counter. Seattle Justice Center, Seattle, Washington, NBBJ Architects, 2002. (Photo: Christian Richter)

10-11. Cutaway rendering of public lobby showing long clerks counter at ground level. United States Courthouse, Seattle, Washington, NBBJ Architects, 2004.

easy-to-navigate system. Each step, from security checkpoint to destination, has its own issues and attributes, and these are always evolving. Some areas along the path include electronic equipment, such as screening devices or public-access computer terminals; others involve seating systems and quiet alcoves. And the corridor portions of the path itself do far more than simply provide a passage: They also serve as places to linger and confer.

The installation of metal detection and X-ray screening devices for security on a retrofit basis has interfered with the circulation patterns in many facilities. Freestanding equipment has been placed in lobbies that were not designed to accommodate it, and secondary public entrances to the building have been closed off to ensure a single control point. The result is congestion, noise, and queuing that may extend to the sidewalk or steps outdoors as people wait to be admitted.

New design and construction for the screening checkpoint must anticipate the need to accommodate people inside, out of the weather, without undue congestion or overcrowding. There are different points of view regarding how obtrusive or transparent the screening equipment itself should be. Some guidelines recommend design solutions that make the equipment as integral to the surrounding architecture as possible. The alternative view argues that the security function can actually be enhanced when the process and its equipment are visible for all to see (fig. 10-4).

The best new design for the screening checkpoint also strives to preserve some measure of dignity and decorum in the space. This is a comparatively manageable design problem when the number of people entering through the front door is a trickle. But when the volume swells to one thousand persons or more per hour, and when the facility is located in a region where people wear heavy winter coats that need to be taken off and screened separately, designing for a security process that works, while simultaneously preserving some decorum, requires great skill (figs. 10-6 and 10-7).

Once through the security checkpoint, people move next to the decision point

TODD S. PHILLIPS

Left:
10-12. View of public corridors at ground floor and mezzanine levels featuring extensive natural light. New Queens Civil Court, New York City, Perkins Eastman Architects, 1997. (Photo: Chuck Choi)

Above:
10-13. Single-loaded corridor next to perimeter wall with ample daylight and bench seating outside courtrooms. United States Courthouse, Denver, Colorado, Hellmuth Obata & Kassabaum and Anderson Mason Dale Architects, 2003. (Photo: Maguire Photographics)

10-14. Single-loaded corridor outside courtrooms, Seattle Justice Center, Seattle, Washington, NBBJ Architects, 2002. (Photo: Christian Richter)

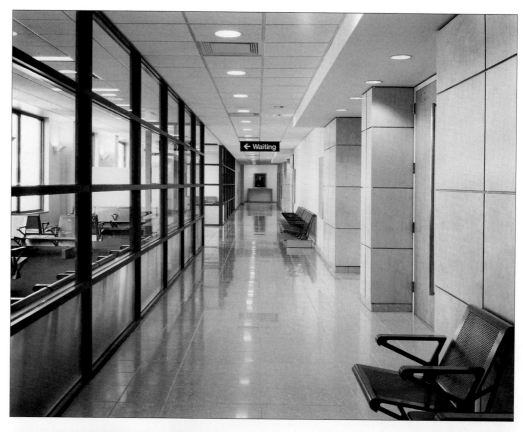

10-15. Public waiting area and transparent partition adjacent to corridor outside courtrooms, Rockland County Courthouse, New York City, Perkins Eastman Architects, 2001. (Photo: Chuck Choi)

10-16. Jury assembly and waiting area at ground level, New Queens Civil Court, New York City, Perkins Eastman Architects, 1997. (Photo: Chuck Choi)

TODD S. PHILLIPS

10-17. Screened courtyard space next to waiting area, allowing natural light at grade in a dense urban setting. New Queens Civil Court, New York City, Perkins Eastman Architects, 1997. (Photo: Chuck Choi)

10-18. Generous, high-volume jury assembly space at top of building with panoramic views to the outdoors. Seattle Justice Center, Seattle, Washington, NBBJ Architects, 2002. (Photo: Christian Richter)

10-19. Portion of jury assembly area with work surfaces for use by prospective jurors who are waiting to be called. Seattle Justice Center, Seattle, Washington, NBBJ Architects, 2002. (Photo: Christian Richter)

10-20. Rendering of large-scale mural by artist Michael Fajans, 82 feet long, with representations of twelve jurors. The mural is conceived in tiers and faces onto the first three levels of the public lobby space. United States Courthouse, Seattle, Washington, NBBJ Architects, 2002.

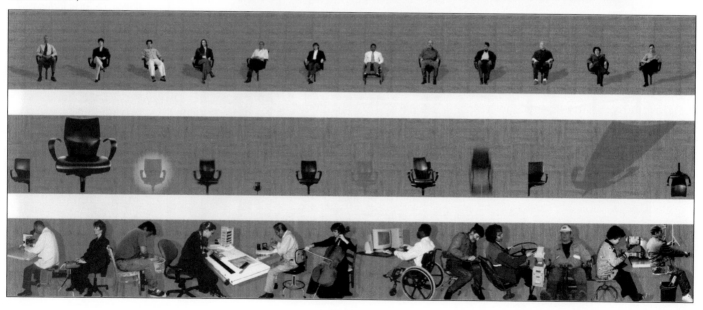

TODD S. PHILLIPS

of the main lobby where signage, information systems, and the layout of the space enable them to choose the correct route to their destinations. The most effective design includes a public information counter that is staffed by court personnel rather than signs, bulletin boards, and/or touch-screen kiosks alone. Many people coming to the courthouse for the first time are unfamiliar with both the building and the justice system. They do not merely have questions, they also have "stories." They want to talk, face to face, with a person.

The provision of information has become an increasingly complicated matter, and it has direct implications for designed space. To serve the growing number of citizens for whom English is not the first language, the court has to provide an array of materials as well as interpreters. The growing number of self-represented litigants calls for information centers that can sometimes include public-access computer terminals, writing counters, and small group assembly spaces for orientation (figs. 10-8, 10-9, 10-10, and 10-11).

Pro se centers in existing facilities tend to be located wherever space for one or more information services can be found. Centers in new facilities are best located on the ground level, as close as possible to the main entrance, and conceived with after-hours and weekend activity in mind.

It is remarkable how many existing court facilities have no adequate waiting space outside the courtrooms. Either none was provided in the beginning or it has been outgrown over time. The corridor, often designed initially for fewer people and as circulation only, has become the makeshift waiting area in

many cases. Crowds of people leaning against corridor walls in stuffy conditions, without windows to provide daylight or view, are common experiences in older buildings. The crowds can become a volatile source of conflict or confrontation, a gauntlet through which others in the courthouse must pass.

Well-designed waiting areas have natural light that is controlled with shading devices, and comfortable seating that is configured to prevent unwanted eye contact or intimidation (figs. 10-12, 10-13, 10-14, and 10-15). They are also designed with sightlines suitable for security monitoring, especially during the peak times of use that represent specific and identifiable risk periods. Proximity to restrooms,

10-21. Like the surfaces underfoot, handrail elements are places where the citizen encounters the building in a direct and physical way. The design, materials, and craft evidenced at this level may have a greater impact than big architectural gestures. Seattle Justice Center, Seattle, Washington, NBBJ Architects, 2002. (Photo: Christian Richter)

10-22. Refined treatment of handrail and balcony details in the entrance rotunda of the United States Courthouse, Denver, Colorado, Hellmuth Obata & Kassabaum and Anderson Mason Dale Architects, 2003. (Photo: Maguire Photographics)

pay phones, and vending machines is a consideration, as well. Furnishings are durable for the high volume of use, yet also of superior quality (figs. 10-16, 10-17, 10-18, and 10-19).

Beyond the many issues of functionality associated with public space are the more elusive aspects that involve a power to educate and resonate at deeper levels. Some courthouse design is overtly, explicitly didactic. Public spaces carry carved inscriptions and images that recall great names, ideas, or events in the national experience. Using a building's surfaces to support a narrative and to edify in these ways is an old technique that extends back at least to the pharaohs. Some of America's best examples in the twentieth century were produced in the Progressive Era and by the Works Progress Administration (WPA) artists in the 1930s and after. The messages may be about the law or the people, or both. The distinctive nature of the courthouse may be emphasized further by the use of architectural elements and symbols associated with justice. The building "speaks" to the citizen, who is brought by its space and explicit messages to a more educated awareness of the place and the process (fig. 10-20).

Other kinds of courthouse design do not depend upon images or inscriptions for their messages or their didactic function. Instead they resonate with the citizen in ways that transcend cultural specifics and touch upon what it means to be human. The architecture may appeal to memory, the mnemonic dimension, and may strike chords with elemental things that are universally recognized. Public space may evoke feelings of safety, shelter, calm, so the architecture alludes to the deontic, the "ought to be,"

TODD S. PHILLIPS

in human relations everywhere.

Ultimately, the expressive power of the courthouse comes from the quality of thought and degree of care invested in how it is shaped and put together. The quality and care are evident in the spatial volumes, the use of light, the selection of materials, the fine-grain detail, articulation, and craft—all of which add up to a message. If the building is done well, it says to the person in its public spaces, "You, your liberty and property, are important ... we care about the truth of things ... this is serious business." The message is that the citizen's interests are uppermost, as evidenced by the attempt to provide a space that puts them first. The architecture is not about the designer's ego or the convenience of the state (figs. 10-21 and 10-22).

The crafting of justice, one person at a time, is intended to be a thoughtful and individualized process. If citizens can sense a basic congruence between the forms, materials, and workmanship of the courthouse, on the one hand, and the truth of what matters most to them as they conduct their business inside it, on the other hand, something approaching an authentic "architecture of justice" will have been achieved.

Although elusive, this dimension of courthouse design is hardly magic. No one doubts the converse—the capacity of badly done buildings to send negative messages—or the power of architecture to denigrate. Most people recognize when they are in cramped, shabby, and demeaning space. It galls them to find matters of great import to them handled in environments that say, in effect, "You are not important enough to warrant a better building." Good courthouse design does not make this mistake; it creates space that is an act of respect for the citizen.

Preserving Public Trust and Confidence

Hard, functional imperatives argue for the best possible treatment of the public in courthouses. The sheer number of people to be served and the growing diversity of interests and capabilities that they represent will continue to demand well-conceived space that works in the most immediately practical sense. ATM machines for paying fines, touch-screen kiosks in shopping malls, and Internet-based resources with downloadable forms will ease some demands upon courthouse facilities in some ways, but they will never eliminate the need for clear and generous lobbies, corridors, counters, and waiting areas.

Nor will even the most generous and considerate technical innovations succeed at the higher task of engendering public trust and confidence in the system. This is the most important role played by those portions of the courthouse that the citizen experiences directly. Architectural space that undermines trust and that alienates is sabotage. If the courthouse overall is a mysterious black box bristling with surveillance cameras, or if its public corridors are an exercise in cold optimization only, it will fail to preserve—and perhaps will even destroy—the bond between the individual and the justice system upon which all depend. It is not a question of precious niceties or mere efficiency. The matters at stake are of the first importance

Daniel Patrick Moynihan and Federal Architecture

NATHAN GLAZER

Daniel Patrick Moynihan, who served in the United States Senate from 1977 to 2001, probably had a greater influence on federal design than any other public figure of the second half of the twentieth century. His influence on courthouse design was particularly profound, both because courthouses specially interested him and because most federal construction was of courthouses during the years of his greatest influence.

Moynihan's retirement from the Senate in 2001 occasioned deep regret among architects, urbanists, and federal officials dealing with architecture and urban design in various departments of government. For decades, Moynihan was the one influential elected official who could be expected to understand and appreciate what they were trying to tell him. He was unique among the members of the U.S. Congress in his high estimate of the role of architecture in government and in his support of high achievement in the buildings of the past as well as in the current work of building for the government. He responded to calls about major buildings in danger, and used his influence to find

new uses that would preserve them. Possibly he was the only member of the Senate who would have known that the massive and magnificent customs house building on the tip of Manhattan (fig. EP-2), abandoned when the Customs Service moved into a new building in the World Trade Center, was designed by Cass Gilbert, the architect of the Woolworth Building and the federal courthouse in New York City. And perhaps he was the only one who cared. Indeed he did succeed in finding new uses for it and in saving it. Notably, he turned much of it into a courthouse.

In his first year in the Senate, walking around Buffalo, we are told by Robert A. Peck, who worked for him, "he spied the dilapidated Prudential [formerly Guaranty] Building, one of the best-known . . . early skyscrapers by . . . Louis Sullivan. Moynihan told Buffalo's mayor that if the city could see to it that the building was rehabilitated, people the world over would come to Buffalo to see it. (The Mayor replied with an eight letter bovine reference)."[1] Moynihan may have been too extravagant in describing what a restored Prudential Building could do for a declining Buffalo, but he did succeed in getting the building restored; crucial in saving it was Moynihan's decision to put his own West New York office into it. When I visited it some years ago, I discovered that his staff maintained for his visits the excellent guide to Buffalo's architecture by Reyner Banham. Looking at it, I could see that it was remarkably well worn. The senator, I was told, made use of it whenever he came to Buffalo.

We are very far from being able to delineate fully the range of Moynihan's various roles affecting federal architecture or the extent of his influence. Few of his official positions gave him any significant or formally recognized platform for intervention in such matters. We can scroll through his various federal posts—assistant to Secretary of Labor Arthur Goldberg in the Kennedy administration, the assistant secretary of labor for research and statistics, assistant to President Nixon for urban affairs, ambassador to India, U.S. ambassador to the United Nations, four times elected senator from New York. They all involved him in major public issues in which he played important public roles: the fate of blacks in the United States and the role of the black family, which he addressed when he was in the department of labor; the problems of the cities, then afflicted by major riots and disorder, when he served President Nixon; the relation of the United States to the developing world, when he was ambassador to India; the cold war and its reach into every corner of the globe, in particular, the Middle East and the Arab–Israeli conflict, when he was ambassador to the United Nations; and a host of major domestic and foreign issues, from saving social security and

reforming welfare to urban transportation and excessive secrecy in government when he was in the Senate. But all along he maintained a strong interest in public architecture and civic design.

This interest emerged at the very beginning of his service in Washington, though it was foreshadowed by his experience in the late 1950s as assistant to Governor Averill Harriman of New York. It was in that position, and directly thereafter, as he worked on a history of the Harriman administration at Syracuse University, that he began publishing the articles in the journal *The Reporter* (then edited by Irving Kristol) that first brought him to some notice. One of them dealt with the epidemic of mortal accidents on the highways and the responsibility of automobile manufacturers and government to do something by way of design to reduce the slaughter.[2] A second dealt with the impact of the interstate highway program on the cities.[3] Moynihan had drawn attention to the role of automobile design in accidents even before Ralph Nader, and he hoped to enter the Kennedy administration in a position to do something about highway building and auto safety—but the automobile industry was powerful enough to veto any such appointment. Having written a

EP-2. An early postcard view of Cass Gilbert's United States Custom House in Lower Manhattan (1899), now home to the United States Bankruptcy Court for the Southern District of New York. (Courtesy of Kathleen Farrell)

thesis on the International Labor Organization, he accepted (somewhat reluctantly) a position as assistant to Secretary of Labor Arthur Goldberg. It was from that improbable position that Moynihan was able to launch a statement, we might call it a manifesto, that has had a remarkable role in influencing federal architecture for the better. To tell the story in Moynihan's own words:

> There's a little story about how [the Guiding Principles for Federal Architecture] came about. In the spring of 1961, the discussion of foreign policy in a Cabinet meeting paused for a moment, whereupon the next most important subject in government came up–office space. Indeed, we hadn't built any office space here in Washington since the federal triangle buildings of the 1920s and 1930s.
>
> The Labor Department, where I served as assistant to Secretary Goldberg, was scattered in seventeen buildings around the city. Then and there, President Kennedy set up something called the Ad Hoc Committee on Federal Office Space. Luther Hodges,

Secretary of Commerce, was co-chairman with Arthur Goldberg.

> When we started, our report had a very detailed inventory—how much office space we needed for this department, that department, and so forth. As we set about this new building boom, we thought we'd put some guidelines in there about what we thought these buildings should look like. So I wrote a little one-page guidelines for federal architecture. One of the rules was that we should avoid an official style. We should seek to do what was the contemporary architecture of the time. There are great moments in architecture, there are lesser moments, but we wouldn't miss any.
>
> The Seagram Building [designed by Mies van der Rohe] had just opened on Park Avenue in New York City. We would say, at any given moment, build whatever the Whiskey Trust is building. Over the years, you won't miss the best.[4]

This is Moynihan's account. But how does something so casually produced become government policy? Moynihan again: "When President Kennedy got the report on federal office space, "[he] had a three-paragraph memorandum that said to the departments, all right, this is our program. Get with it. In his last sentence, he said that we will particularly attend to the proposal on Pennsylvania Avenue."

The report of the Ad Hoc Committee on Federal Office Space of 1962 had extended itself not only to the issue of the quality of federal architecture but also to the condition of Pennsylvania Avenue, then lined on its northern side by shabby and decrepit buildings. Pennsylvania Avenue may not have been part of the original brief of the committee, just as the Guiding Principles for Federal Architec-

NATHAN GLAZER

ture was no part of the original brief. But it is part of the art of government to know when to go beyond what one has been asked to do. Moynihan proposed his guidelines and the rebuilding of Pennsylvania Avenue, and the president gave his approval to both. Robert Peck tells the story: "History has it that President Kennedy noted the dilapidation of the private structures on the north side of the avenue on his inaugural ride to the White House. History does not explain how John Kennedy had failed to notice this condition during all the years he commuted as senator from the Capital to his residence in Georgetown. In light of the fact that the Pennsylvania Avenue proposal appeared amid the banal-sounding 'Report of the Ad Hoc Committee on Federal Office Space,' as did the unsolicited Moynihan contribution of a set of 'Guiding Principles for Federal Architecture,' some think that the whole thing, including the Kennedy apocrypha, was a Moynihan invention."[5]

Perhaps it was. But there was now presidential approval, in the form of Kennedy's note, for the Guiding Principles and the rehabilitation of Pennsylvania Avenue. Does such presidential approval, with nothing more (in the way of an executive order or some entry in the Federal Register or legislation), make federal policy, and policy of such long-lasting effect that it is celebrated as having a major impact on federal architecture forty years after? Both the Pennsylvania Avenue references in the report —there was not yet a proposal nor a project but only some hortatory paragraphs— and the federal guidelines might have, and ordinarily would have sunk without a trace in the wake of President Kennedy's assassination in 1963, but that

would be to count without Moynihan's energy and ingenuity, mere assistant to the secretary of labor that he was at that time.[6]

Moynihan wrote in 1988:

One of the last instructions [Kennedy] left before departing for Dallas was that a coffee hour be arranged for the Congressional leadership in order to display the model of the Pennsylvania Avenue plan and seek their support. Bill Walton [the architect, who was a friend of Mrs. Kennedy and the president], Charles Horsky, [another account has Arthur Schlesinger there too] and I were at lunch discussing this on November 22, 1963, when the White House operator called with the news that the president had been shot. We made our way to the White House; the final word came. We left with this task undone.

It took another twenty-five years. Jacqueline Kennedy made it possible. A day or so after the funeral, President Johnson invited Mrs. Kennedy to the Oval Office and asked what he could do for her. She asked for Pennsylvania Avenue. This became known, and made a claim on the Johnson Administration. The enterprise acquired official if somewhat skeptical sanction, having been wholly informal under JFK. Richard M. Nixon, somewhat in contrast, was genuinely enthusiastic. . . . By the time he left office, the Pennsylvania Avenue Development Corporation had been established by act of Congress, and there has been no turning back.[7]

Moynihan was a master at attributing what he wanted to do to the presidents he served—it gave his efforts greater sanction. Here he underplays his own role in pushing for Pennsylvania Avenue, from whatever position he held, whether as a holdover in the Johnson administration or, a few years later, as advisor on urban affairs to President Nixon. As such, he could do things even Mrs. Onassis couldn't: "Pat, as Nixon's urban advisor, every day could go and take our plans [for Pennsylvania Avenue] from the bottom of George Schultz's desk [director of Office of Management and Budget under Nixon] and put them on the top, which, of course, was the way to getting things done in any administration."[8]

For Pennsylvania Avenue, it was clear: a specific plan was required, and in time one was drawn up. Fortunately, like all first plans, it was later very much revised and in a direction favored by all urbanists and by Moynihan himself. (Moynihan had deferred to Nat Owings of Skidmore, Owings & Merrill, who drew up the somewhat Mussolini-style first plan for Pennsylvania Avenue, because he (Moynihan) did not impose his tastes on architects of reputation and talent.) But how could the very general points made in the Guiding Principles be kept alive when no succeeding president (and perhaps not even Kennedy himself) was very much interested or would think of giving it a place no matter how far down on his agenda? Moynihan was in no position to nurture the Guiding Principles before he entered the Senate in 1977. But he did choose as his first Senate committee appointment the Committee on Environment and Public Works, which gave him some involvement in these issues. However, he was a junior senator, and the committee was much more involved in the issues of the environment. It was not until 1986, according to Robert Peck, when the committee was reorganized following the Democratic recapture of the Senate, that Moynihan had real influence.

At that time Moynihan chose to become chairman of the Subcommittee on Water Resources, Transportation and Infrastructure of the Committee on Environment and Public Works of the Senate. Unwieldy as the title of that position was, it was one of great influence, particularly over the city and the environment-shaping role of major federally funded highways and public transportation.[9]

Moynihan was a master of the arts of publicity as well as government. It would be an interesting enterprise to trace how the ideas of the Guiding Principles were kept alive, even when there was no indication they were being followed anywhere in the federal government. The Guiding Principles said three things. First, they declare that public buildings should be provided "in an architectural style and form which is distinguished and which will reflect the dignity, enterprise, vigor and stability of the American National Government." Wonderful rhetoric, but not very specific. Second, that an official style should be avoided–clearly no more Federal Triangles. Third, that the leading architects of the day should be involved. "Design must flow from the architectural profession to the Government and not vice versa." Perhaps most important was the "Moynihanian" language of the principles: "It should be our task to meet the test of Pericles' evocation to the Athenians, which the President had commended to the Massachusetts legislature in his address of January 9, 1961: 'We do not imitate—we are a model to others.' "[10] Part of the art of moving ahead one's agenda is to quote the president as if it is his views one is promoting, even if the president might not recall just what it was he said.

But the leading architects of the day

were not bidding for government work or being asked to do it in the 1960s and 1970s. They had been called upon to design embassies and chanceries around the world in the 1950s, but that program was drawing to a close in the 1960s. The United States was entering a period of bland and uninspired federal architecture, whose point for the most part was to emphasize efficiency and economy in providing office space—which, after all, is what most government buildings consist of, regardless of their symbolic significance.

The important volume *The Federal Presence*, of 1978, inspired by the Task Force on Federal Architecture of the National Endowment for the Arts with the hope that it would help improve government buildings, concludes with the sad comment that federal architecture has declined: "Today cultural historians, if they consider federal projects at all, find them unimportant. Critics of the building arts consign federal architecture to a second-class status and are virtually unconcerned with those federal policies that affect the use and appearance of public space. Likewise, public concern has been missing. The increasing preference for private over public life has been accompanied by an increase in the physical neglect of the public domain."[11]

The illustrations of the most recent government buildings that close this volume clearly demonstrate the ordinariness of the architecture—their architects are not even named.[12] The Guiding Principles are not much in evidence in federal architecture at the time. But the principles are already apparent in *The Federal Presence*, which quotes Moynihan (on page 540) from an article in the *AIA Journal* in June 1962. (One wonders how that journal

would have known of him that early, before he had published a book or gone to Harvard to head the Joint Center for Urban Studies.) On page 541 there are some powerful lines from Moynihan's introduction to Ada Louise Huxtable's *Will They Ever Finish Bruckner Boulevard?*: "Twentieth-century America has seen a steady, persistent decline in the visual and emotional power of its public buildings, and this has been accompanied by a not less persistent decline in the authority of the public order." The authors of *The Federal Presence* quote the Guiding Principles themselves on page 542, without reference to their author.

How were the Guiding Principles kept alive? David M. Childs of SOM, commenting on his first job—the design for Pennsylvania Avenue in 1968—says that the Guiding Principles, "already six years old, were still very much quoted. They'd gotten to the point where they were beginning to be understood, and they've only become more so as time has gone on. . . . [Moynihan's] call to greatness resounded through a much larger community with such compelling conviction that those reverberations have lasted to today."[13]

In the General Services Administration's oral history of the impact of the Guiding Principles, architect after architect is aware of the principles and happy they are there. The principles helped to inspire the Design Excellence Program, which was formulated by energetic and creative officials of the General Services Administration (GSA) in the late 1980s and early 1990s in order to attract the leading architects of the day to federal building. These officials examined what was wrong with the way the federal government went about designing its buildings, changed the procedures to sweep away a host of requirements that deterred leading architects from considering federal work, and experimented with different approaches.

A key role in bringing the guidelines to bear on courthouse design was played by the Boston federal courthouse (see fig. C-10). There, two very able judges, Douglas Woodlock and Stephen Breyer (soon to become a Supreme Court Justice; author of the Foreword to this book), became, in effect, the clients for the building, with the agreement of the GSA. They hoped that the Boston courthouse would become a model as a federal courthouse and an example of how a federal courthouse could improve the urban environment around it. They asked Bill Lacy, a major figure in promoting good architecture within and beyond the federal government, to guide them in understanding the frontier architecture of the day, and they pioneered a process for building courthouses that was further developed in the Design Excellence Program, which has now resulted in dozens of impressive federal courthouses by leading architects. Examples of the salutary results of Design Excellence appear throughout this book. To note only a few that appear in the color images in this book, these include federal courthouses in Minneapolis (C-5), Portland, Oregon (C-6), Beckley, West Virginia (C-8), Orlando, Florida (C-11), Eugene, Oregon (C-12), and Denver (C-5 and C-6).

Moynihan was rather an inspiration than an active participant. He did not, as far as I know, play a directive role in devising procedures, selecting architects, or in judging their work. He did not, like President Pompidou or Mitterand in France, determine that this design should

be built rather than that. He was almost always present when something was happening on a project that interested him, however. He did not dominate the process, but in his charming and voluble way, he always had a lot to say, a lot of it relevant, but often—in his way, too—somewhat obscure and far from clear to the participants, who included architects and representatives of GSA.

He ensured that the enabling legislation for new federal courthouses in Brooklyn, Manhattan, and Central Islip (see, e.g., figs. 2-19, 2-21, 5-12, and 5-13) required a design competition, and he attended a number of the resultant meetings. His personal intervention, in concert with his colleague from New York, Senator Alphonse D'Amato, was essential in brokering the complex arrangement by which Cass Gilbert's Custom House in lower Manhattan (see fig. EP-2) was saved from demolition through a sharing arrangement between two of the oddest bedfellows ever brought together in such a match: the United States Bankruptcy Court for the Southern District of New York and the National Museum of the American Indian. As a senator from New York, he had a large role in appointing federal judges, several of whom then involved themselves in the building of their new courthouses. He also had a large role in getting the money appropriated for these expensive buildings. He worked tirelessly to get hundreds of millions of dollars of federal money for the new Pennsylvania Station, to be built in the grand post office adjacent to the site of the monumental building that was heedlessly destroyed in the 1960s (fig. EP-3).

But I detect a certain ambiguity in his attitude to modern architecture. "Let the best architects be selected, yes, I will support and applaud them." But I believe Moynihan, like so many of us, was confused by the breathless variety of innovative forms and materials and arrangements that are the trademarks of leading contemporary architects.[14] In contrast, he rather enjoyed, indeed was enthusiastic about, the somewhat classical Ronald Reagan building, the enormous structure that completes, to the degree it will be completed, the Federal Triangle. He placed in it the Woodrow Wilson International Center for Scholars (which he had helped create) and his own office after he retired from the Senate. He would lead his visitors on an appreciative tour of the building, which his persistent political efforts had helped create—even to the point of accepting it being named after a Republican president. Nothing is easy in government, and part of his appreciation was undoubtedly owing to the fact that he had managed to get it done at all, so it could fill a huge hole in the Federal Triangle and replace a surpassingly ugly parking lot. But I think leading architectural critics and modern architects would look askance at the design of this contemporary building and fault it for trying to fit too comfortably into the classically correct Federal Triangle.

Moynihan appreciated the richly, classically detailed older Senate office buildings. When the newest Senate office building, stripped of all classical detailing, had its plastic sheeting removed as it was nearing completion, Moynihan proposed the following resolution: "Whereas the plastic cover has now been removed revealing, as feared, a building whose banality is exceeded only by its expense; and Whereas even in a democracy there are things it is well the people do not

EP-3. Senator Moynihan displaying to President Bill Clinton a model of the planned replacement of McKim, Mead & White's Pennsylvania Station, New York, in the adjacent post office by the same architects. (Photo: courtesy of Maura Moynihan)

know about their government: Now, therefore, be it *Resolved*, that it is the sense of the Senate that the plastic cover be put back."[15]

When it came to distinguished older buildings, there was no ambiguity in Moynihan. Regardless of style, the great structures of the past should be defended, protected, reused. Yes to Cass Gilbert's Beaux-Arts Custom House. Yes to Louis Sullivan's Prudential Building, yes to Daniel Burnham's Union Station in Washington, restored as a rail station (among other things) after the misguided effort to turn it into a visitors center. Yes even to the neo-Gothic armory in Buffalo, burnt down, which Moynihan insisted should be rebuilt rather than replaced by an economical drill hall. One must regret that when the Pennsylvania Station in New York was being demolished in 1962–63, Moynihan was only assistant to the secretary of labor, and his influence was limited to the writing and attaching to a report on government office space the Guiding Principles for Federal Architecture. But in doing so he did more to raise the level of federal architecture, especially federal courthouse architecture, and perhaps public architecture in America generally, than any other public figure of recent memory.

NOTES

CHAPTER 1

1. Richard Pare, ed., *Court House: A Photographic Document* (New York: Horizon Press, 1978). Authors of various articles about courthouses in this volume are Phyllis Lambert, Richard Pare, Hon. Paul C. Reardon, Calvin Trillin, Henry-Russell Hitchcock, and William Seale.

2. This chapter contains illustrations of many cited courthouses; however, it is impractical to illustrate all of them. The reader is referred to the numerous volumes that address most, or all, of the courthouses in a state, such as those on Kentucky, Louisiana, and Nevada noted in notes 3, 5, and 9, respectively; in addition, see Will Counts and Jon Dilts, *The 92 Magnificent Indiana Courthouses* (Bloomington, IN: Indiana University Press, 1999), Herbert Alan Johnson and Ralph K. Andrist, *Historic Courthouses of New York State* (New York: Columbia University Press, 1977), and Oliver D. Williams, *County Courthouses of Pennsylvania* (Mechanicsburg, PA: Stackpole Press, 2001).

3. Boxes varied. In Kentucky an octagonal courthouse was built in Allen County in 1816; Warren County planned a hexagonal courthouse, but changed it to a square. Documents exist for both in the respective county clerks' offices, with the drawing for Warren County in the Kentucky Museum, Western Kentucky University. See John W. Carpenter and William B. Scott Jr., *Kentucky Courthouses* (Brentwood, Tennessee: JM Productions, 1988), xiv–xv.

4. Hanna Hryniewiecka Lerski, *William Jay: Itinerant English Architect 1792–1837* (New York: University Press of America, 1989), p. 177. John M. Bryan in John M. Bryan, ed., *Robert Mills: Architect* (Washington: AIA Press, 1989, 79), addresses the issue of Mills's South Carolina courthouses, concluding, "Mills modified two courthouses that had been designed by William Jay, designed fourteen others, and strongly influenced seven more for which others were responsible."

5. Carl A. Brasseaux, Glenn R. Conrad, and R. Warren Robinson, *The Courthouses of Louisiana* (Lafayette, Louisiana: University of Southwestern Louisiana Press, 1997), 43–45; 58–61.

6. The steeple was popularized by William Strickland in his Merchant's Exchange in Philadelphia, sometimes called the Philadelphia Exchange (1832–34), and appeared on various public buildings, notably the Tennessee State Capitol at Nashville, completed in 1860 from Strickland's designs. See Agnes Addison Gilchrist, *William Strickland: Architect and Engineer* (Philadelphia: University of Pennsylvania Press, 1950), and Roger G.

Kennedy, *Greek Revival America* (New York: Stewart, Tabori & Chang, 1989), 12, 44.

7. Visual dominance of the urban scene became more of a problem with higher buildings after the Civil War and especially after urban architecture responded to the introduction of the elevator, when most courthouses ceased trying to carry the skyline. State capitols, the first at Boston, began to have gilded domes to sustain their presence as they sank. The city hall in Philadelphia, also a courthouse, made perhaps the last great thrust of the nineteenth century to recapture the skyline from commerce. More often in the cities, the approach of the Boston City Hall was taken, to address the street. This approach is found more often than not with the Second Empire courthouses in cities and continued until the courthouse itself joined the skyscraper genre.

8. State, War & Navy was a huge granite building constructed to hold those three executive branches. The treasury remained east of the White House in the building begun by Robert Mills in the 1830s. As presidential offices moved into the building, it came to be called the Executive Office Building; then, after the New Executive Office Building (John Carl Warnecke, 1970) went up to the north, the Old Executive Office Building (OEOB). The name was changed in 1998 to the Eisenhower Office Building.

9. Myron F. Angel, *History of Nevada with Illustrations and Biographical Sketches of Its Prominent Men and Pioneers* (Oakland: Thompson & West, 1881), 497, as cited in Ronald M. James, *Temples of Justice: County Courthouses of Nevada* (Reno: University of Nevada Press, 1994), 1.

10. The dome of the United States Capitol was completed in 1862, during—and despite—the Civil War. At that time the walls of the California Capitol were rising. So powerful was the symbol of the dome that the commissioners in Sacramento scrapped their plan and changed it to one in the United States Capitol image. See Henry-Russell Hitchcock and William Seale, *Temples of Democracy: The State Capitols of the USA* (New York: Harcourt Brace Jovanovich, 1976).

11. Pare, *Courthouse*, p. 200.

12. James, *Temples of Justice*, 13–14; passim.

13. It should be noted that the 1901 Pan-American Exposition in Buffalo, New York featured in part Spanish Renaissance architecture.

14. The courtroom is being abandoned in the court's move to necessary increased space in another building. The court will now occupy a very decorative hearing room from the 1930s, being restored and adapted to the new

use by Schooley-Caldwell, Architects (see fig. 1-34).

15. Henry N. Cobb, FAIA, conversation with the author, Cambridge, Massachusetts, November 16, 1991.

CHAPTER 4

1. As described to the author by a close student of its development, Dr. Christine Mengin, Associate Professor of history of contemporary architecture, University of Paris. Dr. Mengin is undertaking a comparative study of the United States and French courthouse building programs.

CHAPTER 6

1. *Presentation of Portrait of the Honorable Frank J. Murray*, 762 F. Supp. XCVIII, CVI (D. Mass. 1990).

2. *Scott v. Sanford*, 19 How. (60 U.S.) 393 (1857).

3. Daniel Bluestone, *Constructing Chicago* (New Haven: Yale University Press, 1991), 181.

4. Edward F. Hennessey, "Foreword," in *Courthouses of the Commonwealth*, edited by Robert J. Brink (Amherst: University of Massachusetts Press, 1984), iv.

5. Phyllis Lambert, "Mies Immersion—Space and Structure" in *Mies In America* (edited by Phyllis Lambert, New York: Harry N. Abrams, Inc., 2001), 409.

6. Vincent Scully, *American Architecture and Urbanism* (New York: Henry Holt and Co., new rev. ed. 1988), 290.

7. Ibid.

8. Paul Goldberger, "A Public Work That Ennobles As It Serves," *The New York Times*, August 13, 1995, Sec. 2, p. 30.

9. Ibid.

10. *Supra* note 6 at 203.π

11. *Ceremony in Commemoration of Fifty Years of Federal Judicial Service By The Honorable Learned Hand*, 264 F.2d 3, 28-29 (2d Cir. 1959).

12. Learned Hand, "The Preservation of Personality" in *The Spirit of Liberty*, 3rd ed., (New York: Alfred A. Knopf, 1974), 30, 43.

13. Learned Hand, *The Bill of Rights* (Cambridge: Harvard Univ. Press, 1958), 77.

14. *Supra*, note 8.

15. Daniel Webster, "Mr. Justice Story" in *The Great Speeches and Orations of Daniel Webster* (Boston: Little, Brown & Co., 1894), 532, 533–34.

CHAPTER 7

1. Mary P. Kelsey and Donald H. Dyal, *The Courthouses of Texas* (College Station: Texas A & M University Press, 1993); Herbert Alan Johnson and Ralph K. Andrist, *Historic Court-*

houses of New York State (New York: Columbia University Press, 1977). An excellent source of county courthouse images can be found in the work of Calvin Beale of the United States Department of Agriculture Economic Research Service, available at www.ers.usda.gov/Briefing/Population/Photos.

CHAPTER 8

1. The federal Design Guide, once widely available on CD-ROM and otherwise, is no longer a public document, since 9/11, for security reasons. It is made available only to firms doing current federal work. The current version of the National Center for State Courts *Planning and Design Guide* can be obtained by writing the center at 300 Newport Avenue, Williamsburg, VA 23185.

2. Examples are Fred J. Maroon and Suzy Maroon, *The Supreme Court of the United States* (New York: Thomasson-Grant and Lickle, 1996), and Yosef Sharon, *The Supreme Court Building, Jerusalem* (Jerusalem, 1993 [no publisher noted]).

3. Paul Byard, "Representing American Justice: The United States Supreme Court," in Barbara S. Christen and Steven Flanders, eds., *Cass Gilbert, Life and Work: Architect of the Public Domain* (New York: W. W. Norton, 2001), 277–78.

4. Reportedly there have been only three murders of federal judges in the history of the republic; all of the victims were known to the author. Only one of these murders had any connection to any criminal proceeding.

5. *Shaping a New Order in the Court; A Sourcebook for Juvenile and Family Court Design*, published by the National Center for Juvenile Justice (Pittsburgh: 1992), 1–2.

6. See, for example, comments of former Family Court Judge Jeffry Gallet in Christen and Flanders, op. cit., 267–69.

CHAPTER 9

1. Elizabeth C. Wiggins, Meghan A. Dunn, and George Cort, *Federal Judicial Center Survey of Courtroom Technology* 8 (Washington, D.C.: Federal Judicial Center, draft edition August 2003).

2. For example, "Around the Nation," *Chicago Daily Law Bulletin*, January 10, 2002: 3.

3. The Courtroom 21 Project, "The Courtroom of the 21st Century," is an international demonstration, experimental, and educational project sponsored by William & Mary Law School and the National Center for State Courts. The project seeks to determine how to use appropriate technology to improve the administration of justice in the world's legal systems. In the law school's McGlothlin Courtroom it includes the world's most technologically advanced trial and appellate courtrooms. The courtroom, designed primarily by the author, as director, and Martin Gruen, as deputy director, is updated continually. The project is also the world center for courtroom and related research, often concentrating on the human implications of courtroom technology use. This article is informed by the trial and appellate experience gained from working in the Courtroom 21 Project.
See www.courtroom21.net.

4. See *United States v. Yates*, 391 F3d 1182 (11th Cir. 2004; holding testimony of prosecution witnesses in Australia unconstitutional), vacated and in banc consideration ordered, 2005 U.S. App. LEXIS 5065 (11th Cir. March 30, 2005).

5. See Fredric Lederer, *The Potential Use of Courtroom Technology in Major Terrorism Cases*, 12 W&M Bill of Rts.J. 887 (2004); Fredric Lederer, *The New Courtroom: the Intersection of Evidence and Technology: Some Thoughts On the Evidentiary Aspects of Technologically Produced or Presented Evidence*, 28 S.W. U.L. Rev. 389 (1999).

6. The experiments involved civil personal injury cases in which expert testimony was presented on the issue of damages, and the only differing evidence was that of opposing medical experts testifying for the different parties; there was no statistically significant difference in damage verdicts whether the experts testified in person or remotely.

7. In a jury trial the judge explains the law—"instructs"—the jury.

8. In April 2004, the Courtroom 21 Project demonstrated a successful mediation of a multiparty international construction contract dispute. Remote participants from Australia, England, and Norway joined the United States party and a mediator in the McGlothlin Courtroom to resolve the dispute.

EPILOGUE

1. Robert A. Peck, "Daniel Patrick Moynihan and the Fall and Rise of Public Works," in Robert Katzman, ed., *Daniel P. Moynihan: The Intellectual in Public Life* (Baltimore: Woodrow Wilson Center Press and Johns Hopkins University Press), 87.

2. Daniel P. Moynihan, "Epidemic on the Highways," *The Reporter*, April 30, 1959.

3. Daniel P. Moynihan, "New Roads and Urban Chaos," *The Reporter*, April 14, 1960.

4. In "Vision and Voice: Design Excellence in Federal Architecture—Building a Legacy," U.S. General Services Administration, December 2002, 9–10. This publication, which comes from the Center for Design Excellence and the Arts in the Office of the Chief Architect, Public Buildings Service, of the General Services Administration, is an appreciation of Moynihan's role in federal architecture based on more than thirty interviews with architects and others.

5. Peck, op. cit., 82. Peck served on Moynihan's staff when he was senator, but long after these events. His paper on Moynihan's role in public works was part of a tribute to Moynihan on his seventieth birthday, delivered in his presence. One would think that Moynihan would have corrected it if it were incorrect. The story of the origins of both the Guiding Principles and the Pennsylvania Avenue proposal, as we know it, is from Moynihan. Historians in the future may be able to find a paper trail or add other recollections. But the matter is already forty-two years old.

6. Charles M. Atherton, in "Vision and Voice," p. 14.

7. Daniel P. Moynihan, "Foreword," in Carol M. Highsmith and Ted Lamphair, *Pennsylvania Avenue: America's Main Street* (Washington, D.C.: AIA Press, 1988), 10–11.

8. David M. Childs, in "Vision and Voice," 15.

9. Peck, op. cit., 69.

10. The Guiding Principles for Federal Architecture may be found, among other places, in "Vision and Voice," op. cit., 4–5.

11. Lois Craig and the staff of the Federal Architecture Project, *The Federal Presence; Architecture, Politics and Symbols in United States Government Building* (Cambridge, Mass.: MIT Press, 1978), 545.

12. Ibid, 539–544.

13. Childs, op. cit., 125.

14. A hint as to what his attitude might have been to frontier contemporary architecture may be gleaned from his comments when, as chairman of the board of the Hirshhorn Museum and Sculpture Garden on the Mall in Washington, D.C., he accepted as a gift from the Institute of Scrap Iron and Steel the sculpture *Isis* by Mark di Suvero. On that occasion, Moynihan said that he accepted this "splendid gift," continuing, "I recall that on the occasion that Margaret Fuller declared, 'I accept the universe,' Carlyle remarked that she had better." He went on, in what must be intended as parody, "*Isis* achieves an aesthetic transubstantiation of that which is at once elusive yet ineluctable in the modern sensibility. "Transcending socialist realism with an unequaled abstractionist range, Mr. Di Suvero brings to the theme of recycling both the hard edge reality of the modern world and the transcendant fecundity of the universe itself. . . ." And so on. In William Safire, *Lend Me Your Ears: Great Speeches in History* (New York: W. W. Norton, 1992), 208.

15. Peck, op. cit., 89.

INDEX

Note: Page numbers in italic type indicate illustrations. Color plates are indicated by a "C" in parentheses following the page number.

A

Abend Singleton, Charles Evans Whittaker United States Courthouse, Kansas City, Missouri (with Ellerbe Becket), *18* (C-3), 76, 105, *106*, 114–15
accessibility: as architectural theme, 63, 71–73; federal requirements for, 96, 98, 211; technology and, 197–98
acoustics, 96, 173, 193
Ad Hoc Committee on Federal Office Space, 226–27
Adair County Courthouse, Kirksville, Missouri, 175
adaptation, of courthouses, 179–81, 204
additions/annexes, 70–71
adjudication space, shortcomings of, 202–3
administration, technology and, 191
Administrative Office of the United States Courts (AOC), 84, 181
African Americans, 157
AIA (American Institute of Architects) headquarters competition, 149
AIA Journal, 229
Albany, New York, State Court of Appeals, 171
Alcorn County Courthouse, Rienzi, Mississippi, *37*, *38*
Alfonse D'Amato United States Courthouse, Islip, New York (Meier and Spector Group), 72–73, *73*, 85–86, *86*, 93, 104, *105*, 142–43, *143*, 230
Allen County Courthouse, Fort Wayne, Indiana, 54
alternate dispute resolution (ADR), 95, 201
The American Architect and Building News (journal), 50
American Institute of Architects. *See* AIA headquarters competition; *AIA Journal*
American Sign Language (ASL), 191
Americans with Disabilities Act (ADA), 71, 98, 197, 211
AMX courtroom control panel, *199*
Anatomy of a Murder (film), 174
Anderson Mason Dale, United States Courthouse, Denver, Colorado (with Hellmuth, Obata & Kassabaum), *30* (C-24, C-25), 93, *214*, *215*, *218*, *223*, 230
appellate courtrooms, 138, 170–72, 200
appellate courts, 178–82; adaptation of trial courts for, 179–81; expressive requirements of, 179; general design considerations for, 178–79; staff space requirements for, 181; types of, 178
arbitration, 201
Architectural Alliance, United States Courthouse, Minneapolis, Minnesota (with Kohn

Pedersen Fox), *18* (C-4), *115*, 115, 230
The Architectural Record (journal), 50
Architectural Review (journal), 50
arraignment courts, 96, 172–73
art in public buildings, 79
Art Moderne, 57–58, *59*
Ashley McGraw, Onondaga County Courthouse, Syracuse, New York (with Ricci-Greene), 70–71, *71*, *72*
Asplund, Gunnar, Göteborg Courthouse addition, Sweden, 138–42, *139*, *141*
assistive technologies, 197–98
authority, as architectural theme, 142–43

B

bailiffs, 99
Banham, Reyner, 225
Barnstable County Courthouse, Barnstable, Massachusetts, *42*, 43, 165
Bartholomew County Courthouse, Columbus, Indiana, 46
Bassford, Edward Payson, Old Ramsey County Courthouse and City Hall, St. Paul, Minnesota, *49*
Beaumont, Texas, Jefferson County Courthouse, 57, *58*
Beaux-Arts classicism, 53–55, 57, 111, 136–37, 142
Beckley, West Virginia, Robert C. Byrd United States Courthouse and Federal Building (Stern, SEM Partners, and Einhorn Yaffee Prescott), *21* (C-7), *117–18*, 117–18, 230
bench, judge's, 96
Benjamin, Asher, 42–43
Bexar County Children's Courtroom, San Antonio, Texas, *191*
Blashfield, Edwin Howland, 54, 138
Blossom & Blossom, In re (experimental trial), 195
Bohlin Cywinski Jackson, United States Courthouse and Post Office addition, Scranton, Pennsylvania (with RicciGreene), *26* (C-17), 68, *69*, 73, *79*, 79, 147–49, *148*
Bohlin, Peter, 68
Bonfire of the Vanities (Wolfe), 65
Bordeaux, France, High Court (Rogers), *24* (C-14), 63, 126, *127*, *127–28*, 129
Boston, Massachusetts: city hall, 46; Edward W. Brooke Courthouse (Kallmann McKinnell & Wood), *17* (C-2), 76, *76*, *77*, 113; Government Center, *114*; John Joseph Moakley United States Courthouse and Harborpark (Pei Cobb Freed), 9–12, *22* (C-9, C-10), 60, *67*, 67, 76, 79, 85, *120*, *120*, *149–50*, 149–51, 163, 230
Bourbon County Courthouse, Paris, Kentucky, 175
Bradburn, J. H., Jefferson County Courthouse, Boulder, Colorado (with Fentress), 106, *107*
Breyer, Stephen G., 60, 164, 230

Bronx, New York: Bronx Borough Courthouse (Garvin), *180*, 180; Bronx Housing Court (Viñoly), *20* (C-6), *116*, 117; Criminal Courthouse (Viñoly), *65–66*, 65–66; Law Building, former, 180, *181*; Merola Courthouse, 65; models of, *66*
Brooklyn, New York: courthouse projects, 143–47, *144*; gallery, courthouse annex (Kliment and Halsband), 146–47, *147*; United States Courthouse (Pelli/HLW), 73, *74*, 102–3, *104*, *146*, 230; United States Courthouse renovation (Gruzen Samton), *104*; United States Post Office and Courthouse (Kliment and Halsband), 144, *144*
Brown County Courthouse, Wisconsin, 175
Browning Day Mullins, Dierdorf, United States Courthouse, Hammond, Indiana (with Pei Cobb Freed), *102*
builders, 42–43
building materials, and security concerns, 108
Bulfinch, Charles, 43
Burlington County Courthouse, Mount Holly, New Jersey, 41, *42*
Burnham, Daniel, Union Station, Washington, D.C., 231
Burnham, George, Cumberland County Courthouse, Portland, Maine (with Lowell), 55, *56*
Byard, Paul, 179

C

cafeterias, 100, 173
California, courthouse guidelines of, 178
campus plans, 87, 102, 105–6. *See also* ensembles
Carpenter, James, ceiling lens, United States Courthouse, Phoenix, Arizona, 79, *79*
Cary, Cooper, 83
ceiling heights, 101, 169, 199
centralized courthouses, 102–3, *102–3*
ceremonial spaces, 100–101
chambers, judges', 90, *94*, 94, 173, 203
Charles Evans Whittaker United States Courthouse, Kansas City, Missouri (Ellerbe Becket and Abend Singleton), *18* (C-3), 76, 105, *106*, 114–15
Charleston County Courthouse, Charleston, South Carolina, 39
Charlotte County Courthouse, Charlotte, Virginia (Jefferson), 110, *111*
Charlton, Dimetrious F., Marquette County Courthouse, Marquette, Michigan (with R. W. Gilbert), *174*, 174–75
Chester County Courthouse, West Chester, Pennsylvania, 174
Chicago, Illinois: Everett McKinley Dirksen Federal Building and Courthouse (Mies van der Rohe), 13–14, *14*, 84, 112, *160*, 160; Federal Building (Henry Ives Cobb), 13–14, *14*, 158–59, *159*; World's Columbian Expo-

ton, *32* (C-27, C-28), 93, *211–12*, *215–17*, *219–21*